Criminal Appeals

Scottish Criminal Law and Practice Series

Series Editor

The Rt Hon the Lord McCluskey, LLD

Criminal Appeals

Lord McCluskey
Retired Senator of the College of Justice

Paul McBride QC

Second edition

Edinburgh
Butterworths
2000

United Kingdom	Butterworths, a Division of Reed Elsevier (UK) Ltd, 4 Hill Street, EDINBURGH EH2 3JZ and Halsbury House, 35 Chancery Lane, LONDON WC2A 1EL
Australia	Butterworths, a Division of Reed International Books Australia Pty Ltd, CHATSWOOD, New South Wales
Canada	Butterworths Canada Ltd, MARKHAM, Ontario
Hong Kong	Butterworths Asia (Hong Kong), HONG KONG
India	Butterworths India, NEW DELHI
Ireland	Butterworth (Ireland) Ltd, DUBLIN
Malaysia	Malayan Law Journal Sdn Bhd, KUALA LUMPUR
New Zealand	Butterworths of New Zealand Ltd, WELLINGTON
Singapore	Butterworths Asia, SINGAPORE
South Africa	Butterworths Publishers (Pty) Ltd, DURBAN
USA	Lexis Law Publishing, CHARLOTTESVILLE, Virginia

© Reed Elsevier (UK) Ltd 2000

A CIP Catalogue record for this book is available from the British Library.

First published in 1992

ISBN 0 406 982562

Typeset by Phoenix Photosetting, Chatham, Kent
Printed by Thomson Litho Ltd, East Kilbride

Visit us at our website: http://www.butterworthsscotland.com

'An appellate court is a group of people who, in the cool of the evening, undo what a better man did in the heat of the day'

Ian Richard Scott
Barber Professor of Law
The University of Birmingham

Preface

When we started thinking about a second edition of this book, it seemed that it would be a straightforward task to update the statutory and case references and make minimal alterations to the text. Alas, it proved to be much more difficult than that.

The excellent recodification in the Criminal Procedure (Scotland) Act 1995 of the statutory law previously contained in the Criminal Procedure (Scotland) Act 1975 and the many substantial amendments made to it from 1980 onwards had made it necessary to think about bringing out a new text for the busy practitioner. However, the enactment of the 1995 Act proved to be but the prelude to a fresh wave of amending legislation, accompanied by a growing volume of judicial decisions that broke new ground and created many new perspectives on legal remedies in the criminal courts.

In Chapter 1, paragraph 1.06, we have summarised the principal changes effected by the amending legislation. Throughout the text, and notably in Chapters 5 and 7 we have tried to take account of the case law that has recently developed around the statutory reforms. The substantive law itself will continue to develop as the full effects of the Crime and Punishment Act 1997, the Human Rights Act 1998 and the Scotland Act 1998 are worked out.

Fortunately, however, there is good reason to hope that the *procedure* governing the preparation for and conduct of appeals will be adequate for whatever lies ahead; it should need little alteration unless the seeking of remedies derived from the European Convention on Human Rights necessitates further new forms. So we judged that this would be the best moment to publish a second edition.

We have tried to ensure that the index to the contents is as comprehensive as we can make it. The intention is that the busy practitioner should be able to go to the index confident that it will guide him quickly to the appropriate text. We have been greatly helped by several very busy people who spend their whole professional lives working with the procedures that we have attempted to describe and explain. Sheriff Charles Stoddart allowed us to see the material that is prepared to assist the judiciary to keep abreast of the changes in the law, both procedural and substantive. The Crown Agent, Andrew Normand, kindly gave us access to much of the material that he and his staff use every day when preparing for and conducting criminal appeals. Patrick Wheatley, solicitor-advocate, revised Chapter 2 and made many valuable suggestions about the presentation of the material. George Marple and Ian Martin of the Justiciary Office kindly read some of the draft and saved us from errors and omissions of which we might otherwise have been guilty. Mrs Elizabeth Strachan of the Judges' Library has been unfailingly helpful. If errors remain, we have only ourselves to blame.

The law is stated as at 11 August 2000

John McCluskey
Paul McBride
11 August 2000

Contents

Table of Statutes

xi

Table of Orders, Rules and Regulations

Table of Cases

Abbreviations

Case Reports

AC	Law Reports, Appeals Cases (House of Lords and Privy Council) 1890–
Adam	Adam's Justiciary Reports 1894–1919
Crim LR	Criminal Law Review (England) 1954–
EHRR	European Human Rights Reports 1979–
Irv	Irvine's Justiciary Reports 1851–68
JC	Justiciary Cases 1917–
R(J)	Justiciary Cases in Rettie's Session Cases 1873–98
SC	Session Cases 1907–
SCCR	Scottish Criminal Case Reports 1981–
SCCR Supp	Scottish Criminal Case Reports Supplement 1950–1980
SLT	Scots Law Times 1893–1908 (preceded by year and volume number), and 1909 (preceded by year)
SLT (Sh Ct)	Sheriff Court Reports in Scots Law Times 1893
White	White's Justiciary Reports 1885–93

Text books

Alison: Archibal Alison *Practice of the Criminal Law of Scotland* (1830)
Renton and Brown: R W Renton and H H Brown Criminal Procedure according to the Law of Scotland (6th edn, 1996, by G H Gordon)

Legislation

CP(S)A 1975	Criminal Procedure (Scotland) Act 1975 (c 21)
CP(S)A 1995	Criminal Procedure (Scotland) Act 1995 (c 46)
Criminal Procedure Rules	Act of Adjournal (Criminal Procedure Rules) 1996, SI 1996/513
HRA 1998	Human Rights Act 1998 (c 42)
RTOA 1988	Road Traffic Offenders Act 1988 (c 53)

Websites

The following websites are a useful resource and allow access to opinions of the Scottish courts, the House of Lords in respect of European Convention cases, and the European Court of Human Rights. They also allow access to legislation of both the Scottish and Westminster Parliaments:

- European Court of Human Rights   www.echr.coe.int/
- House of Lords   www.parliament.the-stationery-office.co.uk

- Scottish Executive Justice Department (Courts Group) (formerly the Scottish Courts Service)   www.scotcourts.gov.uk/

- Scottish Parliament   www.scottish.parliament.uk/
- Stationery Office   www.hmso.gov.uk/

1. Introduction

1.01 How to use this book

This book is intended to be of use to practitioners at all levels in the criminal courts. It is designed to provide answers to the principal questions the practitioner has to ask when preparing a criminal appeal:

(1) Is there a right to appeal at this stage?
(2) Is there a time limit within which I have to act?
(3) Do I have to seek leave to appeal? If so, from whom and when?
(4) What is the first step to be taken ?
(5) How soon can I do it ? When is the last day for doing it ?
(6) Is there a style or form I should use? Where do I find it?
(7) What should I be saying in the form? Who has to sign it?
(8) How do I frame the grounds on which the appeal is based?
(9) What other documents do I have to submit?
(10) To whom do I send the completed appeal documents?
(11) What is the next step? When am I supposed to take the next step?
(12) Can I seek relief for any procedural errors and omissions?
(13) How can I get a time limit extended if I have missed it?
(14) Can I alter the grounds of appeal at any stage?
(15) Can the Crown appeal against conviction, sentence or incidental, procedural rulings?
(16) What about interim liberation: bail?
(17) How do we ask for the penalties, disqualifications or the like to be suspended meantime?

The answers to most questions are to be found in the legislation, including Acts of Adjournal. The problem in practice is to find the quickest way to the governing enactment, and then to understand it and operate it. So this book aims to make the statutory provisions more swiftly accessible and, both by illustrating how they have been applied in reported cases, and, where it might help, by rephrasing them to help to make them more readily understood. As no practitioner acts for the accused and the prosecutor at the same time, the ordinary appeal procedures for accused and convicted persons (chapters 2 and 3) are kept separate from those used by the Crown (chapter 4). The rapidly developing field of European law (whether from the European Union or from the European Convention on Human Rights), the *nobile officium*, the new Scottish Criminal Cases Review Commission, and fundamental nullity may all be of interest to both sides, as are powers of the court, and these are all dealt with in separate chapters. The whole basis of appeals after conviction (or acquittal) is miscarriage of justice. This developing concept is sufficiently important to merit fuller consideration (in chapter 7) along with a discussion of the related topic of grounds of appeal, including appealing on the basis of fresh evidence. Chapter 8 (bail appeals and interim relief) examines what appellants can do to avoid being incarcerated or disqualified while the appeal is still live. The appendix contains styles for use in certain appeals; sometimes the forms are prescribed by statute or by Act of Adjournal. The authors' intention is that the contents of much of the book, particularly chapters 2, 3, 4, 6 and 8, should be looked up in much the same way that information is sought in a railway timetable. We have tried to make the index more comprehensive than is usual, in the hope that it will afford immediate access to the relevant part of the text, and from there, if necessary, to the governing section of the Criminal Procedure (Scotland) Act 1995 or of the Act of Adjournal (Criminal Procedure Rules) 1996.

Each paragraph in the book has been given a separate heading; but the heading is not designed to be a précis of the paragraph itself. It is there merely to help the busy practitioner to find his way quickly to the text he needs. Information is sometimes referred to more than once: this is also done in order to help the practitioner to find quickly what he needs to know.

1.02 Courts of first instance

Proceedings in a court may be proceedings at first instance or proceedings on appeal. Criminal proceedings at first instance may be described broadly as those proceedings that are initiated by a prosecutor against an accused person in order to place that person before a trial court on a criminal charge or charges, and include the trial itself and any proceedings incidental thereto. The steps taken at first instance may include incidental steps such as obtaining warrants to detain persons in custody, or to search premises, vessels or persons to obtain material that might be presented as evidence. The prosecutor may obtain a warrant to cite witnesses for precognition even if no person has been charged: cf the Criminal Procedure (Scotland) Act 1995 (c 46), section 140. In ordinary procedure, the steps taken will include formal steps such as the serving upon the accused person, usually in compliance with a tightly prescribed format and within a statutorily regulated timetable, of a formal intimation and statement of the criminal offences which he is alleged to have committed, often accompanied by other incidental information as to the intended place and time for trial, and notices as to possible penalties and previous convictions. In some instances there may also be served notice of the witnesses who may be adduced for the prosecution and of productions that may be referred to in evidence. If the criminal proceedings are not abandoned they will normally lead to a trial (at a 'trial diet') before a court which determines all questions of fact and law and pronounces a verdict of guilt or an acquittal. The defence has rights both at common law and under statute to take certain incidental steps in proceedings at first instance, e g to challenge the relevancy or competency of the indictment, complaint or proceedings: see also sections 290 and 291 of the 1995 Act (right to request identification parade, to apply to have witnesses precognosced on oath). In some cases the court of first instance may – subject to appeal in certain instances - end the proceedings, in whole or in part, before evidence of fact is adduced, by holding as a matter of law that the case, or part of it, should not proceed further. In relation to a limited number of relatively incidental matters the court of first instance has a power to review, that is to say, to reconsider, its own decisions (eg on bail: section 30(2) of the 1995 Act), but such reconsideration is not an appeal properly so called.

The courts of first instance are the district courts, the sheriff court and the High Court of Justiciary. The district courts exercise summary jurisdiction within district or island areas ('commission areas'): sections 6 and 7 of the 1995 Act. They consist of one stipendiary magistrate or of one or more justices,[1] and each such court has a legally qualified clerk/assessor. They exercise an original but fairly limited jurisdiction;[2] but when the district court is constituted by a stipendiary magistrate it has the summary jurisdiction and powers of a sheriff: see section 7(5) of the 1995 Act. In the sheriff court, the sheriff, or sheriff principal, sits alone to exercise summary criminal jurisdiction at first instance. Accordingly criminal summary jurisdiction at first instance is that exercised by a judge, a justice or justices, sitting without a jury, whether in the district court or in the sheriff court, in proceedings instituted by summary complaint. Solemn jurisdiction at first instance is exercised by a judge alone in the preliminary stages and by a judge and jury at the final, or trial, stage, such proceedings being raised by petition. The sheriff, or sheriff principal, exercises solemn jurisdiction at first instance. The High Court of Justiciary also exercises solemn jurisdiction at first instance when a Lord Commissioner of Justiciary in Scotland[3] sits with a jury[4] for a trial (there may be a trial with two or more judges presiding – section 1(5) of the 1995 Act), or, before the trial, deals with preliminary matters. Any judge exercising solemn jurisdiction sits without a jury in order to determine preliminary matters under the preliminary diet procedure, devolution issues procedure or human rights procedure, or to consider European Union questions. A jury that has delivered a verdict after trial has no effective continuing function once the verdict has been recorded in the minute of proceedings. Accordingly the trial judge in dealing with sentence is effectively sitting without a jury, and sometimes actually too, for example if the case is continued for sentence.

1   Criminal Procedure (Scotland) Act 1995, s 6(2).
2   CP(S)A 1995, s 7.
3   CP(S)A 1995, s 1(2).
4   The form of the Lockerbie trial in Holland was prescribed by a unique Order in Council: High Court of Justiciary (Proceedings in the Netherlands) (United Nations) Order 1998 (SI 1998/2251).

1.03   The appeal court

With relatively few exceptions, decisions made by a court of first instance can be brought under review in the High Court of Justiciary, sitting as an appeal court. The Court of Session has no supervisory jurisdiction in criminal matters: *Reynolds v Christie*.[1] There is no appeal to the House of Lords in criminal matters[2]. Accordingly, in criminal appeal procedure in Scotland, all appeals from courts of first instance are taken to the High Court of Justiciary, and there is no further appeal from the High Court of Justiciary sitting as an appeal court, except in relation to European Convention on Human Rights matters.[3] Following the coming into force of the Scotland Act 1998, an appeal may lie to the Judicial Committee of the Privy Council against a determination of a devolution issue, as defined in Part I of Schedule 6 to the 1998 Act.[4] Exceptions to the general rule that decisions are appealable include the provision that there is no appeal against a sentence fixed by law[5]. Certain decisions may not be immediately appealable, for example a refusal of bail at an early stage,[6] or decisions as to admissibility of evidence in the course of trial. Other examples are considered in their context. A convicted person needs leave to appeal in most cases. The right of the Crown to appeal is more limited than that of an accused or convicted person and may have to be exercised differently. However, in almost all instances where an appeal is competent, both the time for taking an appeal and the method of appealing are strictly regulated by statute, by Act of Adjournal or by law and practice; and the right to appeal, or the right to advance a particular ground of appeal, may be lost if the prescribed procedural steps are not

taken properly and on time. If the right to appeal or the procedures for appealing are not expressly regulated by law, or some
extraordinary circumstance has arisen in which the interests of
justice appear to warrant a review, it may be possible to petition
the High Court of Justiciary to exercise its *nobile officium*[7] to bring
proceedings under review.

1   1988 SLT 68, OH.
2   See *Renton and Brown* (6th edn.) para 28–01, n 2.
3   See Chapter 5 below.
4   Cf Sch 6, Pt II, para 13.
5   Criminal Procedure (Scotland) Act 1995, s 106(2).
6   CP(S)A 1995, s 23(2).
7   Its inherent and overriding power to intervene in extraordinary circumstances:
    see Chapter 6.

1.04   Private prosecutions

The overwhelming majority of prosecutions are public prosecutions; but private prosecutions may be competent. Private prosecutions, though extremely rare, do occur. The subject falls outwith
the scope of this book.[1] A private prosecutor may appeal in the
same way as the Crown.[2]

1   It is dealt with in *Renton and Brown* 3–09 to 3–15.
2   See Chapter 4 below.

1.05   Legislation governing appeal procedure

Most of the legislation governing appeal procedure was consoli-
dated in the Criminal Procedure (Scotland) Act 1995, the structure of which is a great improvement on its predecessor, the
Criminal Procedure (Scotland) Act 1975. The legislation passed
since the 1995 Act came into force, although effecting very substantial alterations to the law and procedure, has largely employed
the technique of amending the 1995 Act by alteration, addition,
repeal or wholesale substitution. Thus almost everything that
matters in the way of primary legislation regulating appeal procedure is now to be found within the four corners of an updated
copy of the 1995 Act. **In the text of this book, the Criminal
Procedure (Scotland) Act 1995, *as amended by any legislation since it was enacted*, may be referred to as 'the 1995
Act'**; and, because that is virtually the only statute that matters in
this field, it has been decided in most instances, unless the context
renders it desirable to do otherwise, to refer to any section of the

1995 Act simply as section N (or to s N, in footnotes). Any other statutes are referred to as fully as is necessary. It has not been thought necessary to include in this text detailed footnotes to explain when, how or why any amended section in the 1995 Act has come to be amended.

1.06 Summary of the most important legislative changes since 1992

In order to give a rather simplified view of the principal changes made to appeals procedures by legislation since the first edition of this book (1 May 1992) the changes are summarised in this paragraph: the section – *printed in italics* – of the amending statute precedes the summary in the text of the current provision. In some instances, there has been further amendment, but it has not been thought necessary to specify every amending section if the current section is in the Criminal Procedure (Scotland) Act 1995, as amended. Where appropriate, references to sections of the 1995 Act, in their current wording, are printed **in bold** after the summary. The sections in their current (amended) form are most conveniently found in *Renton and Brown's Criminal Procedure Legislation* (W Green/Sweet & Maxwell).

Prisoners and Criminal Proceedings (Scotland) Act 1993
section 42: The Lord Advocate may appeal against a sentence in solemn proceedings, and the prosecutor may do so in summary proceedings: **sections 108 and 175(3)(b), 4 and 4A.**
section 43: Procedure for prosecutor to consent to set aside conviction: **section 188.**

Criminal Justice (Scotland) Act 1995
section 3: No bail pending appeal in attempted murder, culpable homicide, rape or attempted rape proceedings after previous conviction for such offences: **section 26.**
section 5: High Court not to admit a convicted person to bail before a note of appeal has been lodged, unless reasons are stated in the application for bail and there are exceptional circumstances to justify bail: **section 112(2).**
section 13: First diets in sheriff and jury cases: **section 71.**
section 42: Leave to appeal has to be obtained both in solemn (**sections 106 and 107**) and in summary cases (**sections 175, 180 and 187**)
section 43: Reduction of quorum: in High Court to two, for sentence appeals **sections 103(3) and 173(2).**

section 46: In new prosecutions (allowed after successful appeal) the accused is not to be charged with an offence more serious than that of which he was convicted in the proceedings from which he has appealed successfully (**sections 119(2) and 185(2)**) or receive a sentence that could not have been imposed in the earlier proceedings (**sections 119(3) and 185(3)**).

Sections 51 and 52, as also amended in 1997: new provisions allowing appeals (and prescribing procedures therefor) against determinations by the court in proceedings of the kind introduced by *sections 47–50*: these are findings relating to insanity in bar of trial, a finding (after an examination of facts) that an insane accused did the act or made the omission constituting the offence charged, and the making of certain medical orders. The Lord Advocate is also given rights of appeal on points of law in relation to such determinations (cf Part VI, **sections 62 and 63**).

Proceeds of Crime (Scotland) Act 1995

This Act consolidates provisions relating to the confiscation and forfeiture of the proceeds of criminal conduct, following amendments made by the Proceeds of Crime Act 1995. For procedural appeal purposes, confiscation orders, suspended forfeiture orders and other such orders are treated as sentences. A decision by a court to make an order declaring a 'gift' or an 'implicative gift' to be (or not to be) caught by the confiscatory provisions of the Act is appealable to the High Court: *section 5*. The procedure is also the same as for a sentence appeal: *section 6*. The timetable for appealing may be affected if there is a postponement of sentence: *section 10*. Compensation claims – by persons suffering loss as a result of an order that should not have been made – are regulated by Court of Session procedure: *section 17*. Actual forfeiture etc may be delayed if there is an appeal. There are provisions for recalling orders made under the Act and they are appealable to the High Court under *section 27*. Restraint orders (to prevent disposal of or intromitting with property) are subject to civil procedure: Part III.

Crime and Punishment (Scotland) Act 1997

This Act presents problems for the practitioner. Some of its parliamentary and political history is summarised in the editorial notes on the 1997 Act in *Renton and Brown's Criminal Procedure Legislation*. Apart from difficulties in interpretation, which may arise as a consequence of some hasty drafting in the dying days of the then administration, it was foreseen that if there were to be a change of government some of the legislative changes being enacted might

not be to the liking of the new administration. Accordingly most of
the Act was not brought into force at once and the Act provided (*section 65*) that the Secretary of State might by order made by statutory instrument bring it into force in whole as he saw fit. Parts of it
have been brought into force, and parts not. The 1997 Act was
partly amended and partly repealed by the Crime and Disorder Act
1998. The alterations to the relevant provisions as currently made
and as relating to appeals are noted in the text.

The Human Rights Act 1998

The Scotland Act 1998
The effects of both of these Acts in relation to criminal appeals
are considered in Chapter 5 of this book.

1.07   Acts of Adjournal

The Criminal Procedure (Scotland) Act 1995, section 305
enables the High Court, by Act of Adjournal, to regulate the practice and procedure of the courts in relation to criminal procedure.
Section 305 also empowers the High Court by Act of Adjournal
to modify, amend or repel any enactment, including any enactment contained in the 1995 Act itself (in so far as that enactment
relates to matters with respect to which an Act of Adjournal may
be made under section 305). Clearly, having regard to the limits
placed upon the High Court's power by section 305 and having
regard to the Human Rights Act 1998 and the Scotland Act 1998,
an Act of Adjournal is potentially open to challenge as being ultra
vires ie beyond the scope of the powers conferred in the statute.[1]
Today's practitioner is fortunate because the Act of Adjournal
(Criminal Procedure Rules) 1996 revoked all the previous Acts of
Adjournal having effect in this branch of the law.[2] Any relevant
amendments made since then are referred to in the text. **For
brevity, the 1996 Act of Adjournal, as amended, is referred
to as 'the Criminal Procedure Rules'.**

1   *HM Advocate v Dickson* 1999 SCCR 859 – unsuccessful challenge.
2   See Act of Adjournal (Criminal Procedure Rules) 1996, SI 1996/513, s 3 and
    Sch 3.

1.08   Reports of cases

Following the publication of the three Reports of the Thomson
Committee, the Criminal Justice (Scotland) Act 1980 made

substantial changes to the law and practice of criminal procedure in Scotland. The Third Report (December 1977, Cmnd 7005) is still a useful guide to the thinking behind the legislation. Almost coinciding with the coming into force of the various provisions of the 1975 Act, the Law Society of Scotland and Butterworths began to publish the excellent Scottish Criminal Case Reports, edited by Sheriff Sir Gerald Gordon, CBE, QC, LLD. These reports have become an indispensable tool for the serious practitioner. They are published within a few weeks of the judgments reported and contain full background material, and critical, informative commentary. A supplement, for the years 1950 to 1980, of cases decided by the High Court but not reported, is also published in the SCCR series; and the separately published *SCCR 1981–90 Index* includes cases reported in the supplement and also in Justiciary Cases and Scots Law Times. There are cumulative indexes in the 1995 and 1999 volumes. In this book it has been decided primarily to give this reference to SCCR in respect of cases referred to. If the case is reported elsewhere, and many are not, the reference to the other reports can be obtained from case citators. In the oral hearing in the appeal court, the court expects to be referred to the report in Justiciary Cases, if there is one, as the opinions therein have been revised by the judges who wrote them. The Scots Law Times reports are now comprehensive and up to date and enjoy the advantage of being available on CD-ROM. References to pre-1981 cases are seldom necessary on points of procedure because of the comprehensiveness of subsequent reforms of the law relating to criminal appeals. Some of the pre-1980 cases, however, relate to forms of procedure (suspension, advocation, petitions to *nobile officium*) which pre-date the recent legislative reforms. Others relating to fundamental nullity are commonly referred to. Human rights cases decided in the European Court of Human Rights, which sits in Strasbourg and was reconstituted in 1998, are usually also reported in the European Human Rights Reports: a typical citation, including the official identifying number of the case would be, for example, *Maxwell v United Kingdom* (1994) 19 EHRR 97. Scottish cases decided in Strasbourg are usually reported in SCCR and SLT. Cases decided in the Court of Justice of the European Communities, if originating in Scotland, are also usually reported in the domestic reports; they are also reported in the European Court Reports, ECR.

1.09   The role of advocacy in appeals

The principal aim of the advocate is to persuade the judge to see the
issue from the perspective which is most favourable to the client. As
Dr Johnson put it, 'A lawyer is to do for his client all that his client
might fairly do for himself if he could'; adding – in support of the
view that the advocate should advance any argument that may succeed, even if he himself would not necessarily be persuaded by it –
'An argument which does not convince yourself may convince the
judge to whom you urge it; and if it does convince him, why, then
. . . you are wrong and he is right'.[1] It is clear, and is now widely
understood, that a significant proportion of the cases that come
before appeal courts raise issues that could be resolved either way.
Judges make law: Lord Reid said, 'The jurist may ask what I mean
by law . . . the practical answer is that the law is what the judge says
it is . . . There was a time when it was thought almost indecent to
suggest that judges make law - they only declare it . . . But we do
not believe in fairy tales any more'.[2] In the second Reith Lecture,[3]
Lord McCluskey gave many examples to illustrate how evenly balanced the arguments could be.[4] In 'The Law Lords'[5] Alan Paterson
quotes the opinions of many senior judges as to the proportion of
appeals in the House of Lords that could be decided either way:
their estimates range from 10 per cent to 'almost every case'. No
one would estimate that so many of the cases heard on appeal by
the High Court of Justiciary were evenly balanced. But some are;
and the court can be persuaded to change its collective mind.
Striking examples may be found in *Morrison v HM Advocate*[6] and
Leggate v HM Advocate[7] in both of which benches of seven judges
unanimously overruled unanimous decisions by benches of five
judges pronounced within the preceding three years. In *Ross v HM
Advocate*[8] a bench of five judges overruled (at least in part) a decision which for nearly 30 years had effectively excluded the defence
that an accused who at the material time was acting under the influence of drugs, administered to him without his knowledge, lacked
the necessary *mens rea*. The trend continues: cf *Thomson v Crowe*[9]
The matter is discussed illuminatingly in the article by Professor Ian
Willock in 2000 SLT (News) at page 19. The truth is that judicial
perspectives do change. Experience and reflection and different sets
of circumstances cast new light on old problems and traditional
solutions. The European Convention on Human Rights is forcing
changes[10]. Judges sitting in the criminal appeal court now have far
more experience of the workings of the criminal law than their pre-
decessors had. So the role of advocacy and the value of scholarship
have not diminished. Advocacy in the appeal court is the act of per-

suading the court, by the skilful presentation of relevant principle and thoroughly researched precedent and authority, to adopt a favourable perspective on the case before it and, if necessary, to change its collective mind and alter the law. The value of adequate research cannot be overemphasised. One has only to read Sir Gerald Gordon's critical comments on decided cases to realise that important case law is sometimes ignored in the delivering of judicial opinions, particularly if they are delivered *extempore*. The failure to notice the relevant authorities is at least in part the responsibility of those who plead before the court. Since the European Convention on Human Rights began to play such a large part in our law, it has become commonplace to refer to the 'jurisprudence' (i e the reported cases) of the European Courts and of foreign courts, notably in the USA and the Commonwealth.

1 Quoted by Alan Paterson, '*The Law Lords*' from Boswell, *A Journal of a Tour of the Hebrides*.
2 'The Judge as Law Maker' (1972) 12 JSPTL 22.
3 'The Clanking of Medieval Chains'.
4 Cf 'Law, Justice and Democracy' by Lord McCluskey (1987) Sweet & Maxwell/BBC Books.
5 Chapter 8.
6 1990 SCCR 235.
7 1988 SCCR 391.
8 1991 SCCR 823.
9 1999 SCCR 1003.
10 See *Burn, Petitioner* 2000 SCCR 384.

1.10 Advocacy and preparation

It is bordering on tautology to speak of advocacy *and* preparation. Good advocacy is nine-tenths preparation. In our tradition the basis of the oral debate that takes place in court is trust. The court trusts the professionals appearing before it to have prepared thoroughly and to present the fruits of their labours ethically. The court of criminal appeal consists of experienced judges and they face a formidably large calendar of cases on most days when the appeal court sits. They depend to a very high degree upon the quality of the advocacy of those who appear before them. In his memorandum to HM Government, commenting upon Government proposals to extend rights of audience in the higher courts, the then Lord Justice-General, Lord Emslie, stated, 'I cannot emphasise too strongly in particular the very great extent to which, in the adversarial systems of the so-called common law countries, the higher courts are dependent upon the quality of professional performance exhibited by those who practise before them'. Speaking in the House of Lords debate on the second reading of the Law Reform (Miscellaneous Provisions) (Scotland) Bill 1989 (enacted with amendments in 1990) he said:[1]

'The strength of any court is not merely a reflection of the quality of its judges. It is, to a very significant extent, also a reflection of the quality of those who plead before it. The Court of Session in particular – I can speak of that from long experience – is heavily dependent on the quality of its advocates and furthermore upon the mutual respect which exists between Bench and Bar and in the relationships of advocates to each other, relationships which involve a high degree of trust.

These observations point to the qualities that an advocate (whether a member of the Faculty of Advocates or a solicitor-advocate) in the High Court should try to display. Above all, he must prepare his case thoroughly. That involves mastering the facts of the case and its procedural history. It is of the utmost importance that the advocate has a good knowledge of criminal procedure. A vital part of the process of preparation, however, is the selection of those arguments which are stateable and the discarding of those which are not. Of course, if the sifting judges have decided (see 1.23 below) that a ground is 'arguable' it should usually be presented to the Court. But the whole balance of an appeal submission can be destroyed by the inclusion in it of any unstateable argument, which serves only to irritate the court: judges are only human. Brevity is another goal in the preparation process. The papers that go to the judges are voluminous. They contain all the written material that has had some bearing upon the presentation and decision of the case, as well as judges' reports, minutes of proceedings and the like. It is seldom that all such material needs to be referred to by the advocate. In preparing his submissions the advocate should identify any parts of the documentation to which it is necessary or helpful to draw attention, and select the logical order for such reference. This process of selection must be fair in the sense that anything that is material must be included, even if it is adverse to the submission. Ideally, the advocate ought to prepare so that when he comes to present his submissions they contain a logical and comprehensive narrative of the relevant circumstances such that the court could adopt it as the basis of its written judgment. If one needs a style for a submission, particularly for the introductory part, it may be found in any of the recent opinions delivered, particularly after making *avizandum*[2], by the Lord Justice-General or the Lord Justice-Clerk; they are self-contained, in the sense that they refer concisely to all the relevant facts and history and summarise all the arguments and authorities referred to. A submission modelled on such an opinion would be likely to be well received. Research into the relevant law must be thorough. It is the duty of the advocate to draw the court's attention to any relevant authority, including any adverse to the submission he is advancing; and the advocate in preparing the submission must try to ensure that he does not miss any case that is, or may be, in point. The court has ready access to the usual Scottish textbooks and case reports; but if it is intended to refer to any book or report not usually cited it is helpful to prepare photocopies for the use of the court, and even more helpful if they are bound together in some way and indexed. It is to be hoped that practitioners will come up with inventive new ways of putting material before the court by using computer technology. In any event, a list of the books likely to be referred to should be prepared to allow the court staff to ensure that the judges have the necessary books to hand.

It is good practice, if the circumstances warrant it, to consider approaching the Crown before the hearing to see if agreement can be reached, or if any concessions are to be made, which can help to focus the submission at the hearing itself on to the real issues. It is essential to ensure that any submission that it is proposed to advance is adequately covered by the grounds of appeal – in whatever form they are placed before the court. The court is likely to refuse to entertain submissions on any ground of which due notice has not been given; and while, even without notice, the court may deal with matters that suggest that the case is vitiated by some fundamental irregularity,[3] it is proper practice to give notice of any such point when it comes to light; in at least some such cases further inquiry, by the Crown or by the court, into the circumstances might be necessary. It has become increasingly common for the court, at some form of preliminary hearing, to invite or even ordain the parties to prepare, exchange and lodge notes of intended argument with reference to the authorities to be relied on, and perhaps specifying any passages in the transcript of evidence to which reference is to be made.

1   H L Official Report; 30 January 1990, cols 183 and 184.
2   This term describes the process of taking the case away to think about it and to formulate the formal opinions.
3   See Chapter 6; 6.35 and 6.36.

1.11   Advocacy in court

If the submission has been properly prepared, the presentation of the argument should be relatively straightforward. The advocate can assume that the judges will have read the papers and can offer to confine his summary of the facts and circumstances to the salient, material facts. In some cases it will be sensible to ask the court if it would like particular documents or passages in them to be read or merely summarised or referred to. In some cases it will be essential to read out material that has to be placed before the court in order to make the submission fully intelligible. That, of course, is a matter of judgment, a judgment that should be made before the advocate rises to his feet. An advocate's ears are as important as his tongue. If, between his ears, he has a well-calibrated mind he will be able to detect which of his points are being favourably received and which are hopeless; he will also be able to pick up, adopt and develop a favourable line of argument that has been suggested from the bench. The court as currently constituted does not sit silently recording counsel's speeches. It responds, asks questions and debates the issues with counsel. The test of a good advocate is how well his preparation and properties of mind enable him to engage in that forensic debate. Normally, the advocate is given only one opportunity to speak. So he must anticipate his opponent's argument and try to meet it in advance. In particular he must refer to and attempt to distinguish (or to challenge) any authorities which are against his submission and which his opponent is likely to found upon. In some cases the advocate may be called upon to reply to some part of the submission made in response to his opening submission, so it is necessary to concentrate on that submission and to be ready to reply, if asked. It is perfectly proper to request an opportunity to reply to a point that has emerged since the end of the first submission, but only if the advocate has something new to say.

1.12 Assisting the court

In presenting his submission the advocate is endeavouring to inform the court as to the facts and the law. When statutes are referred to in court for the first time they should be described by reference to their short title (including the date) and their chapter number; although this will be unnecessary in the case of the most common criminal procedure statutes, such as the Criminal Procedure (Scotland) Act 1995. If the version of the statute to be referred to is in *Renton and Brown's Criminal Procedure Legislation*, as it commonly will be, the appropriate page reference should be given. The page reference should be given if the official bound volumes of statutes are being used. As a part of his preparation the advocate must ensure that what is placed before the court is the statute as amended and in force at the material time. The same detail is required for statutory instruments. Reported cases should, where possible, be placed before the court by reference to the official reports, such as the Justiciary Cases; but the SCCR are most commonly referred to. If the case is not reported (or not fully reported) in the official reports, counsel should refer to the best available report and should be in a position to assure the court that the case is not reported in official reports. All references to statutes, statutory instruments or reported cases should be enunciated clearly and the advocate would be wise to check that the judges have had an adequate opportunity to record the reference, and, if necessary, have found the report, before the pleader starts reading excerpts from it. Textbooks and articles in learned journals may properly be referred to but it is important to ensure beforehand that the judges have access to such material or copies of the relevant pages. If there is no printed list of the names of cases it is a matter of courtesy to spell out any very unusual names to assist the judges to make an accurate note. Accurate lists of authorities and texts to be referred to should be handed into the court macer in good time before the submissions are heard. It is important for the advocate to make it crystal clear to the court, preferably at the first opportunity, what propositions in law he or she is to advance, and precisely what it is that the court is being invited to do.

1.13 Terminology

A person who appeals against a decision at a preliminary diet or, in summary proceedings, under the Criminal Procedure (Scotland) Act 1995, section 174(1), is referred to as the **appellant** (Form 19.1-A) and his opponent is the **respondent**. A person who appeals after conviction on indictment is properly described as the **appellant**, although in the forms used to give intimation of intention to appeal (Form15.2-A) and in the note of appeal (Form 15.2-B) and in other forms he is variously described as 'the convicted person', 'the applicant'(Form 15.3-B), 'the petitioner' (Form 15.2-D) or 'the appellant'. By the time the case is heard in court he is usually referred to as 'the appellant'. Section 132 provides that, unless the context otherwise requires, 'appellant' includes a person who has been convicted and desires to appeal under this part of this Act. A person who appeals by way of stated case after summary conviction is referred to as the **appellant** even at the stage of the application for a stated case.[1] If he appeals by bill of suspension he should be referred to as the **complainer**. The person (whether he is the accused or the prosecutor) who brings a bill of advocation is called the **complainer**. Those on the other side (including perhaps the co-accused) are **respondents**.[2] A person who petitions the High Court to use the *nobile officium* is a **petitioner** and those answering the petition are **respondents**. It has become common in criminal proceedings to refer to the victim of a crime (eg of assault) as 'the complainer'. Purists would say that, as it is the procurator fiscal in whose name any complaint runs, he is the one who should be described as 'the complainer'. But if the accused appeals by bill of suspension or advocation it is he who is then the complainer, which is very confusing.[3] It would seem sensible to use relatively unambiguous terms like 'the appellant', 'the accused', 'the Crown', 'the victim', where the context allows, especially in the oral presentation of appeals. The judges from whose courts appeals are taken are described simply as the **justice** (or the **justices**), the **sheriff**, the **trial judge**. It is not necessary to preface every, or, indeed any, reference to a judge with the epithet **learned**. The term 'High Court of Justiciary' is usually referred to in the singular.[4] **The Crown** is also commonly referred to in the singular. A person appearing before the appeal court should address the whole court as 'My Lords' or 'Your Lordships', even if one member of the bench is a woman[5]. If a particular judge has asked a question or made a comment and the pleader wishes to refer back to it, he can simply refer to the judge by name[6], or refer, where appropriate, to 'Your Lordship in the chair'. A woman judge is referred to as 'My Lady' or 'Your Ladyship'.[7] In this book, the terms 'advocate' and 'counsel' are used to include 'solicitor-advocate'.

1   Criminal Procedure (Scotland) Act 1995, s 176(1).
2   Cf *HM Advocate v McDonald* 1984 SCCR 229.
3   See Lord Prosser's opinion in *MacPherson v Gilchrist* 2000 SCCR 477 at 481.
4   CP(S)A 1995, s 104(1).
5   No one has yet decided how to address a bench consisting entirely of women; it is obviously a matter deserving much careful thought before a suitably worded Practice Note is promulgated.
6   'Lord Auchtermuchty' will do – not the Uriah Heep-ish 'My Lord Auchtermuchty'.
7   Practice Note of 12 November 1992.

LEAVE TO APPEAL

1.14   The requirement for leave (1995)

The Criminal Justice (Scotland) Act 1995[1] removed the simple, unconditional right of appeal then contained in section 228 (solemn) and sections 442 (summary) of the Criminal Procedure (Scotland) Act 1975. Section 42 of the Criminal Justice (Scotland) Act 1995 Act made it necessary first to obtain leave to appeal. Once section 42 came into force (in relation to offences committed on or after 26 September 1995), leave had to be sought and obtained in accordance with new procedures specified in the same Act. After the consolidation of the legislation in the 1995 Act, further prospective amendments were made by the Crime and Punishment Act 1997[2] and certain parts of the 1997 Act have been brought into force. The present statutory position is now to be found in sections 106, and 107 (solemn) and 175, 180 and 187 (summary) of the 1995 Act, as amended. Leave is required for any appeal under these sections. A party to a summary prosecution does not require leave to appeal if he appeals to the High Court by bill of suspension against a conviction in the circumstances detailed in section 191[3]. However, if, under section 191, a party to a summary prosecution appeals to the High Court by bill of suspension, a different form of leave, to be obtained from the High Court itself, is required under section 191(2); because, if the alleged miscarriage of justice is already referred to in an application for a stated case under section 176(1), then, until the appeal to which the application relates has finally been disposed of or abandoned, the appellant cannot proceed with his appeal by way of bill of suspension without leave of the High Court. The provisions in sections 106, 107, 175, 180 and 187 apply to appeals following verdict. They do not apply to devolution issues raised in the course of proceedings before verdict and appealed at that stage, as in *Starrs v Ruxton; Ruxton v Starrs*[4]. Accordingly leave in terms of these sections is not required at that stage in order to appeal on a devolution issue. If, however, a devolution issue is raised before trial and is determined in the court in which it has been raised, and no appeal is taken at that stage, then, if an appellant seeks to raise the point again in an appeal against the verdict, he would have to include it in his grounds of appeal. It would then be subject to the ordinary 'sifting' process (see 1.18 below). In certain circumstances, if a devolution issue is raised by preliminary diet procedure, leave may be required under the provisions of section 74.[5] The procedure in relation to raising devolution issues on appeal is discussed in Chapter 5.

---

1   s 42.
2   As amended by the Crime and Disorder Act 1998, Sch 8, para 119.
3   See 3.09 below.

4   1999 SCCR 1052.
5   See 3.01–3.04 below.

1.15   Solemn cases

In solemn cases the basic right of appeal available to a person convicted on indictment is contained in the Criminal Procedure (Scotland) Act 1995, section 106. Subsection (1) lists the matters that may be appealed against, but only with leave. In short, they are the conviction itself, the sentence passed on conviction, and various orders that may be made instead of imposing a sentence of fine or imprisonment.

1.16   Summary cases

The right of appeal available to a person convicted, or found to have committed an offence, in summary proceedings is contained in the Criminal Procedure (Scotland) Act 1995, section 175, though without prejudice to any right of appeal by bill of suspension under section 191. Under the section he may also appeal to the High Court against conviction, sentence or other order made in place of a fine or imprisonment.

1.17   Obtaining leave to appeal: solemn or summary

The Criminal Procedure (Scotland) Act 1995, section 107 regulates leave to appeal in solemn cases. In summary appeals the corresponding provisions are contained in sections 180 and 187. From the practitioner's point of view, however, once the appeal has reached the Clerk of Justiciary in the ordinary way (under section 110, 179(8) and (9) or 186(4)(a)) the responsibility for initiating procedure for putting the matter to a judge passes to the Clerk of Justiciary. The practice is governed by Practice Note No 1 of 1995.[1]
Although that Practice Note expressly relates to the statutory provisions as introduced by the Criminal Justice (Scotland) Act 1995, it still governs the practice and procedure for applying the successor provisions of the Criminal Procedure (Scotland) Act 1995, as amended. In short, therefore, any person who seeks leave to appeal to the High Court against conviction and/or sentence (or other sentence-type disposal) simply does so in the normal manner, whether his appeal is under solemn or summary procedure. When the papers appropriate to the case reach the Clerk of Justiciary, it is the Clerk of Justiciary who takes the steps necessary to place them (with appropriate additions) before the judges.

1   Practice Notes are printed in Vol. 2 of Renton and Browns *Criminal Procedure Legislation*.

1.18 'Sifting'

The process that begins when the Clerk of Justiciary places the papers before judges for decisions about leave to appeal and ends when leave is granted or refused is known colloquially as 'sifting'. No party has any right to be heard orally or even to be present when the sifting judges consider and make their decisions. The proceedings do not take place in public. The statute confers no express right upon the sifting judges to summon parties to appear before them to make submissions. In *Martin v United Kingdom*[1], the European Court of Human Rights decided that the system for seeking and obtaining leave to appeal did not discriminate against an accused person simply by reason of the fact that he had no right to appear and present oral submissions to the sifting judge or judges. Regardless of whether the appeal is from solemn or from summary proceedings the sifting process within the Justiciary Office and the High Court itself is, for practical purposes, the same. The only real difference lies in the documentation that the Clerk of Justiciary sends to the sifting judges. That depends upon the character and source of the appeal. There are two possible stages, the 'first sift' and the 'second sift'. At the first sift, the leave decision is taken by one judge of the High Court in chambers. If the single judge *grants* leave in respect of all the grounds of appeal the Clerk of Justiciary intimates the decision by letter to the appellant or to the solicitor who lodged the appeal, setting out in the letter of intimation any comments that the sifting judge may have made in writing. The appellant or his solicitor need take no further action on receipt of the intimation. The letter of intimation may give notice of the date and time fixed for the hearing of the appeal. That is the only notice of the diet that the Clerk of Justiciary will give in such a case. Alternatively, the letter intimating the grant of leave may simply state that the date of the hearing will be notified in due course. The Clerk of Justiciary will then assign the appeal to a court roll in the ordinary way and intimate that diet.

1   1999 SCCR 941.

1.19 Refusal by first judge; further appeal; and time for appealing

The first sifting judge may conclude that no proposed ground of appeal is arguable; he must then *refuse* leave. In that event, the Clerk of Justiciary's letter of intimation will simply inform the appellant or his solicitor, as the case may be, that the application for leave to appeal has been refused, and the reasons given by the single sifting judge will be stated in an appendix to the letter. The letter will also inform the recipient that the appellant has the right to appeal against the refusal of leave and that he may exercise that right by intimating an appeal to the Clerk of Justiciary within 14 days from the date of the intimation to the appellant of the refusal of leave. The 14 days run from the date of 'intimation'. Section 7 of the Interpretation Act 1978 applies: accordingly, unless the contrary is proved, intimation is deemed to have been effected at the time at which the letter giving intimation would be delivered in the ordinary course of post (first class). Therefore the 14-day period runs from the end of the first weekday after the date of first class posting. The period prescribed for an appeal is mandatory. Accordingly, a late application for leave to appeal after refusal by the single sifting judge cannot be dealt with by the *nobile officium*.[1] Leave may be granted in respect of one matter, one ground of appeal, but refused in respect of others. If the appellant wishes to appeal against a refusal, whether in whole or in part, he sends a letter to that effect addressed to the Deputy Principal Clerk of Justiciary, Parliament House, Edinburgh EH1 1RQ. It is quite common for the letter intimating an appeal against refusal of leave to be more than a mere formal intimation that the decision is appealed. It may contain further representations, perhaps supported by counsel's opinion and/or other material. The letter may comment critically upon the reasons given for the refusal, upon the trial judge's report, or upon any errors or omissions, such as failing to deal expressly with a discrete ground of appeal.

The appeal is then placed by the Clerk of Justiciary before the High Court in chambers with all the documents, including such additional material, but without parties being present. This is the second sift. In fact, what happens is that the necessary quorum of judges (two for sentence-only appeals; three for convictions etc) is assembled as soon as the business of the court allows, and they determine in chambers, whether or not, on the basis of all the material before them, leave should be granted in respect of all or any of the grounds of which the first sifting judge has decided are not arguable. If the first sifting judge has concluded that one or more of the proposed grounds of appeal may be argued but that others are not arguable, then the Clerk of Justiciary will intimate that result accordingly. The appellant then has the same right to appeal the part refusal(s) to the High Court in chambers; as before, he has to do so by letter, within 14 days of intimation. The two or three judges who consider the appeal at the second sift do not review any decision made at the first sift to *grant* leave to appeal. What they have to decide is whether or not to grant leave in respect of any grounds of appeal which the judge at the first sift has *refused* as not arguable. They can, of course, add to the matters to be considered at the appeal, if, for example, they notice a point of competency that has not yet been raised. The result of the second sift is intimated by the Clerk of Justiciary in the same manner as was the result of the first sift; but there is no right of appeal against the result of the second sift, either in whole or in part.

1 *Connolly, Petitioner* 1997 SCCR 205. But see *HM Advocate v Wood; HM Advocate v Cowie* 1990 SCCR 195.

1.20   The documents

As has been pointed out, the appellant has no right to appear in person and to argue his case orally. In solemn cases the documents that have to be placed before the judge of the High Court for the purposes of considering whether or not to grant leave to appeal are, as listed in the Criminal Procedure (Scotland) Act 1995, section 107(2):

(a)   the note of appeal lodged under section 110(1)(a);

(b)   in the case of an appeal against conviction or sentence in a sheriff court, the certified copy or, as the case may be, the record of the proceedings at the trial; in High Court cases a copy of the relevant parts of the Book of Adjournal are added to the papers;

(c)   where the judge who presided at the trial furnishes a report under section 113 of this Act, that report; and

(d)   where, by virtue of section 94(1) of this Act, a transcript of the charge to the jury of the judge who presided at the trial is delivered to the Clerk of Justiciary, that transcript; though an appeal will not necessarily succeed where no transcript is available, the recording machinery having failed.[1] In nearly all appeals against conviction on indictment the Justiciary Office orders a copy of the judge's charge and supplies copies free of charge to the parties.

It is clear, of course, that other documents will be required, depending upon the points which may have to be considered. Thus, for example, the indictment itself will be placed before the sifting judge. Similarly, the sift papers may have to include some of the documentary and other productions produced at the trial court (and retained by that court in terms of section 106(5)). These may include any schedule of previous convictions, and reports, such as social inquiry reports or testimonials or letters from employers, which may have been placed before the court below. It is not unusual to submit, especially at the stage of the second sift, a note or opinion of counsel supporting the application for leave to appeal by reference to specific matters which are said to be arguable and explaining why and how they fall to be treated as arguable. It is quite common for such material to contain a skeleton argument and references to decided cases bearing upon the grounds of appeal. In practice, material of this kind is treated as amplifying the matters contained in the note of appeal itself and is considered by the sifting judges. As explained in Chapter 3, the appellant in summary proceedings appeals by note of appeal against sentence or other appealable disposal and by stated case against conviction or against both conviction and sentence etc. Leave to appeal, when the appeal is or includes an appeal against the conviction or finding, is regulated by section 180. When the appeal is by note of appeal against sentence etc, but not against conviction, the matter of leave to appeal is governed by section 187. In an appeal against conviction (or conviction *and* sentence) the documents to be placed before the sifting judge must include those specified in section 180(2), namely the stated case and the complaint, productions and any other proceedings in the cause, as detailed in section 179(8). In an appeal against sentence etc only, the documents are those sent to the Clerk of Justiciary in terms of section 186(4)(a), namely the note of appeal, the sentencing judge's report, a certified copy of the complaint, the minute of proceedings and any other relevant documents, such as social inquiry reports.

1   As in *Carroll v HM Advocate* 1999 SCCR 617.

1.21   The note of appeal

A note of appeal must, as required by the Criminal Procedure (Scotland) Act 1995, section 110(3), identify the proceedings, contain a full statement of all the grounds of appeal, and be in as nearly as may be the form prescribed by the Criminal Procedure Rules, namely Form 15.2-B. This form has to be signed by the appellant or by his counsel or solicitor. It is important to ensure that the grounds of appeal are stated properly. What the Act requires is a *full* statement of *all the grounds* – see section

110(3)(b). Effectively, the same fullness in the statement of the grounds is required in an appeal by way of stated case[1] or by note of appeal in summary proceedings against sentence.[2] Whatever the character of the intended appeal, each distinct ground of appeal should be identified separately. The best practice is to number them so as to distinguish each from the others. This is because any judge or judges before whom the documents are placed for sifting must consider each separate ground and, if refusing leave in respect of any ground, should give distinct reasons in writing for the refusal in respect of that ground. As already noted, it is perfectly competent for the first sifting judge to conclude that some of the grounds are arguable and to allow the appeal to proceed in respect of those grounds but to refuse leave in respect of others because he does not consider them to be arguable. If he refuses leave in respect of any ground he must give reasons for such refusal; but even if he grants leave in respect of any specified ground he has the right to make such comments in writing as he considers appropriate. He may also choose to *add* to the grounds of appeal (section 107(7)) and if he does so will certainly comment, as provided for in the Act, in order to explain why he thinks that a matter not raised by the appellant may afford an arguable ground of appeal. It follows that the whole documentation, including the first sifting judge's decisions and the reasons therefor or comments thereon, and any comments by or on behalf of the appellants (which will go to the second sift judges if the appellant applies to the High Court for leave to appeal), will be more readily intelligible if the grounds of appeal are laid out in an orderly manner, using numbered paragraphs for discrete points or grounds. Those acting for an appellant who is applying for leave to appeal are well advised to frame the grounds of appeal with care. For, apart from the fact that a ground which is not specified can not be advanced at any oral appeal hearing, (except by leave of the High Court on cause shown)[3] – it is important that the note of appeal should reveal as clearly as may be what the *arguable* point is. The whole purpose of the exercise is to satisfy the sifting judges that there is a point to be argued. Accordingly the appellant's lawyer's professional duty is to try to demonstrate to the sifting judges exactly why the point advanced should be regarded as arguable. Although it is not necessary to set out the argument in full or to refer to any case law, this is sometimes done and it can be valuable in demonstrating that the point advanced is not frivolous and is truly arguable.

1   Criminal Procedure (Scotland) Act 1995, s 176(1)(b).

2   Criminal Procedure (Scotland) Act 1995, s 186(1).
3   CP(S)A 1995, s 107(8).

1.22 The leave decision

If the sifting judges consider that the documents placed before them by the Clerk of Justiciary in terms of the applicable statutory provisions disclose arguable grounds of appeal, leave to appeal is *granted* in respect of the ground or grounds considered arguable. Leave may be granted in respect of a ground of appeal which has not been advanced by the appellant if the sifting judge thinks that the documents disclose an arguable ground, even though the appellant or his advisers were not aware of it. If, for whatever reason, an appellant does not want to advance the ground of appeal so identified by the sifting judge there is no obligation upon him to advance that ground at the hearing of the appeal. If, however, the point noticed by the sifting judges is one that appears to render the proceedings in the court below fundamentally null, the court will decide the matter at the hearing, not at the sifting stage. There is no provision for the sifting judges to add a ground of appeal against sentence if the appellant has chosen to not to appeal against sentence or to add a ground of appeal against conviction in a case where the appeal has been taken against sentence only. If the sifting judges, when considering a conviction-only appeal, detect what may be thought to be a fundamental nullity in relation to a sentence (or a conviction) that has not been appealed, the appropriate course would appear to be for them to make appropriate comments in writing and instruct the Clerk of Justiciary to intimate the comments to the appellant for his consideration and action. In terms of Rule 19.18 of the Criminal Procedure Rules[1], the judges may, before deciding to grant or refuse leave, remit to the judge at first instance for a report or supplementary report. As the court also has power to extend the time for initiating appeal proceedings[2], there should be no difficulty in dealing with an unusual situation of this character speedily and informally.

1   Act of Adjournal (Criminal Procedure Rules) 1996, SI 1986/513.
2   CP(S) A 1995, s 103(5) (solemn) s 181 (summary).

1.23 Arguable grounds

Precisely what is meant by the word 'arguable' in the leave to appeal provisions of the Criminal Procedure (Scotland) Act 1995 is somewhat difficult to say. In the House of Lords, when the Bill was being discussed in committee, the purpose of the new leave provisions was said by the then Lord Advocate (Lord Rodger of Earlsferry) to be to 'allow the High Court to filter out frivolous and unmeritorious appeals quickly and simply', adding that 'only appeals that are clearly without merit - those which are unarguable is the way it is expressed – would be refused leave to appeal.'[1]. The words of the statute and even the explanation given in Parliament do not provide a crystal clear guide to the meaning and application of the adjective 'arguable'; and there is no significant case law about it. The best way to persuade judges that a point is 'arguable' is to formulate stateable arguments in favour of it, in other words, to show that there is an argument to be presented. One consequence of the introduction of a requirement for leave to appeal was that the statutory provision for disposing summarily of frivolous appeals[2] was repealed in 1995.

1 Cf 560 HL Official Report, 16 January 1995, cols 480–481.
2 Criminal Procedure (Scotland) Act 1975, s 256.

1.24 Consequences of refusal

If leave to appeal is not granted, a warrant is granted to apprehend and imprison him if the sentence imposed on him was one of imprisonment and he is out on bail.[1] If such a warrant is granted by the first sifting judge, it does not take effect until after the expiry of the 14 days allowed for appealing to the second sift.[2] If an appeal is taken to the second sift, it does not take effect then either, pending the decision at the second sift. If leave to appeal is granted at the second sift the warrant granted by the first sifting judge falls. The second sift judges do not grant a warrant when they grant leave to appeal. If leave to appeal is finally refused at the second sift, the appeal is at an end and a warrant, if appropriate, is granted by the second sift judges.

1 Criminal Procedure (Scotland) Act 1995, s 107(1)(b)(ii) (solemn), ss 180(5)(b)(ii); 187(2) and 187(1)(b)(ii) (summary).
2 CP(S)A 1995, s 107(3) (solemn); ss 180(3) and 187(2) (summary).

1.25 European Convention on Human Rights

In *Martin v United Kingdom*[1] a person whose application for leave to appeal against sentence had been refused at the sifting stage applied to the European Court of Human Rights, complaining that his right to defend himself had been violated. He submitted that by not being given the opportunity to present oral argument – at the sift – in support of his application for leave to appeal he had been denied his right under article 6 of the Convention to a fair and public hearing. The Court rejected the argument as manifestly ill founded and rejected the application.

This may not, however, be the last word on the matter of the leave to appeal procedures. The case of *Martin* was decided in the context of an appeal against sentence only. The Court did not decide anything about the adequacy of the procedure in an application for leave to appeal against conviction where the appellant seeks to raise issues about the evidence or other matters that night not be fully dealt with in the papers, including the judge's report or note. Nor has the Court been asked to pronounce upon the adequacy of abbreviated 'reasons' such as are sometimes given for refusing leave to appeal. Such matters may yet be tested against the case law bearing upon the application of article 6 and the need to give reasons for important judicial decisions. The Court has not yet been asked to consider whether or not the European principle of 'equality of arms' is departed from in circumstances in which, as sometimes happens, the sentencing judge writes a report robustly defending the sentencing or other decision he has made, thus risking a suggestion that he has taken on the role of an advocate supporting the soundness of his own decision. The appellant has no formal right to comment upon such a report, although in practice he may be allowed to do so, at least after the first sift. The appellant will sometimes draw attention to errors contained in or revealed by the report. One possible criticism of the current system is that, despite the practice of allowing the appellant to submit additional material – such as counsel's opinion or detailed argument in a solicitor's letter or a further report or comments upon the judge's report – for consideration by the judges at the second stage of the sifting process, there is technically no *right* to submit material other than that specified in the Criminal Procedure (Scotland) Act 1995 and there is no statutory duty on the second sift judges to consider it, even although in practice they will. The European Court tends to require that the rights of persons be clearly defined and specified in a written law, not just accorded in practice, however well established the practice is. The Thomson Committee, in its third Report[2], having examined experience in England and in Scotland since 1927, concluded: 'We consider it wrong in principle that in order to seek judicial review of either a conviction obtained, or a sentence imposed, under solemn procedure a convicted person should be required to overcome a preliminary test.'[3] There may therefore be room for further argument, in the context of article 6 of the European Convention, about the fairness of the sifting process.

1   1999 SCCR 941.
2   Cmnd 7005 (December 1977) para 2.09.
3   Ie obtaining leave to appeal.

2. Appeals by the accused: solemn jurisdiction

2.01 Right of appeal – with leave

Before trial, a person upon whom an indictment has been served may have a right to appeal against a decision at a first or preliminary diet (see 2.03 below) or, by note of appeal, against the grant of an application to extend the periods mentioned in the Criminal Procedure (Scotland) Act 1995, section 65 (i e the 12 months and the 80- and 110-day periods there prescribed).[1] After trial, any person who has been convicted on indictment, whether in the High Court of Justiciary or in the sheriff court, has the right to apply for leave to appeal to the High Court against the conviction, against the sentence passed on such conviction or against both the conviction and the sentence.[2] A decision whether or not to grant leave to appeal is now made in accordance with the procedures discussed in Chapter 1 at 1.14 ff. The appellant's right to appeal includes the right to appeal, with leave, against any of the various orders that may be made at the time of conviction or sentence (see 2.23 below). A person who has pled guilty may competently appeal, with leave, against conviction, though such an appeal is unlikely to succeed unless the circumstances are wholly exceptional.[3] A person who has pled guilty to an indictment (or complaint) which is vitiated by some fundamental nullity may challenge his conviction on appeal, whether or not the point was taken when it should first have been taken.[4] Fundamental nullity is discussed in chapter 6.

1 Criminal Procedure (Scotland) Act 1995, s 65(8).
2 CP(S)A 1995, s 106.
3 *Boyle v HM Advocate* 1976 JC 32; *Harvey v Lockhart* 1991 SCCR 83.
4 *Sangster v HM Advocate* (1896) 2 Adam 182.

2.02 Sentence fixed by law

A convicted person has, however, no statutory right of appeal against any sentence fixed by law.[1] A person aged 21 or over who is convicted of murder therefore cannot appeal against the sentence of imprisonment for life which is a sentence fixed by law.[2] Similarly, a person who is under the age of 18 years when he is convicted of murder cannot appeal against the sentence that he be detained without limit of time as this sentence is also fixed by law.[3] Where a person is convicted of murder and at the date of conviction is 18 or over but under 21 years of age his sentence is also fixed by law[4] and is not appealable. Although a sentence of life imprisonment for murder cannot be appealed the murderer has a right of appeal[5] against a recommendation made by the sentencing judge under section 205(6) as to the minimum period which should elapse before release. It is, however, at least conceivable that the provisions in sections 106(2) and 205 will be challenged as violating rights introduced by the European Convention on Human Rights. The procedure for such a challenge is discussed in Chapter 5.

1   Criminal Procedure (Scotland) Act 1995, s 106(2).
2   Cf CP(S)A 1995, s 205(1).
3   CP(S)A 1995, s 205(2).
4   CP(S)A 1995, s 205(3).
5   CP(S)A 1995, s 205(6).

FIRST DIETS AND PRELIMINARY DIETS

2.03   Appeals from first diets, preliminary diets

The Criminal Procedure (Scotland) Act 1995, section 72 provides for a preliminary diet to be held to allow the High Court to deal with certain issues that may or must be resolved before the trial. Section 71(2) makes similar provision for first diets in sheriff and jury cases. The issues include matters relating to competency or relevancy, the validity of the citation, pleas in bar of trial or for separation or conjunction of charges or trials and questions as to refusing or allowing the record of proceedings at the judicial examination to be read to the jury.[1] A party can also invite the court to exercise its discretion to order a preliminary diet to consider and deal with any matter which could in the opinion of that party be resolved with advantage before the trial.[2] An objection to the validity of the citation, on the ground of any discrepancy between the record copy of the indictment and the copy served on the accused, or on account of any error or deficiency in the service copy or in the notice of citation must be stated in a notice under section 72(1)(a)(ii) of the 1995 Act and argued at a first or preliminary diet.[3] If it is not taken and argued in this way the accused is held to have passed from and waived the objection. This was made clear in *HM Advocate v McDonald*.[4] Except by leave of the court on cause shown, no application, matter or point mentioned in section 72(1) of the Act may be made, raised or submitted , unless the intention to do so has been stated in a notice under section 72(1) or 71(2). The court, if it orders a first or preliminary diet, may postpone the trial diet: cf sections 71(7), 72(4) and (5).

1   Criminal Procedure (Scotland) Act 1995, s 278(2).
2   CP(S)A 1995, s 72(1)(d).

3   CP(S)A 1995, ss 72(1) and 79(1).
4   1984 SCCR 229.

2.04   Appeal procedure

Appeals against any decision taken at first diets and preliminary diets are governed by the Criminal Procedure (Scotland) Act 1995, section 74 and the Act of Adjournal (Criminal Procedure Rules) 1996, Chapter 9, paragraphs 9.11 ff,[1] although (a) the prosecutor may bring such a decision under review of the High Court by bill of advocation[2] and (b) the full rights of appeal conferred by section 106 are preserved even if the accused does not at the end of the preliminary diet seek leave to appeal against the adverse decision. Leave to appeal to the High Court against a decision at a first or preliminary diet is required and must be sought by way of motion to the judge who has made the decision at the diet. The motion for leave to appeal must be made to the judge at the diet immediately following the making of the decision. The judge has to grant or refuse leave as soon as he has intimated his decision and has been moved to grant leave.[3] The judge may grant leave *ex proprio motu*, that is to say even if there is no motion for leave.[4] Any party who appears at the diet hearing may seek leave to appeal. So, for example, the first of several accused might invite the court at a first or preliminary diet to separate the trials. It would be competent for any of the other accused persons to seek leave to appeal against the decision that followed that application. Again, the motion for leave must be made immediately and on the spot.

1   In this book any reference to a rule is to a rule of the Act of Adjournal (Criminal Procedure Rules) 1996, SI 1996/513, as amended.
2   Criminal Procedure (Scotland) Act 1995, s 131, and see 'Appeals by the Crown' at 4.06 below.
3   Criminal Procedure Rules 1996, r 9.11.
4   CP(S)A 1995, s 74(1).

2.05   Postponement of trial diet pending appeal

If he grants leave the judge must decide if the trial diet should be postponed.[1] It will commonly be necessary to postpone the trial diet if leave is granted because most pre-trial diets are heard in the week before the trial is due to begin and there is little time to complete the appeal process before the date fixed for the trial (see the interaction of the time limits in the Criminal Procedure (Scotland) Act 1995, sections 76(7) and 75). If the court decides at the first or preliminary diet that the original trial diet should be postponed, the court is allowed to discharge it and fix a new diet or give leave to the prosecutor to serve a notice fixing a new trial diet, under section 74. The High Court itself may postpone the trial diet for such period as appears to that court to be appropriate and may direct that the whole or part of the period is not to count in the computation of any time limit in respect of the case.[2] If the decision to postpone is taken by the High Court, the Clerk of Justiciary has to inform the sheriff clerk (in a sheriff court case), all the parties and the governor of any institution in which any of the persons accused on the indictment in the case is detained.[3]

1   Act of Adjournal (Criminal Procedure Rules 1996), SI 1996/513, r 9.11(2).
2   Criminal Procedure (Scotland) Act 1995, s 74(3).
3   Criminal Procedure Rules 1996, r 8.

2.06 Time for appealing

Any appeal to the High Court against a decision taken at a preliminary diet must be *taken* not later than two days after such decision,[1] but leave to appeal must be sought immediately following the decision.[2] It should be remembered, however, that the two-day period is automatically extended by the Criminal Procedure (Scotland) Act 1995, section 75 if the second of the two days falls on a Saturday, Sunday or court holiday; the period is then extended to and includes the next day which is not a Saturday, Sunday or court holiday.

1   Criminal Procedure (Scotland) Act 1995, s 74(2).
2   Act of Adjournal (Criminal Procedure Rules 1996, SI 1996/513, Rule 9.11.

2.07 Note of appeal

The appeal against a decision taken at a first or preliminary diet must be made by way of note in the form contained in Form 9.12. The completed form must be lodged not later than two days after the making of the decision (or such longer period allowed by the Criminal Procedure (Scotland) Act 1995, section 75). If the case was one set down for trial in the High Court the note of appeal has to be lodged with the Clerk of Justiciary; in a case set down for trial in the sheriff court, with the sheriff clerk.

2.08 Procedure on lodging note of appeal; report

Rules 9.13 and 9.14 of the Act of Adjournal (Criminal Procedure Rules) 1996 regulate the procedure in an appeal from the sheriff court and impose certain duties on the sheriff clerk once a note of appeal has been lodged with him. He is required to certify that leave to appeal has been granted and the date and time of lodging Form 9.12. He must, as soon as possible, send a copy of the note of appeal to all other parties or their solicitors. He must request a report from the sheriff on the circumstances relating to the decision appealed against and send the Clerk of Justiciary a certified copy of the indictment, the record of proceedings and any relevant document. The sheriff in turn must, as soon as possible, send his report to the Clerk of Justiciary. The Clerk of Justiciary thereafter has to send a copy of the sheriff's report to the parties or their solicitors, arrange for the appeal to be heard as soon as possible, and make copies of any documents that the appeal court may need.[1]

Appeals from preliminary diets in the High Court are in practice treated in the same way, although if the High Court judge has written an opinion explaining his decision he is not likely to be asked for a separate report. A High Court judge who grants leave would usually write an opinion without being asked to do so and would certainly do so at the request of any party; but it is good practice to ask for a written opinion when obtaining leave to appeal. In any event the appeal court should have an opinion or report from the court below explaining the decision.

It will be observed that in a sheriff court case it is not the indictment itself which is transmitted by the sheriff clerk but a certified copy only.[2] That has the consequence that if the Crown seeks to amend the indictment during the course of the hearing in the appeal court (e g to meet a criticism directed at specification or latitude) it cannot be done there and the Crown would have to undertake to seek leave to amend in the court below. In that circumstance the appeal court or the Clerk of Justiciary has to record in some unambiguous form what has transpired and what has been undertaken. The actual amendment must be effected to the record copy of the indictment that has been lodged (on or before the date of service) with the clerk of court before which the trial is to take place.[3]

1 Act of Adjournal (Criminal Procedure Rules) 1996, SI 1996/513, rule 14(2).
2 Criminal Procedure Rules 1996, rule 9.13(3)(i).
3 See Criminal Procedure (Scotland) Act 1995, ss 66(5) and 96(2).

2.09   Disposal of the appeal from preliminary diet decisions

The appellant may abandon an appeal against a decision at a first or preliminary diet at any time before the hearing of the appeal.[1] He does so by lodging with the Clerk of Justiciary a completed version of Form 9.17 signed by himself or by his solicitor. In an appeal from the sheriff court, the Clerk of Justiciary informs the sheriff clerk. In all cases he informs other interested parties and the case resumes its progress towards trial. If the appeal proceeds, the powers of the High Court in this regard are governed by the Criminal Procedure (Scotland) Act 1995, section 74(4). The accused need not be present at the appeal court hearing.[2] The High Court may affirm the decision of the court of first instance. It may remit the case to that court with such directions in the matter as the High Court thinks fit. This power would allow the High Court, in a sheriff court case where the Crown indicated at the appeal hearing that it was intended to amend the indictment, to direct the court of first instance to allow such amendment, if moved; and, failing such a motion, to dismiss the indictment (or otherwise as the circumstances may require). If the court of first instance has dismissed the indictment or any part of it, the High Court may reverse that decision and direct the court of first instance to fix a trial diet; though such a direction will not be necessary if a trial diet has already been fixed as regards part of the indictment not dismissed at the preliminary diet. In cases from the sheriff court, the Clerk of Justiciary tells the sheriff clerk what the High Court has decided. If what the High Court has decided is to reverse a decision of the court of first instance which resulted in the dismissal of the case and, consequently, to direct the court of first instance to fix a trial diet, that High Court direction is authority for the Clerk of Justiciary or the sheriff clerk, as the case may be, to issue a fresh warrant for citation under section 66 of the 1995 Act. If the trial court has dismissed the indictment and the High Court reverses the decision it is not necessary for the trial court to fix another, or a continued, preliminary diet just for the purpose of requiring the accused to state how he pleads to the indictment.[2] If, in reversing the decision of the court of first instance, the High Court holds that the proceedings were and are incompetent, it will sustain the plea to the competency, as in *K v HM Advocate*,[3] a 110-day rule case. If, as a result of delay occasioned by the taking and hearing of an appeal against a decision at a first or preliminary diet, the trial cannot commence within the 12-month period allowed by section 65(1) (the period from first appearance on petition to commencement of trial) the court has power to extend that period, retrospectively if necessary.[4]

1 Act of Adjournal (Criminal Procedure Rules) 1996, SI 1996/513, rule 9.17.
2 *HM Advocate v O'Neill* 1992 SCCR 130.
3 1991 SCCR 343.
4 *HM Advocate v M* 1986 SCCR 624.

APPEALS AFTER CONVICTION

2.10 Appeals against conviction only

Subject to the right of the Scottish Criminal Cases Review Commission to refer the whole case to the High Court under the Criminal Procedure (Scotland) Act 1995, Part XA, as amended,[1] the only procedure by which a convicted person may appeal after conviction on indictment is that prescribed by Part VIII of the 1995 Act.

1 See Chapter 5 below.

2.11 Intimation of intention to appeal; timing; form

The first step is to lodge with the Clerk of Justiciary written intimation of intention to appeal and send a copy to the Crown Agent.[1] All appeals under the Criminal Procedure (Scotland) Act 1995, section 106 following conviction on indictment are initiated in the Justiciary Office of the High Court, not in the sheriff court. The form to be used for giving written intimation of intention to appeal is Form 15.2-A. The written notice must be given within two weeks of the final determination of the proceedings. For this purpose the final determination of the proceedings normally occurs on the day on which sentence is passed in open court. However, if sentence is not passed at the time of conviction but is deferred under section 202 (which permits the court to defer sentence for a period on conditions) the two-week period begins to run from the date on which sentence is first deferred in open court[2] (a court may defer sentence several times). In 'drug trafficking' cases (as defined in section 49(2) of the Proceeds of Crime (Scotland) Act 1995) in which a confiscation order[3] can be made, the court may, after conviction, require information before coming to a decision as regards making a confiscation order (under section 1 of the same Act) and may therefore postpone its decision for a period to enable the required information to be obtained.[4] If it does so, an intention to appeal against conviction must be intimated within two weeks of the day on which the period of postponement commences,[5] which means the day on which the decision to postpone is made. The two-week period may be extended at any time by the High Court.[6] As Form 15.2-A itself makes clear, an intimation of intention to appeal must be signed by the convicted person or by his counsel or solicitor. This Form, like all prescribed forms and related instructions, is available from the Clerk of Justiciary at the Public Office, Parliament House, Edinburgh EH1 1RQ. Section 127 requires him to furnish such forms and related instructions to any person who demands them, and to officers of court, to governors of prisons and others as he thinks fit. Each prison governor must make the forms and any related instructions available to prisoners desiring to appeal or to make an application (e g for bail or for extension of time) incidental to the appeal. The governor has the responsibility for forwarding to the Clerk of Justiciary any written intimation of intention to appeal prepared by a prisoner.

1 Criminal Procedure (Scotland) Act 1995, s 109(1).
2 CP(S)A 1995, s 109(4).
3 For appeal purposes this is a sentence: s 1(8) of the Proceeds of Crime (Scotland) Act 1995.
4 See s 10 of the Proceeds of Crime(Scotland) Act 1995.
5 s 10(4)(a) of the Proceeds of Crime (Scotland) Act 1995.
6 CP(S)A 1995, s 111(2); see 2.31 below.

2.12 Note of appeal; form; timing; content

Within six weeks of lodging intimation of intention to appeal, the convicted person may lodge a written note of appeal with the Clerk of Justiciary.[1] The six-week period may, before it expires, be extended by the Clerk of Justiciary, if, for example, there has been a delay in making the transcript of the judge's charge available. The six-week period may also be extended by the High Court itself.[2] The written note of appeal must be in the form prescribed by Rule 15.2 of the Act of Adjournal (Criminal Procedure Rules) 1996, namely Form 15.2-B, and signed by the convicted person, his counsel or solicitor. All the grounds of appeal must be fully stated in the form. It is not competent for an appellant to found any aspect of his appeal on a ground not contained in the written note of appeal, unless the High Court, on cause shown, grants leave.[3] Accordingly, although the section says that the convicted person 'may' lodge a written note of appeal, it is clear that he *must* do so if he intends to proceed with the appeal. The grounds of appeal must be stated with sufficient specification to identify the particular criticism of the conviction which the appellant hopes to present to the High Court;

if they are not so stated the appeal court will usually refuse to entertain submissions related to an unspecific ground.[4] As has already been made clear, a failure to state the grounds properly may well result in refusal of leave to appeal: see 1.21 above. If a ground of appeal passes the sifting stage, section 110(5) allows the appellant to present submissions in support of all grounds of appeal that have been accepted as 'arguable'. The note of appeal must identify the proceedings which have resulted in the conviction of the appellant. Form 15.2-B makes it clear what details are required. The note of appeal effectively supersedes the written intimation in Form 15.2-A.

1 Criminal Procedure (Scotland) Act 1995, s 110.
2 See 2.30 below.
3 CP(S)A 1995, s 107(8).
4 High Court of Justiciary Practice Note of 29 March 1985 – see 2.27 below.

2.13 Written presentation of appeal

The appellant has the right to present his case and his argument to the appeal court either orally or in writing.[1] If he prefers to present it in writing he must so inform the Clerk of Justiciary at least four days before the diet (i e the date) fixed for the hearing of the appeal, lodge with the Clerk of Justiciary three copies of 'his case and argument' and send a copy to the Crown Agent. The High Court must consider the material submitted.[2] This method of proceeding by written presentation, dating from 1926, is unknown in modern practice and is not regulated in any way by the Criminal Procedure Rules. It is not clear what is meant by 'his case'. It is, however, clear that if an appellant opted to present his argument in writing instead of orally the appeal court would study the written material presented.[2] (What does sometimes happen is that a party appellant comes to court on the day of his appeal and asks if the court, instead of listening to an oral presentation by him, will instead read some notes or other written material which he has prepared or collected. Such requests are invariably granted.)

1 Criminal Procedure (Scotland) Act 1995, s 115.
2 The details of the procedure are to be found in CP(S)A 1995, s 115.

2.14 Bail pending appeal

The High Court has a discretion to admit the appellant to bail pending the determination of the appeal on his application at any time after he has lodged a written intimation of intention to appeal.[1] The application is made on Form 15.2-D. This is more fully treated in Chapter 8.

1   Criminal Procedure (Scotland) Act 1995, s 112.

2.15   Record of trial

The whole proceedings at a trial have to be recorded mechanically or by shorthand[1]. Any party interested (which is defined to include the convicted person) is entitled to be furnished with a transcript of the notes or part thereof if he pays the appropriate charge fixed by the Treasury.[2] Normally no transcript, except of the judges charge, is made unless the Clerk of Justiciary so directs, after the court has decided that it wishes to see a transcript. The appeal court, at a procedural hearing, commonly leaves it to the parties to agree which parts are to be transcribed and may instruct them to attempt to reach agreement. The proceedings at a first or preliminary diet are proceedings at the trial for the purposes of the application of section 93.[3] In exceptional circumstances the court may be able to determine the appeal even if, for mechanical or other reasons, no transcript – even of the judge's charge to the jury – exists.[4]

1   Criminal Procedure (Scotland) Act 1995, s 93.
2   CP(S)A 1995, s 94(2).
3   Act of Adjournal (Criminal Procedure Rules) 1996, rule 9.10 and CP(S)A 1995, s 93.
4   See the discussion in *Carroll v H.M. Advocate* 1999 SCCR 617.

2.16   Documentary productions

A party interested in an appeal, whether against conviction or sentence (being one of those parties listed in section 94(9)), has the right to obtain from the Clerk of Justiciary a copy of any documentary production lodged by or for any party to the appeal upon payment of the appropriate charge fixed by the Treasury.[1]

1   Criminal Procedure (Scotland) Act 1995, s 94(a).

2.17   Appeals against sentence only

The only procedure by which a person may appeal against a sentence passed on conviction on indictment is that prescribed in the

Criminal Procedure (Scotland) Act 1995, Part VIII and the Act of Adjournal (Criminal Procedure Rules) 1996. There is no right of appeal against any sentence fixed by law – but see 2.02 above.

2.18 Note of appeal: form; timing; content

The first step in taking an appeal against sentence only is to lodge with the Clerk of Justiciary within two weeks of the passing of the sentence in open court a written note of appeal. The two-week period may be extended at any time by the High Court.[1] The written note of appeal should also be in the form prescribed Form 15.2-B. The procedural requirements are effectively the same as in appeal against conviction: see 2.12 above.

1   Criminal Procedure (Scotland) Act 1995, s 111.

2.19 Stating and amending the grounds

As the note of appeal is the principal document that the appellant places before the appeal court when the appeal is against sentence alone, it is important that it should contain properly and fully formulated grounds of appeal. But as the convicted persons often obtain the forms direct from the prison authorities, complete them without legal advice and cause the completed forms to be sent direct to the Justiciary Office, the grounds of appeal are often badly stated. A solicitor who is instructed to act for a person who has already completed and sent Form 15.2-B himself should, at the earliest possible moment, take steps to ensure that, if necessary, amended grounds are presented in place of those contained in the Form 15.2-B that the prisoner has caused to be lodged. In practice, when an appeal form is sent direct from a convicted person who is in prison the Justiciary Office sends a copy of that completed form to the agents who acted for him in the proceedings giving rise to the appeal. . This procedure allows the grounds to be amended and properly stated at an early stage. If amended grounds are submitted promptly by agents the amended grounds are simply substituted for those submitted by the convicted person.

2.20 Written presentation of appeal against sentence

As in the case of an appeal against conviction, the appellant has the right to present his argument orally or in writing. There are no special considerations affecting appeals which are taken against sentence alone. Accordingly the considerations discussed at 2.13 above apply.

2.21 Record of Proceedings

In some, but not all, cases on appeal against sentence alone a transcript of the proceedings is available. In those cases in which the trial judge's charge to the jury is before the appeal court the transcript of the whole proceedings in relation to sentencing, in so far as it was completed on that one occasion, will be before the appeal court. But if sentence is deferred for any reason there will usually be no transcript of the proceedings at the deferred diet. Nor will there be a transcript of proceedings at a diet under the Criminal Procedure (Scotland) Act 1995, section 76 at which an accused pleads guilty. In practice, the appeal court seldom orders a transcript of the record of proceedings in relation to sentence-only appeals. It would not be incompetent to seek to lay such a transcript before the appeal court or for the appeal court to require one if the High Court thought that an examination thereof would be of assistance to the appeal court; but this is virtually unknown in practice.

2.22 Appeals against both conviction and sentence

The methods and forms of appeal which apply to appeals against both conviction and sentence, in indictment cases, are the same for most practical purposes as those which apply to appeals against conviction. Reference should be made to 2.03 to 2.09 above for descriptions of the relevant methods and Forms. A person who has appealed against both conviction and sentence may abandon the appeal in so far as it is against conviction and may proceed with it against sentence alone.[1] Form 15.6 specifically allows for this. An appellant can use Form 15.6 to abandon his appeal against sentence while proceeding with his appeal against conviction.

1 Criminal Procedure (Scotland) Act 1995, s 116(2).

2.23 Other appealable orders

In addition to the more familiar sentences, namely the imposition of a fine, of imprisonment or detention, the giving of an admonition or an absolute discharge, the making of a probation order, community service order or restriction of liberty order[1] or orders for the forfeiture of property there are other less common orders which are appealable by note of appeal in the same manner as ordinary sentences. They are:

(1) recommendations as to the minimum period which should elapse before the Secretary of State releases on licence a person convicted of murder: Criminal Procedure (Scotland) Act 1995, section 205(4);

(2) hospital orders, interim hospital orders, guardianship orders or orders restricting discharge: sections 58–60;

(3) disqualification from holding a driving licence: e g ss 248–248C;

(4) compensation orders: ss 249–253;

(5) recommendations for deportation[2];

(6) a confiscation order under Part I of the Proceeds of Crime (Scotland) Act 1995 made in relation to a drug-related offence;

(7) statutory disqualifications: several statutes empower courts to declare persons convicted of statutory offences to be disbarred or temporarily disqualified from holding or continuing to hold certain permits or licences or from entering certain licensed premises without the express consent of the licensee.

(8) an 'order' subjecting a person convicted of a sexual offence to notification requirements under Sch I to the Sex Offenders Act 1993.[3]

1 Recently introduced: see Criminal Procedure (Scotland) Act 1995, s 245A.
2 Immigration Act 1971, s 6; and CP(S)A 1995, s 132; cf *Caldewei v Jessop* 1991 SCCR 323.
3 See *MacPherson v Gilchrist* 2000 SCCR 477.

2.24 Appeals in respect of contempt of court

There is no appeal to the High Court of Justiciary against a sentence imposed for contempt of court in civil proceedings.[1] The remedy in such a case must be sought in the Court of Session. If a contempt finding is made in criminal proceedings the appeal must go to the High Court. The Criminal Procedure (Scotland) Act 1995, section 130 provides that it shall not be competent to appeal to the High Court by bill of suspension against any conviction, sentence, judgment or order pronounced in any proceedings on indictment in the sheriff court. It was formerly held competent to proceed by way of bill of suspension to the High Court against a sentence of imprisonment imposed by a sheriff, during the course of a jury trial, on a witness whom he held guilty of contempt of court for prevarication.[2] That decision was overruled by a bench of five judges in *George Outram & Co Ltd v*

Lees.[3] Application to the High Court of Justiciary by petition to the *nobile officium* is the appropriate method of appealing in such circumstances. This method was held to be competent in the case of two Crown witnesses who, having been cited to give evidence at a trial in the High Court of Justiciary, entered the witness box but refused either to take the oath or to give evidence.[4] They had been detained in custody till the conclusion of the trial when they were brought before the presiding judge and sentenced to three years' imprisonment each.[5] An accused person may also be found guilty of contempt of court, e g by swearing at witnesses or at the judge or refusing to leave his cell or to plead when brought to court.[6] In a solemn case, if the accused has not been convicted of any charge contained in the indictment but is found guilty of contempt, the only appropriate method of appealing would be by petition to the *nobile officium*. Although the definition of sentence in section 307(1) appears to have the effect that the provisions of section 106 do not apply to any sentence passed for contempt of court, it is not unlikely that the court, when hearing an appeal against sentence, would hear submissions about any additional penalty imposed on the appellant for contempt if the matter has been raised in the note of appeal and has passed the sifting process.

1   *Cordiner, Petitioner* 1973 JC 16.
2   *Butterworth v Herron* 1975 SLT (Notes) 56.
3   1992 SCCR 120.
4   *Wylie v HM Advocate* 1966 SLT 149.
5   The maximum period is now two years: Contempt of Court Act 1981, s 15(2).
6   *Dawes v Cardle* 1987 SCCR 135.

2.25   Leave to appeal – after conviction

This whole matter is fully discussed in 1.14 to 1.24 above.

2.26   Grounds of appeal

In Chapter 7 consideration is given to the meaning of the term 'miscarriage of justice'. The term 'grounds of appeal' is used in this text to describe the detailed criticisms which are specifically related to the particular appeal. The expressions 'ground of appeal' and 'ground' were used in the Criminal Appeal (Scotland) Act 1926.[1] Thus the High Court was directed (subject to a proviso) to allow the appeal 'if they think that the verdict of the jury should be set aside on the ground that it is unreasonable or cannot be supported having regard to the evidence, or that the judgment of the court before whom the appellant was convicted should be set aside on the ground of a wrong decision of any question of law or that on any ground there was a mis-carriage of justice'. The word 'ground' was virtually synonymous with 'basis'. The words 'grounds of appeal' have changed their context in the more recent statutory provisions, but not their meaning. The grounds of appeal, therefore, consist of specific and distinct statements of the particular criticisms of the conviction or sentence that the appellant intends to present at the oral hearing of the appeal. All the grounds of appeal should be stated at the same time in Form 15.2B. Each ground should be fully and separately stated.[2] Fresh evidence as the basis of appeal is considered in chapter 7.

1   ss 1 and 2.
2   Criminal Procedure (Scotland) Act 1995, s 110(3).

2.27   Specifying the grounds

The best guide as to how *not* to frame grounds of appeal is that contained (expressly and by inference) in the High Court of Justiciary Practice Note of 29 March 1985. It is in the following terms:

'29 March 1985
Appeals in solemn procedure and appeals against sentence in summary procedure
   All too often the time of the appeal court is wasted, and proper disposal of appeals is hampered, where the grounds stated in notes of appeal are wholly unspecific. In appeals against conviction, for example, it is common to find grounds stated thus:
(i) "Misdirection" without any specification whatever;
(ii) "Insufficient evidence" without any specification of the particular point, if any, which is to be taken, e g the absence of corroboration of evidence identifying the appellant as the perpetrator of the crime, or an alleged insufficiency of evidence to establish that the crime libelled, or a crime within the scope of the libel, was committed;
   In appeals against sentence, for example, the ground of appeal is more often than not equally uninformative, e g "sentence excessive in the circumstances" or merely "severity of sentence". No hint is given of the circumstances to be relied on and it often happens that at the hearing the court is told of allegedly relevant circumstances which, it is said, were not before the judge or sheriff or which, it is said, the judge or sheriff ignored.
   It will be appreciated that the consequence of the statement of unspecific grounds of appeal is that the trial judge or sheriff is unable to

report upon them, and the appeal court is at a grave disadvantage in preparing for and hearing appeals without the benefit of the observations of the trial judge or sheriff upon the proposition which the appellant submits to the court without notice.

This practice note is intended to remind practitioners that grounds of appeal must be stated with sufficient specification to identify the particular criticism of the conviction or sentence which the appellant hopes to present at the hearing. In the case of notes of appeal lodged after the issue of this practice note the appeal court may be expected, save in exceptional circumstances and on cause shown, to refuse to entertain any appeal upon any unspecific ground.'

2.28 Criticism of unspecific grounds

The practice note reflects the concern of the court, repeatedly expressed,[1] that adequate notice of the points to be argued must be given in the note of appeal. This has now become of the utmost importance because of the need to obtain leave to appeal, as fully discussed in chapter 1. In *Moffat*, simply because of the seriousness of the consequences of the conviction under review (18 years' imprisonment for each of two accused) the court entertained submissions that went beyond the stated grounds of appeal but added, 'the tabling of stated grounds of appeal does not open the door to a free for all'. The court has also[2] criticised the practice of including in the note of appeal grounds of appeal which are departed from at the start of the hearing. It was stated[3] that, 'Since the judge's charge should now be available timeously, practitioners have a professional responsibility to see that criticisms of a judge's charge can be read out of the charge and do not stem from recollections which can be imperfect and unjustified'. To make unchecked and unwarranted criticisms of a judge's charge was said to constitute 'an unwarranted public criticism of the judge's professional competency and result in a waste of time and money'. These observations are still apt even although leave to appeal has to be sought.

1 E g *Moffat v HM Advocate* 1983 SCCR 121.
2 *McAvoy v HM Advocate* 1982 SCCR 263.
3 *McAvoy v HM Advocate* 1982 SCCR 263, 271.

2.29 Framing grounds of appeal – general

From some examples quoted in some detail in chapter 7 it is clear that the characteristics of a well-drawn ground of appeal are as follows:

Accuracy: any description of events or quotation from the proceedings should be accurate.

Stateability: if the ground of appeal is stateable, that is enough. Of course frivolous points should not be advanced and are unlikely to pass the sifting process; but it is bad advocacy to advance only those submissions which are bound to succeed. Between the frivolous and the unanswerable lies an unmapped territory in which knowledge of the law, experience, instinct and good judgment are the only guides.

Clarity: the ground should be clearly stated in language as simple and non-technical as can be achieved.

Brevity: the purpose of a ground of appeal is to give written notice of the point to be argued, not to argue the point in writing. The ground should be stated as shortly as is consistent with giving full notice of the circumstances said to have caused a miscarriage of justice. However, as it is important now to demonstrate that the points are arguable, the tendency has been to state the ground more fully than in the past, and to refer to relevant authority. Unnecessary repetition should be avoided, although it may be necessary where, for example, one error gives rise to several distinct grounds of appeal, e g (a) that the judge allowed the jury to hear inadmissible evidence; (b) that he later misdirected the jury by telling them they could take it into account; and (c) that without the inadmissible evidence there was insufficient evidence in law to support his conviction.

Explanatory: if the appellant's advisers intend to draw attention to a particular case or statutory provision it is helpful to give its reference. Similarly, references to pertinent parts of the charge or other written material can assist the court to focus more swiftly on the true issues.

Responsibility: those who frame grounds of appeal and present them and submissions in support of them have a responsibility not just to the appellant, but also to the appeal court, the court of first instance and, in some cases, to persons such as other accused or witnesses or court staff: grounds of appeal should not cast imputations upon the character or conduct or professional competence of others without a solid justification. Those who frame grounds of appeal are professionally responsible for their contents.

2.30 Late amending of the grounds of appeal

The written note of appeal, whether against conviction or sentence or both, must, as already noted, contain a full statement of all grounds of appeal.[1] It is not competent for an appellant to found any aspect of his appeal on a ground which is not contained in the note of appeal unless on cause shown he obtains the leave of the High Court[2]. In the case of an appeal against conviction the appellant and his advisers will have had six weeks or more to consider and frame the grounds of appeal and will have had adequate opportunity to study a transcript of the charge to the jury. In practice, the six week period allowed for lodging grounds of appeal against conviction[2] is split up by the Justiciary Office into the 'first' and 'second' three-week periods, in terms of the power contained in section 110(2). The second three-week period does not start to run until the transcript of the judge's charge has been obtained. The Justiciary Office then sends the appellant, or his solicitor, a letter with copies of the indictment proceedings and charge, giving a date some three weeks ahead on or before which the note of appeal (Form 15.2-B) must be lodged. That period may be further extended by the High Court if good grounds are presented to it for so doing.[3] Upon receiving the note of appeal the Clerk of Justiciary immediately takes steps to intimate the grounds to all the interested parties, including the trial judge and the Crown Agent, and gives notice to the Secretary of State if the appellant is in custody.[4] and to obtain the judge's report. He sends a copy of the note of appeal to the Crown Office, to the Legal Aid Board and to the Criminal Records Office. If the note of appeal has come direct from prison, a copy is sent to the solicitor who acted for the appellant with a standard letter asking if he still acts for the appellant; this gives the solicitor an opportunity to substitute amended grounds for those prepared by the convicted person. If the note of appeal comes from a solicitor, copies are sent to the prison where the appellant is detained. The judge who presided at the trial must furnish a report to the Clerk of Justiciary 'as soon as is reasonably practicable'.[5] In practice, if the report is not received within three or four weeks the Justiciary Office will take steps to see that the report is prepared. The High Court can order the report to be furnished or, if it thinks fit, can hear and determine the appeal without obtaining the report.[6] On receiving the report the Justiciary Office sends a copy to the appellant or his solicitor, as well as to the Crown Office. In a case referred under Part XA of the 1995 Act by the Scottish Criminal Cases Review Commission the Clerk of Justiciary sends a copy to the Commission.[7]

1   Criminal Procedure (Scotland) Act 1995, s 110(3)(b).
2   CP(S)A 1995, s 110(1)(a).
3   CP(S)A 1995, s 111(2).

4   CP(S)A 1995, s 110(1)(b) and s 110(6).
5   CP(S)A 1995, s 113(1).
6   CP(S)A 1995, s 113(3).
7   CP(S)A 1995, s 113(2)(c).

EXTENSION OF TIME LIMITS

2.31   The time limits – application for extension

It has already been noted[1] that any period prescribed ·by the Criminal Procedure (Scotland) Act 1995, sections 109(1) and 110(1)(a) may be extended by the High Court. The application form (solemn appeals) is Form 15.2-C which may be signed by the convicted person, or by his solicitor or counsel. The form itself specifies an obvious and necessary requirement of the application, namely that it must state fully the reasons for the failure to lodge the written notice or note within the prescribed time. The application form is checked by Justiciary Office staff to ensure that it has been completed correctly and contains all the relevant information and, usually on the day following receipt (provided it is in order), is put before a single judge of the High Court (normally the bail judge)[2] in chambers together with the indictment, the list of previous convictions and, in High Court cases, the copy book of adjournal. Unless there is some unusual feature about the application the single judge will usually grant it without the need for any appearance by the appellant or his lawyer. The reasoning of the court in *Clayton, Petitioner*,[3] (a summary case), would apply equally to a solemn case; thus even a very long delay in appealing (in that case, nearly two years) may be excused. If the appellant has to be represented, for example because the judge seeks further information or explanation, the appellant may appear personally or by counsel or be represented and appear by a solicitor alone. After the judge has considered the application and decided to grant or to refuse it the applicant is notified of the result on Form 15.3-A. If the application is refused, the Clerk of Justiciary sends with the refusal an application form (Form 15.3-B) to enable the applicant to exercise his right[4] to have his application determined by the High Court as fully constituted for the hearing of solemn appeals. If the applicant does not apply properly within five days, the refusal by the single judge is final.[5] If he duly applies for his application to be determined by the full court he has to state on the form if he desires to be present at the hearing of that application. If he is not to be legally represented he is entitled to be pre-

49

sent at the hearing and does not need leave to be present; if he is to be legally represented at the hearing he is not entitled to be present, unless the court gives leave.[6] If he expressly seeks leave to be present, the Clerk of Justiciary places his request before the High Court in chambers and notifies the applicant of that court's ruling on the matter. As for a full hearing (2.44 below), leave is automatically granted as a matter of course. If (whether with or without leave) the applicant is to be present at the hearing the Clerk of Justiciary must notify (a) the applicant, (b) the governor of the prison in which the applicant is in custody, and (c) the Secretary of State.[7] The single judge who refused the application may sit on the full court.[8]

1   See 2.30 above.
2   Criminal Procedure (Scotland) Act 1995, s 103(5).
3   1991 SCCR 261.
4   CP(S)A 1995, s103(6).
5   CP(S)A 1995, s 105(2).
6   CP(S)A 1995, s 105(3).
7   CP(S)A 1995, s 105(5).
8   CP(S)A 1995, s 105(6).

ABANDONMENT

2.32   Express and deliberate abandonment by notice

An appellant may abandon his appeal by lodging with the Clerk of Justiciary a notice of abandonment (Form 15.6)[1] which must be signed by the appellant himself. He does not need leave of the court to abandon his appeal, but he must be sure to abandon in the manner prescribed by the Criminal Procedure (Scotland) Act 1995, section 116(1) before the case calls in court. If he does so the appeal is deemed to have been dismissed by the court.[2] But the time for lodging the notice ends when the case is called.[3] The court then becomes master of the procedure, and has a discretion to refuse to permit the appeal to be abandoned. It may choose to hear the appeal and even to exercise its powers[4] to increase the sentence appealed against, as in *Grant v HM Advocate*[5] where the sentences appealed against were substantially increased. (There is no such power if the appeal is against conviction alone.) An appellant who has appealed against conviction and sentence[6] (or other disposal) may abandon the appeal against conviction and proceed with his sentence appeal.[7] Section 118(3) allows the court to reduce the sentence if it sets aside the verdict in an appeal against conviction.

1 Criminal Procedure (Scotland) Act 1995, s 116(1).
2 CP(S)A 1995, s 116(1).
3 *Ferguson v HM Advocate* 1980 JC 27.
4 CP(S)A 1995, s 254(3)(b).
5 1985 SCCR 431.
6 'Sentence' includes for this purpose a decision specified in CP(S)A 1995, s 106(1)(bb), namely a decision not to depart from the requirement to impose the minimum sentence prescribed by s 205B.
7 CP(S)A 1995, s 116(2).

2.33 Finality of abandonment

A statutory abandonment is final[1] subject to two possibilities:

(1) the power of the Scottish Criminal Cases Review Commission under the Criminal Procedure (Scotland) Act 1995, Part XA of the 1995 Act, to refer a case to the High Court is not affected by a statutory (or a deemed) abandonment;

(2) it is impossible to rule out an exercise of the *nobile officium* to permit an appeal to proceed after statutory abandonment.[2]

Where the appellant's legal representatives know that the appeal is to be abandoned (in whole or in part) they should so intimate to the Clerk of Justiciary and without delay lodge the notice of abandonment as soon as possible.

1 *Biondi v HM Advocate* 1967 SLT (Notes) 22.
2 *McNab, Petitioner* 1994 SCCR 633.

2.34 Deemed abandonment

If an appellant has lodged a written intimation of intention to appeal but fails to lodge either a note of appeal or an application for extension under the Criminal Procedure (Scotland) Act 1995, section 111(2), the Justiciary Office prepares a letter stating that as no note of appeal has been lodged and no application for extension of time received the proceedings are deemed to have come to an end. Such a letter goes to the Crown Office, the Criminal Records Office, the Legal Aid Board, the prison governor, the trial judge, the sheriff clerk (in the case of a sheriff court appeal) and the convicted person and his solicitor. If that evokes no response from the convicted person the appeal comes to an end. The convicted person may respond by choosing to apply for an extension of time and, if an extension is granted, to present a late note of appeal.

2.35   Abandonment by non-appearance

'Where no appearance is made by or on behalf of an appellant at the diet appointed for the hearing of an appeal and where no case or argument in writing has been timeously lodged, the High Court shall dispose of the appeal as if it had been abandoned'.[1] Accordingly, when an appellant fails to appear, the Advocate Depute will, in the absence of any plausible explanation for the non-appearance, move that the appeal be refused 'for want of insistence' and, if it is appropriate to do so – the appellant being on bail – the Advocate Depute will ask the court to grant a warrant for the arrest of the appellant. As is made clear in *Ferguson v HM Advocate*[2], if a notice of abandonment is not lodged prior to the calling of an appeal when the case calls in the appeal court and counsel seeks leave from the court for the appeal to be abandoned it is open to the court to refuse such a motion and thereafter deal with the appeal; the court then has power to increase the period of imprisonment or vary any other sentence that was imposed in the court of first instance; for although, where an appellant fails to appear personally in court , the provisions of the Criminal Procedure (Scotland) Act 1995, section 112(4*)* allow the court to decline to consider the appeal or to dismiss it summarily, the court also has the power in terms of section 112(4)(b) to consider and determine the appeal or make any other such order as it thinks fit. There are many possible reasons why such a situation may arise. For example, if an appellant has been admitted to bail and has failed to appear, has not managed to notify the reason for that failure to his solicitor or counsel in time for the appeal calling but he has otherwise always obtempered the conditions of bail, counsel may explain to the court his surprise at the non-attendance of the appellant in these circumstances when he has otherwise always attended (e g at consultation) when required to do so, and the court will usually be persuaded to allow the appeal to be continued for enquiry – perhaps until later on the same day – as to why the appellant is not present. If neither counsel nor the appellant is present when the case calls in court that suggests that there has been a breakdown in communication between the Justiciary Office, the Edinburgh agent and the local solicitors in informing them of the date of the appeal. Finally, if an appeal has obvious and substantial merit or raises a point which the court is anxious to deal with because of public interest relating to a particular issue it may continue the appeal for the appellant to be given another opportunity to attend or, as section 112(4)(b) provides, proceed to consider the appeal and determine it.

Although the provisions of section 120(1) appear to be fairly peremptory, when they are taken along with section 112, they give the court flexibility in dealing with the non-attendance of appellants. It must be said, however, that any counsel who has real concerns about the possibility that a sentence might be increased would be well advised to obtain instructions to abandon the appeal before the appeal court sits. To do otherwise is to run a very real risk of the appeal court refusing leave for the appeal to be abandoned and the appellant's sentence being increased.

1   Criminal Procedure (Scotland) Act 1995, s 120(1).
2   1980 J C 27.

2.36   Agents withdrawing from acting

It is open to agents and counsel to withdraw from acting for the appellant. The reasons why that may happen are varied but may include such matters as the appellant's failure to accept certain advice about the progress of an appeal or to accept his lawyers' refusal to advance a ground of appeal that the appellant thinks is of merit. Since the leave to appeal provisions have been introduced the occasions on which agents and counsel withdraw from acting have substantially reduced. This is because, if leave to appeal is granted, legal aid now is almost automatically granted, and if a High Court judge has decided that an appeal is 'arguable' it is very difficult for the appellant's advisers to say that the appeal is wholly without merit. Accordingly it is now recognised that the duty of counsel is to present an appeal where the appellant insists upon it if legal aid has been granted. Although it is usual to support in submissions any ground that has been held to be 'arguable', it is not uncommon for the appellant to accept advice that not all the grounds that have passed the sifting process should be argued. If, however, in an extreme situation, there has been a breakdown of confidence between the appellant and his counsel it is of the utmost importance that both the court and the Crown are informed as soon as possible that counsel is to withdraw from acting. The agent should make arrangements to instruct another counsel immediately. To do this reduces the risk that the court and the Crown prepare for an appeal only to find counsel appearing and indicating that the appeal cannot proceed because he is withdrawing from acting. Such behaviour is disapproved of by the court as it wastes the time of everyone concerned. If the appellant has indicated that he wishes to present the appeal himself, without the benefit of counsel, the court would require to be satisfied that agents have properly withdrawn from acting, notified all parties and given timeous intimation to the appellant in advance of the hearing indicating that he should present the appeal himself. A copy of these letters should be sent both to the Crown and to the Clerk of Justiciary as soon as possible.

The normal and proper procedure to follow is to advise the appellant of the situation as early as possible and, unless he instructs abandonment, then, whether or not he has been told orally, for the solicitor to send him at his bail and/or his last-known address a recorded delivery letter telling him clearly and simply of the situation (and possibly the reasons for it), advising him of the date and place of the diet fixed for his appeal hearing and of his rights and duties in relation to abandonment or to continuing with the appeal in person or instructing new agents and reminding him of his duty to surrender his bail. The appeal court requires to be satisfied that timeous intimation has been given to the appellant so any such letter should be sent as long before the hearing as circumstances allow. A copy of the letter should be sent to the Clerk of Justiciary as soon as possible.

2.37   Consequences of abandonment

If the appeal has passed the sifting process but is later abandoned, or if it is abandoned before a sifting decision is taken to grant or refuse leave, then once it is clear that the appeal has been wholly abandoned the effect is the same as if the appeal has been determined and dismissed by the court. Intimation of the (deemed) dismissal goes to the Crown Office, the appellant's agent, the prison governor (where necessary), the Criminal Records Office, the judge or sheriff and the sheriff clerk (to enable him to release Crown productions). The Clerk of Justiciary checks if the appellant was on bail pending the determination of the appeal. If the appellant was on bail, a warrant is issued to apprehend him and convey him to prison to serve the remainder of his sentence; the warrant can be executed immediately. Thus an appellant on bail who has attended Parliament House on the day fixed for the hearing but chooses to abandon the appeal without going into court can surrender himself to the court (the clerk will provide the form for him to sign) and the warrant can be executed at once. Otherwise the Crown Office receives the principal warrant from the Clerk of Justiciary and a copy of the interlocutor recalling bail. If the ex-appellant is then in custody in connection with some other matter, the principal warrant and a copy of the interlocutor are sent direct to the governor of the prison where the ex-appellant is held.

JUDGE'S REPORT

2.38 Report to be furnished timeously

The judge who presided at the trial leading to the appellant's conviction (or who passed sentence following the appellant's plea of guilty to any charge on indictment) receives from the Clerk of Justiciary a copy of the written note of appeal.[1] It is then his duty to furnish the Clerk of Justiciary with a report in writing giving the judge's opinion on the case generally and on the grounds of appeal contained in the note of appeal.[2] He must furnish his report 'as soon as is reasonably practicable', but this term is not defined. If the Clerk of Justiciary does not receive it within about four weeks, action is taken by him to obtain the report. If necessary, the High Court can order it to be furnished and may specify a period within which that must be done.[3] The judge cannot decline to furnish a report even if the grounds of appeal are inadequate in some way, such as failing to meet the requirements of the Practice Note of 29 March 1985.[4] The Clerk of Justiciary sends a copy of the report to the convicted person or to his known solicitor. A report will be called for in the same way in a case referred to the High Court by the Scottish Criminal Cases Review Commission.[5] The judge's report is available only to the High Court, the parties, and if appropriate the Commission;[6] but copies are in practice made available to those who report proceedings of the High Court and also, if requested, to legal periodicals. There have been recent examples of appeals in which no report has been produced even after many months, and would-be appellants have resorted to petitioning the *nobile officium* in an attempt to obtain the report so as to allow the appeal to proceed.[7]

1 Criminal Procedure (Scotland) Act 1995, s 110(1).
2 CP(S)A 1995, s 113(1).
3 CP(S)A 1995, s 113(3).
4 *Henry v Docherty* 1989 SCCR 426.
5 See Chapter 5, para. 5.30 below.
6 CP(S)A 1995, s 113(2)(c).
7 See Appendix, Style 7.

2.39   The judge must report

The Criminal Procedure (Scotland) Act 1995, section 113 provides that the report has to give the judge's opinion on the case generally and on the grounds contained in the note of appeal. In summary cases, where the trial judge has to draft a stated case and different statutory provisions apply, sheriffs have declined to state a case in circumstances in which the statement of matters which the appellant desired to bring under review disclosed no relevant ground of appeal[1] or failed to specify or focus the issue sufficiently clearly and unambiguously to enable the sheriff to understand what the point of the appeal was.[2] In solemn cases, it is clear that the judgment as to the adequacy of the grounds is one for the High Court to make[3] and the reporting judge must furnish a report, regardless of the judge's opinion of the shortcomings of the grounds of appeal.[4] If he does not report, or prepares and sends what purports to be a report but which the High Court regards as inadequate, he will be required by the High Court to provide a (supplementary) report containing the information which the High Court needs and any other information which the judge considers is relevant to the appeal.

1   *McQuarrie v Carmichael* 1989 SCCR 370.
2   *Durant v Lockhart* 1986 SCCR 23; *Galloway v Hillary* 1983 SCCR 119.
3   *Smith v HM Advocate* 1983 SCCR 30.
4   *Henry v Docherty* 1989 SCCR 426.

2.40   Contents of the judge's report

There are no rigid rules as to the contents of the report. The statutory requirement that it should contain 'the judge's opinion on the case generally *and* on the grounds contained in the note of appeal' itself opens a wide door, despite the circumstance that in solemn cases the jury alone determines all questions of fact, including credibility and reliability.[1] The new provision contained in the Criminal Procedure (Scotland) Act 1995, section 106(3)(b) – which is discussed at 7.28 below – means that, if this ground of appeal is advanced, the judge must comment upon all aspects of the case bearing upon the reasonableness of the verdict. The required comment is likely in many cases to necessitate substantial reference to the evidence, and even the expressing of the judge's views about the witnesses, including their credibility and reliability. But, even under the legislation in force before 1997, there was no barrier to the judge's expressing an opinion on any aspect of the case and indeed – given that he had to give his opinion on the grounds contained in the note of appeal, regardless of his view as to their relevancy – he might have been obliged to do so if a ground of appeal of the kind now authorised by section 106(3)(b) was stated. Thus in *Rubin v HM Advocate,* above, the additional ground of appeal contained the assertion 'That the evidence of the Crown witness number 15 ... was *and is* [emphasis added] so deficient with regard to its character, quality and strength as to render it insufficient to substantiate or materially corroborate the Crown case'. Another appellant had a similarly worded ground of appeal. Such a ground would clearly necessitate some comment on matters of fact and evidence.[2] In *Mitchell v HM Advocate*[3] (and in the later associated case of *Chapman v HM Advocate* (unreported) both trial judges in their respective reports made comment about the evidence. It is clear that, in any particular case, such opinions might assist the High Court to decide if a miscarriage of justice has occurred. If the final judgment about whether or not a miscarriage of justice has occurred is one that has to be made against the whole known background of the case – and it is – then the trial judge's opinion about the quality and coherence of the evidence is a factor, but not necessarily a decisive one, to be taken into account in making the necessary assessment of the quality or sufficiency of the evidence and the reasonableness of the jury's verdict. Comments upon the witnesses are not necessary or appropriate where the issue is purely one of sufficiency.[4]

1   *Rubin v HM Advocate* 1984 SCCR 96.
2   *Rubin* at 103 per the Lord Justice-General.
3   1989 SCCR 502.
4   *Horne v HM Advocate* 1991 SCCR 248 at 253.

2.41   The report and the evidence

The purpose of the report is to assist the High Court to appreciate the background against which the appeal is taken and the context in which the grounds of appeal arise. Clearly this is absolutely necessary at the sifting stage. If leave is granted and the case is put out for hearing, the judges in the appeal court will not have the evidence before them but, at least where an appeal is taken against conviction, they will have a transcript of the judge's charge to the jury. The trial judge in preparing his report should be able to make reference to parts of the charge if there can be found there any account of the evidence or of any other circumstance which is relevant to any ground of appeal. Whatever needs to be added should be added with such economy as the author can command.[1] If one issue in the appeal is the sufficiency of the evidence the High Court will expect to find all the evidence upon which the Crown is able to found referred to in the judge's charge. Thus in *McGougan v HM Advocate*[2] the court expressed surprise that, while the trial judge's report referred to certain evidence in which corroboration might be found, the charge to the jury did not refer to some of that evidence. That, taken along with a misdirection, was enough to persuade the court that a miscarriage of justice had occurred.

1   *Horne v HM Advocate* 1991 SCCR 248 at 252 per Lord Justice-Clerk Ross.
2   1991 SCCR 49 at 53, 54.

2.42   The report and alleged misdirections

As in the case of judges' reports on sentence (cf 2.43 below) the report should be more concerned to explain the circumstances in which the direction complained of came to be given than to justify or defend them. The court of appeal can read what was said to the jury and needs only to be advised fully and accurately as to its context. If the reporting judge considers that the transcript is inaccurate in any material particular he should point out the inaccuracy. If he considers that the alleged misdirection ought for completeness to be considered along with other passages in the charge he should direct attention to them. If he thinks on reflection that the direction given was faulty he may well choose to say so in his report; but unless it is clearly wrong he is perfectly entitled to leave it to the court of appeal to assess the charge as a whole. The real issue is whether or not a miscarriage of justice has occurred; and that is not a matter for the reporting judge to decide.

2.43   The report and sentence

The purpose of the report when dealing with a sentence or order appealed against is to explain why the sentencing judge acted as he did. It is also very important for him to disclose fully, but concisely, what information was placed before him and what representations were made to him, which of these matters he considered of real or of little or of no importance and whether or not he took into account any other circumstance known to him and considered relevant – by him – such as the prevalence of the type of offence in the locality. If he has pronounced sentence immediately after trial and the appellant has also appealed against conviction then the appeal court will have the charge to the jury and also the transcript of the sentencing proceedings. So if, when imposing sentence, the trial judge has publicly and fully explained why he was imposing the sentence imposed, the report may be short and may explain the sentence by reference to the contemporary transcript. It is proper for a judge, who on mature reflection has come to the conclusion that the sentence he imposed was too severe, to say so and to indicate the lesser sentence he now feels he should have imposed.

THE HEARING

2.44   Obligation or entitlement to be present

An appellant who has been admitted to bail and who is at liberty must, unless the High Court otherwise directs, appear personally in court on the day or days fixed for the hearing of the appeal: Criminal Procedure (Scotland) Act 1995, section 112(3). An appellant who is in custody is entitled to be present; but he is not obliged to be present[1] – unless he has been admitted to bail and is back in custody on another matter. The High Court can always excuse attendance.[2] In practice all appellants who are in custody (whatever the reason) are brought to court on the day or days appointed for the hearing of the appeal. Leave to attend is necessary if an appellant in custody wishes to attend any High Court proceedings preliminary or incidental to the appeal itself; but in practice leave is always given and appellants in custody are brought to court for matters not dealt with by a single judge under section 103. If an appellant is in custody, the Clerk of Justiciary, who will have prepared a list of appeals and appellants several weeks before the week in which the appeal is to be heard, notifies all the persons specified in section 117 of the probable date of the hearing. This notification enables the Secretary of State to take the necessary administrative measures to ensure that the appellants will be able to appear and also be able to consult their legal advisers (if any). Appellants appearing from custody must appear in 'ordinary civilian clothes'.[3] Appellants who are neither on bail nor in custody include those who were admonished or given an absolute discharge but are appealing against conviction, persons who received a non-custodial sentence such as a fine, those who have completed their sentences, those on deferred sentence, those who have escaped from custody and those who have died. Appellants who have received a non-custodial sentence are entitled but not obliged to be present and their counsel may present their appeals in their absence.

1   *Manuel v HM Advocate* 1958 JC 41.
2   Criminal Procedure (Scotland) Act 1995, s 112(3) and (4).
3   CP(S)A 1995, s 117(6).

2.45 Transfer of rights of appeal of deceased person

Until 1997, if an appellant died his appeal died with him.[1] Now, in terms of the Criminal Procedure (Scotland) Act 1995, section 303A,[2] where a person convicted of an offence has died any person may, subject to the provisions of that section, apply to the High Court for an order authorising him to institute or continue any appeal which could have been or has been instituted by the deceased. The application has to be lodged with the Clerk of Justiciary within three months of the death or at such later time as the court may, on cause shown, allow. Where the Scottish Criminal Cases Review Commission makes a reference under section 194B the application must be made within a month of the reference.[3] Section 303A provides that the person in whose favour an order under that section is made shall be afforded the same rights to carry on the appeal as the deceased enjoyed at the time of his death. Where the applicant for an order is an executor of the deceased or 'otherwise appears to the court to have a legitimate interest' the court makes an order authorising the applicant to proceed with any appeal that the deceased could have or has taken. Persons who are said to be interested in this matter are the executor of the deceased or people who otherwise appear to the court to have a legitimate interest. Applications are currently before the court in respect of cases in which appellants have died. In one case, *Gormley,* the parents of the deceased, who had been convicted of culpable homicide, were allowed to continue with his appeal against conviction. In their petition they narrated that he had died intestate and without issue.

1   *Keane v Adair* 1941 JC 77.
2   Inserted by s 20 of the Crime and Punishment Act 1997.
3   Criminal Procedure (Scotland) Act 1995, s 303A(3).

2.46 Obtaining of forms

It is important to remember that in terms of the Criminal Procedure (Scotland) Act 1995, section 127 the appropriate forms and instructions in relation to intimations of intentions to appeal, notes of appeal and various incidental procedures under the Criminal Procedure Rules must be made available to any person who demands them, including, in particular, prisoners who are unrepresented. The governor of a prison is required to cause the forms and instructions above referred to to be placed at the disposal of prisoners desiring to appeal or to make any application to the court relating to an appeal. Further the governor of a prison is required, if requested to do so, to forward on the prisoner's behalf to the Clerk of Justiciary any intimation note or notice in respect of an appeal.

3. Appeals by the accused: summary jurisdiction

APPEALS AGAINST SENTENCE

3.01 Right of appeal

Before trial, an accused person upon whom a complaint has been served has a right of appeal (but only with leave of the court of first instance) against a decision of that court relating either to any objection which he has taken to the competency or relevancy of the complaint or the proceedings, or in relation to a denial issued by or on behalf of the accused that he is the person charged by the police with the offence.[1] He may also appeal by note of appeal against the grant of an application under the Criminal Procedure (Scotland) Act 1995, section 147(2) – to extend the 40 days' maximum detention period prescribed by section 147(1).[2] After trial, any person who has been convicted on a summary complaint, whether in the sheriff court or the district court, has the right to appeal to the High Court against the conviction, against the sentence or against both conviction and sentence, but only with leave granted in accordance with section 180 (conviction etc) or section 187 (sentence).[3] His right of appeal includes the right to appeal against any of the various orders that may be made at the time of conviction or sentence (see 2.23 above). As in solemn cases (see 2.01 above), a person who has pled guilty may competently appeal against conviction. The accused's right to appeal to the High Court by bill of suspension against a conviction is preserved to the extent specified in section 191. As to appeal against sentence by bill of suspension, see 3.09 and 3.40 below.

1   Criminal Procedure (Scotland) Act 1995, s 174.
2   CP(S)A 1995, s 147(3).
3   CP(S)A 1995, s175(1): see 1.14 ff above.

3.02 Appeal before trial

The right to appeal before trial in respect of matters of competency, relevancy or the identity of the accused is contained in the Criminal Procedure (Scotland) Act 1995, section 174. The procedure is regulated by the Act of Adjournal (Criminal Procedure Rules) 1996, Rule 19(1) and Form 19.1-A.[1] A plea in relation to such matters may, prior to pleading, be stated by or on behalf of the accused at the first calling of the case whether he is present or absent but legally represented (by counsel or solicitor).[2] Such a plea, if not taken then, may not be taken later, except with the leave of the court; leave may be granted only on cause shown.[3] Leave of the court which has decided the issue raised by such a plea (prior to pleading to the charge) is required for an appeal, and leave must be applied for immediately[4] under section 144 against the decision.[5] Such leave may be granted on the motion of the accused or by the court *ex proprio motu* (i e on its own initiative). If leave is refused, the refusal of leave is not appealable.[6] The appeal must be taken not later than two days after the decision of the court of first instance.[6] If leave is granted by the court, the case cannot proceed to trial at once, as otherwise permitted by section 146(2);[7] the presiding judge may adjourn[8] the case to a diet for trial or some other fixed diet. Once the appeal has been taken, the High Court may postpone the trial diet (if one has been fixed) for such period as to that court seems appropriate, and has a discretion to direct that the whole or any part of that period is not to count towards any time limit applying in respect of the case.[9] If the High Court makes an order postponing the trial diet under section 174(2), with or without a direction, the Clerk of Justiciary intimates to all the persons specified in Rule 19.1(9) of the Criminal Procedure Rules 1996, i e to the appropriate clerk of court, to any accused who are not parties to the appeal, or to their solicitors, and to the governor of any institution in which any of the accused is detained.

1   See 3.03 below.
2   Criminal Procedure (Scotland) Act 1995, s 144 (1) and (2).
3   CP(S)A 1995, s 144(5).
4   Act of Adjournal (Criminal Procedure Rules) 1996, Rule 19.1(2).
5   Without prejudice to any rights of appeal under CP(S)A 1995, s 175(1) (after conviction, but with leave, or acquittal) or s 191 (suspension or advocation).
6   CP(S)A 1995, s 174(1).
7   CP(S)A 1995, s 174(3).
8   CP(S)A 1995, s 174(3) and s 146(3).
9   CP(S)A 1995, s 174(2).

3.03   Appeal procedure (pre-trial)

The procedure governing such an appeal is that prescribed by the Act of Adjournal (Criminal Procedure Rules) 1996, rule 19.1. An accused whose plea to competency or relevancy has been repelled must state to the court which has repelled the plea how he pleads to the charge or charges set out in the complaint before he applies for leave to appeal. If he pleads guilty, he can still competently appeal to the High Court after conviction (by stated case or by bill of suspension): *Harvey v Lockhart*.[1] In this case an appeal was successfully taken by way of stated case even although the appellant had tendered a plea of guilty following the dismissal of his plea to the competency. The court said that it would have been better if leave to appeal had been sought before the plea was tendered. It may, in an unusual case, be necessary where questions of competency and/or relevancy are raised before trial to have them resolved before trial by having a preliminary proof so that a proper basis in fact may be provided for taking the necessary decisions: *MacNeill v Sutherland* (the 'beef on the bone' case).[2] The provisions of rule 19.1 apply expressly only to objections stated to the competency or relevancy; but the Criminal Procedure (Scotland) Act 1995, section 174(1) allows an appeal also against the ruling of the court of first instance in relation to a denial by the accused that he was the person charged by the police with the offence. If leave to appeal is granted, the clerk of court enters the necessary details in the minutes of proceedings. The appeal must be by way of note of appeal in the form of Form 19.1-A. This form needs no explanation, except to note that it does not deal explicitly with an appeal in respect of a ruling against a person whose objection is that he is not the person charged by the police with the offence. However, the necessary details in connection with such an appeal can go under heads (2) and (3). Only two days are allowed for lodging the note of appeal with the clerk of the court that granted leave,[3] subject, however, to the automatic extension allowed by section 194(1) if the second of the two days falls on a Saturday, Sunday or court holiday prescribed for the relevant court. Once the note of appeal is lodged, that clerk sends a copy to the respondent or his solicitor, requests a report from the presiding judge and transmits the note of appeal, and certified copies of the complaint, the minutes of proceedings and relevant documents, to the Clerk of Justiciary. The presiding judge must send his report as soon as possible to the Clerk of Justiciary who furnishes copies to the parties or their solicitors. The Clerk of Justiciary arranges for the appeal court to hear the appeal as soon as possible and it is his responsibility to copy any documents that that court may need. The sheriff or justice who hears a debate on a preliminary plea should reach a conclusion on each and every point debated before him, even if he disposes of the case by upholding only one of the submissions made to him.[4] If he does not decide each point, the High Court may remit the matter to him to deal with the other points. There may, however, be circumstances in which it will be appropriate to reserve a question of relevancy or competency for disposal at the trial.

1   1991 SCCR 83.
2   1998 SCCR 474.
3   Criminal Procedure (Scotland) Act 1995, s 174(1).
4   *MacNeill v Sutherland* 1998 SCCR 474.

3.04   Disposal of the appeal (pre-trial)

Any appeal against a preliminary diet decision may be abandoned at any time prior to the hearing of the appeal.[1] Form 19.1-B should be used. When the minute of abandonment is lodged, the Clerk of Justiciary informs the appropriate clerk of court and the respondent or his solicitor that the appeal has been abandoned,[2] and the procedural process at first instance resumes, as near as may be, just as if no appeal had been taken. In disposing of an appeal the High Court may affirm the decision of the court of first instance or may remit the case to it with such directions in the matter as the High Court thinks fit.[3] In a case where the court of first instance has dismissed the complaint, or any part of it, and a successful appeal is taken by the prosecutor against that decision, the High Court will, if necessary, direct the court of first instance to fix a trial diet. In that situation, the accused will not have pled in common form; but there is no statutory provision requiring that a special diet be fixed to allow him to plead.

1   Act of Adjournal (Criminal Procedure Rules) 1996, SI 1996/513, Rule 19.1(10).
2   Criminal Procedure Rules 1996, Rule 19.1(12).
3   Criminal Procedure (Scotland) Act 1995, s 174(4).

3.05   Appeal after conviction – quorum; methods

The principal method of appeal against sentence alone is by note of appeal (see 3.39 below); but the Criminal Procedure (Scotland) Act 1995, section 175(9) preserves the right of a convicted person to proceed by way of a bill of suspension in respect of any alleged fundamental irregularity relating to the imposition of the sentence. In cases where the sentence is not the only issue, the principal method of appeal after conviction is by stated case. But in some circumstances, discussed below,[1] an accused may choose to proceed by bill of suspension.[2] There are also certain special methods of seeking review, or the like. They are discussed elsewhere. They are (1) petitions to the *nobile officium*;[3] (2) references to the Court of Justice of the European Communities.[4] (3) devolution/human rights issues.[4] The quorum consists of three High Court judges (section 173(1)) or two, if the appeal is taken against sentence only (section 175 (2)(b)) or against an absolute discharge or admonition or any probation or community service order or any order deferring sentence, (section 175(2)(c)) or in relation to any proceeding connected therewith (section 173(2)).

From time to time appeals that may competently be heard by two judges are in fact heard by three, usually for reasons of convenience, or because it has been recognised that a point of general interest may be in issue. A court of two judges may decide to send a case to a court of three judges.[5]

1   See 3.06 ff.
2   Criminal Procedure (Scotland) Act 1995, s 191(1).
3   See Chapter 6.
4   See Chapter 5.
5   *Bain v Wilson* 1998 SCCR 454, a case raising points of competency and statutory construction.

3.06   Choice of method of appeal (against conviction or conviction and sentence)

Although, in some circumstances, more than one method of appeal may be open to a party,[1] usually one method is competent and appropriate and others are not. The Criminal Procedure (Scotland) Act 1995, section 175(5) gives a right of appeal to the High Court, but only with leave granted in accordance with section 180 (conviction etc) or section 187 (sentence etc), to any person who in summary proceedings has been convicted, or found to have committed an offence. The stated case has to be lodged before a decision is made by the High Court to grant or refuse leave to appeal. The appellant may thus bring under review any alleged miscarriage of justice in the proceedings, by applying for a stated case, against conviction alone, or against both conviction and sentence. This right to appeal by stated case is, however, conferred without prejudice to any right of appeal under section 191. Section 184(2), which provides that once the stated case has been lodged with the Clerk of Justiciary[2] the appellant shall be held to have abandoned any other mode of appeal which might otherwise have been open to him, is specifically made subject to section 191, so that, if section 191 applies, this deemed abandonment does not occur. Section 191 allows an accused to appeal to the High Court by bill of suspension against a conviction (which, for this purpose, includes conviction and sentence) on the ground of an alleged miscarriage of justice in the proceedings if an appeal under section 175 would be incompetent or would in the circumstances be inappropriate, for example where the judge in the summary proceedings has died before completing the stated case. If an application for a stated case has already been made and in that application (or in any duly made amendment or addition to it)[3] the same alleged miscarriage of justice is referred to, the appeal by bill of suspension cannot proceed without the leave of the High Court until the appeal by way of application for a stated case has been finally disposed of or abandoned.[4] The effect of these provisions is that, if an appellant raises the same point of alleged miscarriage of justice both in a stated case and in a bill of suspension, the bill cannot proceed (without leave of the High Court) until the stated case has been disposed of, whether by the court[5] or by abandonment by minute.[6] Section 191(4) provides that the provisions of section 191 are to be without prejudice to any rule of law relating to bills of suspension or advocation in so far as such rule of law is not inconsistent with the section. And section 191(4) provides that the provisions regulating appeals shall, subject to the provision of Part X of the Act (Appeals from Summary Proceedings), be without prejudice to any other mode of appeal competent. The result of these provisions is that in deciding which method of appeal to adopt the appellant and his legal advisers have to be familiar with the old (pre-1980) law as well as the current statutory procedures. On the other hand, the preservation of some pre-1980 appeal procedures means that there may be a choice of instruments for raising matters which an appellant desires to bring under review.

1   E g advocation or note of appeal, as in *Lafferty v Jessop* 1989 SCCR 451 – though there was no conviction in this case.
2   Criminal Procedure (Scotland) Act 1995, s 179(9).
3   Under CP(S)A 1995, s 176(3).
4   CP(S)A 1995, s 191(2).
5   CP(S)A 1995, ss 183, 190, 191.
6   CP(S)A 1995, s 184.

3.07   General rule governing choice of procedure

Appeal by stated case is the normal method of appeal by a person who has been convicted in summary proceedings and who seeks to appeal against his conviction on its merits. In *Handley v Pirie*[1] the High Court, though allowing an appeal brought by way of a bill of suspension, said:

'We ... wish to cast no doubt upon the general rule, which will be enforced, that a challenge of a conviction on its merits will, save in exceptional circumstances, only be entertained when the matter is brought before the court by a stated case in which the considered views of the trial judge will be expressed.'

In that case, however, the crucial circumstances were said to be 'instantly verifiable' and the only point to be divided was 'a crisp issue of competency' which could be resolved by applying the terms of the statute to the known and agreed facts and circumstances which were set out in the minutes of procedure. The only point falling to be decided in that case resolved itself into a simple question of law, i e 'Did the trial begin on 3 November 1975 when the accused appeared at the diet ordained for trial and pleaded not guilty or on 28 November 1975, the date to which the trial was adjourned, no evidence having been led after the recording of the plea?' If, as a matter of law, the trial had begun on 3 November it was not in dispute that the conviction could not stand; if the trial had begun on 28 November it was not in dispute that the conviction must stand. Thus neither the facts nor the merits of the case itself were in issue, the trial judge's view of them was irrelevant, and the only 'fact' that needed to be known was instantly discoverable from the minutes of procedure. The general rule clearly enunciated in *Handley v Pirie* is still applicable and any exceptions to it must derive from the statutory provisions referred to. Accordingly, if, for any reason, a convicted person considers that a method of appeal other than by stated case might be adopted, he must decide (1) if appeal by stated case is competent or incompetent, (2) if the alternative contemplated is competent, and (3) (if both methods under consideration are competent) which of them is the more appropriate. In practical terms, appropriateness and competency tend to raise the same or similar considerations.

1   1976 JC 65, 1977 SLT 30 overruled – but not in this respect – by *Ruxton v Borland* 2000 SCCR 484.

3.08   Competency of proceedings by stated case

As stated in the preceding paragraphs, appeal by stated case is competent against conviction or against both conviction and sentence and is effectively the only competent process for reviewing the merits of a conviction. Until he has been convicted, an accused person cannot appeal by stated case. Others, for example witnesses dealt with for contempt, or an accused person acquitted of the charge(s) in the complaint but punished for contempt, or a solicitor found guilty of contempt,[1] have no right to appeal by stated case; the appropriate procedure for them is to raise a bill of suspension. Similarly, if a conviction has been recorded but the whole proceedings have been vitiated by some essentially procedural or jurisdictional flaw and are inept, that matter ought to be brought before the court by bill of suspension. If the whole proceedings are incompetent and, as a result, fall to be treated as entirely null and void, then any acquittal or conviction therein or any sentence pronounced is incompetent. That kind of incompetency has been held to be not properly reviewable by stated case because the essence of the ground of appeal is that what purports to be a conviction (or acquittal or sentence) is in law and in reality nothing of the kind. It is just a sham. The person 'convicted' accordingly does not qualify for the statutory description of 'any person convicted in summary proceedings', because those proceedings were inept, null and void. This was the situation in *MacNeill v MacGregor*.[2] When that case first called in court the accused's solicitor tendered a plea of guilty in the absence of the accused; the plea was accepted and duly recorded and sentence was imposed. On the next day the same solicitor appeared and explained that the plea had been tendered in error. The sheriff allowed the plea to be withdrawn and recalled the sentence. The case thereafter proceeded to trial. It was held that the result of the trial (which was an acquittal) could not be challenged (by the prosecutor) in an appeal by stated case because the trial itself, and indeed everything else that had happened since sentence had been passed on the guilty plea, had been ultra vires and inept. The foundation for a stated case did not exist. But if a stated case has been taken and such a flaw later emerges, the court is likely to entertain and decide the invalidity point.[3] Although, as noted in 3.09 below, procedural irregularities, and other irregular proceedings, including oppression, may be able to be brought under review by bill of suspension, it is usually competent in relation to such matters to proceed by way of stated case following conviction.

1   E g as in *McKinnon v Douglas* 1982 SCCR 80.
2   1975 JC 55.
3   See 6.35 ff below.

3.09   Bill of suspension

'Suspension is a competent method of review, available in summary proceedings only[1] when some step in the procedure has gone wrong, or some factor has emerged which satisfies the court that a miscarriage of justice has taken place resulting in a failure to do justice to the accused': *MacGregor v MacNeill*.[2] This case was the sequel to *MacNeill v MacGregor*;[3] in an appeal brought by bill of suspension after the failure of the stated case, the conviction recorded following the plea of guilty tendered in error was quashed. *Renton and Brown* defines suspension more generally:[4]

'Suspension is a process, restricted to criminal cases, whereby an illegal or improper warrant, conviction or judgment issued by an inferior judge may be reviewed and set aside by the High Court.' If the appellant is detained in custody the process becomes one of suspension and liberation. Suspension is not open to the prosecutor: he proceeds by bill of advocation, or by stated case, or by petition to the *nobile officium*. 'A bill of suspension is particularly appropriate when the appeal is based either on defects which appear on the face of the proceedings themselves or on irregular or oppressive conduct on the part of the judge or the prosecutor'.[5] Thus, more generally, where there has been some material procedural irregularity, some jurisdictional defect or some clear departure from the rules of natural justice or other such circumstance which it appears may have affected the proceedings and resulted in justice not having been done to the appellant, he may competently appeal by bill of suspension against the conviction or purported conviction or against a sentence or purported sentence,[6] or against a warrant or purported warrant.

Suspension is competent, and appears to be the more appropriate form of appeal, where what is suggested is that the summary trial judge should have declined jurisdiction because of some personal connection with the accused or the case and the related principle that justice must be seen to be done.[7] Alleged oppressive conduct by the trial judge can competently be brought under review by bill of suspension.[8] The procedure was properly and successfully used in *Stewart v Lowe*[9] where the sheriff, after trial, convicted the accused without having given the accused's solicitor any opportunity to make submissions. Where there has been a plea of guilty it would be competent, and probably more appropriate, to proceed by bill of suspension, but quite exceptional circumstances would be required to suspend a conviction following upon a plea of guilty.[10]

Procedure by bill of suspension is available only where there is a conviction or sentence to suspend[11] (apart from the exception that exists in respect of incidental warrants, such as search warrants, which do not form part of the case).[12] A decision by the sheriff to allow evidence to be obtained by letter of request or on commission under the Criminal Procedure (Scotland) Act 1995, section 272 is not appealable, either by bill of suspension or by petition to the *nobile officium*, but if it results in unfairness that issue may be raised in an appeal against conviction.[13] It is competent for a convicted person to present a bill of suspension to the High Court if the judge who convicted him cannot sign the stated case because of illness or death and by means of such a bill to bring under review any matter which might otherwise have been brought under review by stated case.[14] If, before the case concludes, the accused seeks to bring under review alleged irregularities in the preliminary stages of a case, being irregularities that seriously put at risk the prospects of there being a fair trial, he may proceed by bill of advocation.[15] There is no time limit for bringing a bill of suspension but it should be done as soon as possible: acquiescence in the judgment complained of may be inferred from undue delay: *Low v Rankine*[16] and *McPherson v Henderson*,[17] in which the imposition of a period of disqualification was challenged by means of a bill of suspension 20 years after the event. The challenge failed on other grounds, but the court appeared to suggest that the appellant might have been barred by acquiescence. What might amount to undue delay is judged in the light of the whole circumstances and any judgment on such a matter is, to some extent, discretionary.[18]

1 *Butterworth v Herron* 1975 SLT (Notes) 56, to the contrary effect, was overruled in *George Outram & Co Ltd v Lees* 1992 SCCR 120.
2 1975 JC 57, per LJC Wheatley.
3 1975 JC 55.
4 para 33.01.
5 Thomson Report (Third Report) (Cmnd 7005), para 9.01.
6 See proviso to the Criminal Procedure (Scotland) Act 1995, s 175(9) (fundamental irregularity).
7 See *Harper of Oban (Engineering) Ltd v Henderson* 1988 SCCR 351; *Robertson v MacPhail* 1989 SCCR 693; and *McPherson v Hamilton*; *Penman v Hamilton* 1990 SCCR 270.
8 See *Kane v Tudhope* 1986 SCCR 161; *Bradford v McLeod* 1985 SCCR 379 (sheriff stating on a social occasion before trial of miners that he would not grant legal aid to miners).
9 1991 SCCR 317.
10 *Pirie v McNaughton* 1991 SCCR 483; *Dirom v Howdle* 1995 SCCR 368. However, see Editor's comments at p 87 in *Harvey v Lockhart* 1991 SCCR 83, an unusual case in which the accused took a plea to the competency of the proceedings, pled guilty when it was repelled, did not then apply for leave to appeal, was sentenced and then successfully appealed by stated case.
11 *Durant v Lockhart* 1985 SCCR 72.
12 Cf *Morton v McLeod* 1981 SCCR 159 at 164, per Lord Cameron, and Editor's commentary in *Durant v Lockhart* 1985 SCCR 72.
13 *Lang, Petitioner* 1991 SCCR 138.
14 CP(S)A 1995, s 176(4).
15 *Durant v Lockhart* 1985 SCCR 72; see 3.12 ff below.
16 1917 JC 39. See also *Love v Wilson* 1993 SCCR 325 and *Storie v Friel* 1993 SCCR 955.
17 1984 SCCR 294.
18 Trotter, *Summary Criminal Jurisdiction* p 66; *Watson v Scott* (1898) 2 Adam 501; *Macfarlan v Pringle* (1904) 4 Adam 403; *Muirhead v McIntosh* (1890) 2 White 473.

3.10   Bill of suspension – style and procedure

The bill is prepared and signed either by a solicitor or by counsel.[1] If the solicitor does not practise in Edinburgh he may (but no longer needs to) appoint an Edinburgh agent to act for him.[2] The signed bill is lodged in the Justiciary Office. An order for service is craved and there may be a crave for interim liberation, if the accused is in custody, or for any other interim order, such as interim suspension of disqualification. The bill is dealt with in the first instance by a single judge. He may, if he thinks the bill discloses no substantial ground, remit the case to a quorum of the High Court who may refuse the bill. In the normal case an order for service will be granted and the bill may be served by any officer of law.[3] The prosecutor is the respondent. Where a bill contains a prayer for interim suspension of any order or for interim liberation, the judge before whom the bill is laid for a first deliverance must assign a diet at which counsel, or a solicitor who has a right of audience in the High Court of Justiciary, may be heard on the interim prayer.[4] The Clerk of Justiciary must forthwith give notice of that diet to the parties.[5] An application to suspend a driving disqualification has to be made by requesting interim suspension in the prayer of the bill: the provisions of the Act of Adjournal (Criminal Procedure Rules) 1996, Rule 19.10 apply. Rule 19.10(4) applies to bill of suspension procedure the main rules, contained in Rule 19.9, applicable to appeals by way of stated case: cf Rule 19.9(2), (8), (9) and (10). The application must be dealt with within seven days. Such matters are dealt with by a single judge whose decision is final. Where a bill of suspension contains a prayer for interim suspension of any order or for interim liberation, the judge assigns a diet to deal with the prayer, and the Clerk of Justiciary gives notice of the diet to the parties.[6] If interim suspension is granted it is not effective until the bill has been served on the respondent, and the complainer or his solicitor has returned to the Clerk of Justiciary the principal bill and first deliverance, endorsed by the clerk of the sentencing court with a certificate that an execution or acceptance of service has been exhibited to him. On certifying the bill, the clerk of the sentencing court must send a certified copy of the complaint and the relative minute of proceedings to the Clerk of Justiciary[7] at the same time as he returns the bill. It is preferable practice to serve the bill and a copy thereof on the clerk of the sentencing court rather than simply attend and hand it in. It is now the practice for the Clerk of Justiciary, when ordering service, to send a copy of the bill to the sentencing judge together with a letter suggesting that he may wish to comment on the terms of the bill. Such comments take the form of a report which is prepared and sent to the Clerk of Justiciary and is used to assist the court in consideration of the bill. It is the duty of the solicitor for the complainer (i e the appellant), or the complainer/appellant himself if not represented, to uplift from the Clerk of Justiciary the complaint, the bill and relative minute of proceedings, to arrange for printing and to return the process to the Clerk of Justiciary not later than seven days before the hearing.[8] In other respects the duties of solicitors, or of party appellants (complainers), are those specified in Rules 19.11, 19.12 and 19.13, discussed at 3.34 below. As with stated cases, the prosecutor, if not prepared to maintain the judgment appealed against, may consent to the setting aside of the conviction. This matter is more fully discussed at 4.15 below. The respondent is not obliged to lodge written answers to a bill of suspension though he may choose to do so.

1   Styles may be found in Trotter, *Summary Criminal Jurisdiction* in Appendix III at pp 537–539. More recent examples are printed in the Appendix, nos 4 and 5.
2   Act of Adjournal (Criminal Procedure Rules) 1996, SI 1996/513, Rule 19.11.
3   Criminal Procedure (Scotland) Act 1995, s 192(5).
4   Criminal Procedure Rules 1996, Rule 19.15. Cf Rule 1.2(1) for wide definition of 'counsel'.
5   Criminal Procedure Rules 1996, Rule 19.15.
6   Criminal Procedure Rules 1996, Rule 19.15.
7   Criminal Procedure Rules 1996, Rule 19.10.
8   Criminal Procedure Rules 1996, Rule 19.12.

3.11   Suspension of warrants and incidental orders

The High Court has power to suspend an illegal search warrant which is *ex facie* valid,[1] but the trial judge cannot do so.[2] An application by bill of suspension (or advocation) to suspend such a warrant is competent both before trial[3] and after trial.[4] The procedure may be used *pendente processu* to challenge as oppressive a warrant granted by a sheriff for the taking of a blood sample (for blood grouping purposes) from an accused person.[5] As in the case of a search warrant, the granting of the warrant can be challenged after conviction.[6] The process of suspension is available to challenge other warrants, such as a warrant to take fingerprints[7] – the procurator fiscal will proceed by bill of advocation, but the same principles apply – a warrant to place an accused person on an identification parade,[8] or a warrant to take a sample of pubic hair.[9] A bill of suspension may still be competent (e g more than 24 hours after the order has been made) to suspend an order made by a court whereby a first offender is ordered to be detained in custody pending the pursuit of inquiries whose purpose is to discover if there is some method of dealing with him other than by imposing a custodial sentence;[10] but the competency of such a bill must now be in doubt, and the correct method of proceeding is by note of appeal presented to the High Court under the Criminal Procedure (Scotland) Act 1995, section 201(4).[11] This can be heard promptly by the bail judge in chambers. Proceeding by bill of suspension would be appropriate for a challenge to an order made in relation to bankers' books.[12]

1 *Bell v Black and Morrison* (1865) 5 Irv 57.
2 *Allan v Tant* 1986 SCCR 175.
3 *Paterson v Macpherson* 1924 JC 38; and *HM Advocate v Gerald Rae* 1992 SCCR 1 (obiter opinion of trial judge) doubted on the Merits in *Birse v HM Advocate* 2000 SCCR 505; cf also *Oldfield, Complainer* 1988 SCCR 371 (bill of advocation) *Mellors v Normand* 1996 SCCR 500.
4 *Bell v Black and Morison* (1865) 5 Irv 57.
5 See *Wilson v Milne* 1975 SLT (Notes) 26.
6 *Hay v HM Advocate* 1968 JC 40.
7 See *Lees v Weston* 1989 SCCR 177.
8 *Currie v McGlennan* 1989 SCCR 466.
9 *McGlennan v Kelly* 1989 SCCR 352 (also a Crown bill of advocation).
10 *Morrison v Clark* 1962 SLT 113.
11 Criminal Procedure (Scotland) Act 1995, s 201(4) applies to both solemn and summary cases.
12 Cf *Jessop v Rae* 1990 SCCR 228 – this was also a Crown bill of advocation.

3.12 Advocation – generally

'Advocation, which is literally the calling up or removal of a cause from an inferior to a superior Court, seems to have been originally not strictly speaking a process of review, but a removal of the cause, at its commencement or during its course, on account of some objection to the jurisdiction of the inferior Judge, or on account of partiality or incapacity on his part, in order to allow it to be proceeded with before the superior Court or before some other tribunal or Judge . . . By degrees advocation came to be used also as a mode of review; as such it is strictly speaking the appropriate remedy for errors committed in the course of and during the dependence of the trial or criminal process, and before final judgment or sentence'.[1]

It was formerly accepted in practice that advocation was the means whereby the prosecutor might seek review, and that an accused would use suspension and not resort to advocation.[2] In 1969, the Lord Justice-General (Clyde) said: 'In modern times this procedure has become very rare, and for practical purposes is really out of date'.[3] In the same case Lord Cameron said: 'The limited sphere of competence of the process of advocation lies in the correction of irregularities in the preliminary stages of a case, though recourse to the process is incompetent until the cause is finally determined, unless in very special circumstances'.[3] Despite these dicta, and despite the provision of various other statutory means of review, the process of advocation has been competently used in a number of cases before the final determination of the cause. In some recent cases the court has taken a very restricted view on the competency of advocation, especially in solemn cases.[4] However it remains competent in very unusual circumstances.[5]

1   *Moncrieff on Review in Criminal Cases* (1877) p 163.
2   See the Thomson Committee (Third Report) chapter 15; see also Trotter, *Summary Criminal Jurisdiction* pp 68–69; Hume ii, 509; Alison ii, 26, para 15.
3   *MacLeod v Levitt* 1969 JC 16 at 19.
4   *HM Advocate v Thompson* 1994 SCCR 40; *Khalid v HM Advocate* 1994 SCCR 47; *McKenna p HM Advocate* 1994 SCCR 51, *McLeay v HM Advocate* 1994 SCCR 116.
5   *HM Advocate v Sorrie* 1996 SCCR 778.

3.13   Advocation by accused

It is now clear that advocation is still available in summary criminal proceedings *pendente processu* (i e before the verdict) to enable an accused person to challenge some procedural irregularity (including any 'order or procedure' in the course of a trial or criminal process in an inferior court)[1] which threatens to deprive him of a fair trial. There must be an act or decision of the court itself which can be made the subject of review: thus alleged oppression by the prosecutor could not be reviewed by advocation[2] In *Durant v Lockhart*,[3] a case had been set down for trial but repeatedly adjourned without the trial being started; the accused took a bill of suspension against the fourth such adjournment and maintained that advocation as a form of review for accused persons was obsolete. In holding the bill of suspension incompetent because there was no conviction or sentence to be suspended, the court, after a brief reference to the history of advocation, concluded that there might be circumstances where procedure by way of advocation would still be open to an accused, and stated:[4]

'Accordingly we conclude that in very special circumstances where grave injustice to an accused would result from an irregularity in preliminary procedure, which injustice could not be reasonably rectified by a bill of suspension brought after the determination of the case, a bill of advocation would be appropriate'.

In *Grugen v Jessop*[5] an accused brought a bill of advocation to bring under review an alleged abuse of process which, it was complained, resulted from a sheriff's decision to continue a partly heard trial for eight days even although the 40-day period[6] had previously expired and had already had to be extended. The High Court dealt with the issue on its merits without suggesting that there was any question mark over the competency of proceeding by bill of advocation in the course of a trial. The High Court took the same approach in *Platt v Lockhart*,[7] raising no issue as to the competency of proceeding by bill of advocation in circumstances in which the accused's complaint was that it was incompetent for a sheriff to allow a new trial to commence against him, the first (partly heard) trial not having been completed owing to the illness of the judge who had been hearing that trial. In *Hoyers (UK) Ltd v Houston*[8] the accused company competently proceeded by bill of advocation, before trial, against an interlocutor and decision of the sheriff allowing an amendment to the complaint by substituting therein the true version of the accused company's name in place of an inaccurate version. The procedure for advocation by an accused person in a summary case is the same as that for a bill of suspension, as described at 3.10 above. A style may be found in *Trotter*, Appendix III, page 539, and more recent examples in the Appendix Nos 1–3. In *HM Advocate v Thomson*[9] it was held that a trial on indictment cannot be interrupted to allow the prosecutor to appeal to the High Court by bill of advocation against a ruling to exclude evidence tendered by the Crown. It was observed, however, that in exceptional cases under the summary procedure, where an irregularity of a procedural nature is alleged at the trial diet, a bill of advocation may be competent while the trial is still in progress.[10] In *Khalid v HM Advocate*[11] a bill of advocation brought to challenge a sheriff's decision to refuse a motion to postpone a trial on indictment was refused as incompetent, it being clear that if the accused were to be convicted he could raise the matter as a ground of appeal. An important test of competency is whether the matter complained of is of such a nature that grave injustice would result to the accused which could not reasonably be rectified by an appeal against conviction.[12]

---

1 Alison ii, 26.
2 *Roselli v Vannet* 1997 SCCR 655.
3 1985 SCCR 72.
4 At 74.
5 1988 SCCR 182.
6 Cf the Criminal Procedure (Scotland) Act 1995, s 147.
7 1988 SCCR 308.
8 1991 SCCR 919.
9 1994 SCCR 40.

10 At 45.
11 1994 SCCR 47.
12 *McKenna v H.M. Advocate* 1994 SCCR 51 (trial on indictment): see the Editor's comments at 54.

3.14 Appropriateness of different methods of appeal

It is clear that circumstances may arise in which it is competent to proceed by stated case but it would also be competent to proceed by suspension or by advocation. The first consideration must be one of timing. In relation to an ordinary trial resulting in conviction and sentence, procedure by stated case or by suspension is not available until the proceedings in the trial court have been concluded. Advocation is available at an earlier stage. If the point to be taken is one that may competently be taken either before or after trial (or even in the middle of an adjourned trial, as in *Grugen v Jessop*),[1] it is a matter of judgment in all the circumstances of the case which method is the most likely to produce the most expeditious result. Thus, for example, the complaint might be that the judge who is to try the case is disqualified by reason of some personal connection with the case or some conduct reflecting on his impartiality – as was alleged in *Bradford v McLeod*:[2] in that case the sheriff attended a social function and it was reported that in the course of a conversation about miners on picket lines he had remarked that he personally would not grant legal aid to miners. On the basis of such a report, agents appearing some months later for miners in a series of trials arising out of picket-line disturbances moved the sheriff to disqualify himself from considering the case. He declined to do so. The convictions of those who were convicted were then quashed on appeal, the appeal having been brought by bill of suspension. Obviously, however, the point, which was known about for some time before the trial, might have been taken before the trial by bill of advocation, if it had been known that the sheriff in question was to preside at the trial. Since 20 May 1999, when the Lord Advocate became a member of the Scottish Executive, with the result that section 57 (2) of the Scotland Act 1998 is applied to his acts, the act of the procurator fiscal in proceeding with the case before the sheriff might have been raised as a devolution issue, under reference to article 6 of the European Convention on Human Rights: cf Chapter 5. Section 6(1) of the Human Rights Act 1998 puts the same restriction on the acts of courts, including sheriffs, with effect from 2 October 2000. The most important rule in making a choice between alternative methods of appealing must be that it is necessary to consider whether or not the point, if not taken at the earliest opportunity, may be lost altogether, in the sense of being regarded as waived by not being taken timeously. This consideration is of vital importance in those cases in which some statutory provision prescribes a point of time (or procedural stage) beyond which the objection cannot be entertained: e g Criminal Procedure (Scotland) Act 1995, sections 72 and 192(3).[3]

1 1988 SCCR 182.
2 1985 SCCR 379.
3 And see Criminal Procedure (Scotland) Act 1995, s 79(1); *HM Advocate v McDonald* 1984 SCCR 229, a solemn case decided under s 108(1) of the Criminal Procedure (Scotland) Act 1975.

APPEALS BY STATED CASE

3.15 Stated case procedure

Any person convicted, or found to have committed an offence, in summary proceedings may, with leave granted under the Criminal Procedure (Scotland) Act 1995, section 180, appeal to the High Court against such a finding or against his conviction or against both conviction and sentence by applying for a stated case. The sections of the 1995 Act governing the procedure in appeals by stated case are those following:

section 175	(right of appeal);
section 176	(manner and time of appeal);
section 177	(procedure when appellant is in custody);
section 178	(preparation of draft stated case);
section 179	(adjustment and signature of case);
section 180	(leave to appeal): cf Chapter 1, paras 1, 14 ff;
section 181	(directions by High Court – if appellant fails to comply with rules);
section 182	(date for hearing; and the powers of the High Court);
section 183	(disposal of the appeal);
section 184	(abandoning, by minute, before lodging the stated case);
section 188	(prosecutor's action to set aside conviction/finding/sentence);
section 190	(disposal where appellant 'insane at the time');
section 192	(miscellaneous, including rule about appellant attending hearing);
section 193A	(applying for interim suspension of sentence).

The Act of Adjournal (Criminal Procedure Rules) 1996 also govern procedure. The principal rules are those contained in Chapter 19 thereof. The following should be noted particularly:

Rule 19.2	(forms for appeals by stated case: Forms 19.2-A,19.2-B, 19.2-C);
Rule 19.4	(extension of time: Form 19.4);
Rule 19.5	(minute for abandoning before lodging case: Form 19.5);
Rule 19.6	(abandoning appeal against conviction, but continuing appeal against sentence: Form 19.6);
Rule 19.9	(applying to High Court to suspend driving disqualification: Form 19.9);
Rule 19.10A	(applying for interim suspension of sentence);
Rule 19.11	(solicitor entering appearance etc);
Rule 19.12	(duty to print and intimate stated case and other documents);
Rule 19.15	(diet for interim suspension);
Rule 19.16	(intimation to sentencing court of result of appeal).

The practitioner would be well advised to refer directly to these statutory provisions in relation to any step which has to be taken and not to rely solely on any summary or paraphrase thereof which appears in this or any other text. In relation to the detailed steps of procedure the text which follows can not take the place of the statutory provisions but may assist the practitioner to obtain easier access to them and see how they are applied in practice.

3.16 Time for applying (section 176)

A stated case must be applied for 'within one week of the final determination of the proceedings'. The convicted person who applies for a stated case is referred to as 'the appellant'. The final determination of proceedings occurs on the day on which sentence is passed in open court,[1] unless sentence is deferred,[2] in which event the proceedings are deemed to be finally determined on the day on which sentence is first deferred in open court.[3] But in either event (sentence passed or first deferred) the final determination is not deemed to occur until the finding and sentence (or order deferred) are entered in the record of proceedings.[4] The one-week period is automatically extended by the Criminal Procedure (Scotland) Act 1995, section 194(1) if the last day of that week falls on a Saturday, Sunday or court holiday (in the convicting court); the period then expires at the end of the next day which is not a Saturday, Sunday, or court holiday in the convicting court. The period of one week starts to run on the day after sentence is passed (or deferred) and entered in the record of the proceedings.[5] The application must be in the hands of the clerk of court within the week; mere posting within the week is not enough.[6] Only the High Court has a discretion to decide that a further period of time may be afforded to the applicant[7] who must apply in writing to the Clerk of Justiciary, stating the grounds for the application, all in accordance with the requirements of section 181. Notification of the application must be made by the appellant or his solicitor to the clerk of the court from which the appeal is taken. That clerk must thereupon transmit the complaint, documentary productions and any other proceedings in the cause to the Clerk of Justiciary.[8] The High Court disposes of an application for further time to comply (section 181(3)) in the same manner as it deals with bail appeals but it may dispense with a hearing: it almost invariably does.

1 Criminal Procedure (Scotland) Act 1995, s 194(3).
2 Cf CP(S)A 1995, s 202.
3 CP(S)A 1995, s 194(3).
4 *Tudhope v Campbell* 1979 JC 24; *Williams v Linton* (1878) 6 R(J)12: see also CP(S)A 1995, s 167(2).
5 *Hutton v Garland* (1884) 5 Couper 274; *Smith v Gray* 1925 JC 8 at 12, per Lord Anderson.
6 *Elliot, Applicant* 1984 SLT 294.
7 CP(S)A 1995, s 181(1).
8 CP(S)A 1995, s 181(2).

3.17 The manner of applying (section 176)

The application, signed by the appellant or his solicitor, should be in the form prescribed by the Act of Adjournal (Criminal Procedure Rules) 1996, Form 19.2-A. It must be lodged with the clerk of the convicting court;[1] and the appellant must, within the same one-week (or extended) period, send a copy to the respondent or the respondent's solicitor. The clerk of court enters in the record of proceedings the date when the application was lodged with him.[2] The appellant has the right to amend any matter stated in the application or to add new matters. He effects such amendment or addition to the terms of the application by intimating in writing to the clerk with whom the application was lodged and must intimate any such alteration to the respondent or the respondent's solicitor.[3] The period allowed for such alteration or addition, after lodging the initial application (unless it is extended by the High Court under the Criminal Procedure (Scotland) Act 1995, section 181), is approximately five weeks. The actual period allowed for alteration/addition, after lodging the initial application, comprises (1) the two weeks or thereby between the lodging of the application and the issue of the draft stated case, plus (2) the three-week adjustment period allowed by section 179(1)), plus (3) an extra day or so, if appropriate, automatically allowed by section 194(1), plus (4) any extension allowed by the sheriff principal.[4]

1   Criminal Procedure (Scotland) Act 1995, s 176(1).
2   CP(S)A 1995, s 176(2).
3   CP(S)A 1995, s 176(3).
4   CP(S)A 1995, s 194(2).

3.18   The content of the application

The written application[1] must contain a full statement of all the matters which the appellant desires to bring under review and, where the appeal is also against sentence, or disposal or order, the ground of appeal against that sentence or order.[2] Clearly, if the appellant desires to bring under review particular points bearing upon sentence (being points upon which the sentencing court should have the opportunity to comment) they must be included and specified in the full statement; it is not enough merely to state (in the words of the form): 'The appeal is also against sentence.' Nor is it enough to write something such as 'sentence too severe for the crime that I committed'.[3] The matters to be brought under review should, if possible, be distinctly specified in separate paragraphs. It must be emphasised that this document is of great importance when the application for leave to appeal is being considered. The High Court will not normally entertain an appeal on a matter not referred to on the application for a stated case, even if there might be enough in the case as stated to show that another matter might have been raised.[4] The application will have provided the basis for the stated case itself; and it will be considered by any sifting judge who has to decide, for leave purposes, if the case is arguable. This is a further reason for stating the distinct grounds in separate paragraphs: leave to appeal may be granted in respect of all, none or some of the grounds. As Form 19.2-A indicates, the appellant should also use that form to crave the court for bail, for interim suspension of an order for disqualification imposed under the Road Traffic Acts, for interim suspension of sentence under section 193A, or for any other interim order in terms of the Criminal Procedure (Scotland) Act 1995, section 177(1). This section refers to bail, sist of execution and 'any other interim order', including an order for disqualification, for forfeiture, or imposing a disability, or ordering the destruction of some item.[5]

1   Act of Adjournal (Criminal Procedure Rules) 1996, Form 19.2-A.
2   Criminal Procedure (Scotland) Act 1995, s 176(1).
3   *Henry v Docherty* 1989 SCCR 426 where it was emphasised that the High Court might refuse to entertain such an appeal: see also 3.19 below.
4   *Walton v Crowe* 1993 SCCR 885.
5   See e g CP(S)A 1995, s 193.

3.19   The statement of matters for review

The requirements in the Criminal Procedure (Scotland) Act 1995, section 176(1)(b) are that the statement should be full and be a statement of all matters which the appellant desires to bring under review and, where appropriate, the ground of appeal against any sentence or order appealed against. It is not competent for an appellant, without leave of the High Court on cause shown, to found any aspect of his appeal on a matter not contained in his application under section 176(1), or in a duly made amendment or addition to that application.[1] This, however, is now subject to the consideration that under section 180(1)(a) and 180(5)(a) the judge(s) considering the application for leave to appeal – commonly referred to as the 'sifting' judges – may make comments in writing. If the comments identify what amount to arguable grounds of appeal those grounds so specified may be argued even although they were not contained in the stated case. The Act of Adjournal (Criminal Procedure Rules) 1996, Rule 19.18 allows the sifting judge, before deciding to grant or refuse leave, to remit the case to the judge at first instance for a report or supplementary report. Accordingly, if the sifting judge is minded to specify as arguable a ground of appeal not contained in the stated case, he can remit for such a report if he thinks that it may shed light on the point that has occurred to him. This is the time to do it, because the power of the sifting judge to remit for report expires when he grants or refuses leave. The High Court itself can always remit for such a report; but greater delay is likely to be caused if the decision to seek an additional report is not taken until the High Court comes to deal with the appeal In *MacLean v Mackenzie*[2] the court allowed the (party) appellant to raise an issue not raised in the stated case: exactly why is not clear, but it appears that the magistrate had acted ultra vires. If a new point does arise at the hearing, including a point raised by the Crown or by the court, and it is recognised as being likely to succeed, as in *Aitken v Lockhart,*[3] the court is more readily persuaded to entertain it. The Practice Note of 29 March 1985[4] applies in terms only to appeals in solemn procedure and appeals against sentence in summary procedure. However, the same general principles apply to the statement of matters which an application for a stated case has to contain.

Section 110(3) of the 1995 Act, dealing with solemn appeals, also contains a requirement for 'a full statement of all the grounds of appeal'. In both solemn and summary appeals the principles are applicable at the sifting stage, although they might be less strictly applied if the sifting judges consider that 'arguable' grounds have been disclosed but are inadequately expressed. However, no appellant should take the risk and hope that the sifting judges will fill any gaps he has left. If the matters to be brought under review are not sufficiently specified, the trial court may be unable to report upon them and the appeal court will be put at a grave disadvantage. The Crown may well found upon the same circumstances as causing an inexcusable disadvantage to the Crown. These considerations are relevant to the basic issue that the sifting judges have to decide: whether or not 'arguable' grounds of appeal are disclosed by the documents specified in section 180(2). In an extreme case, the sheriff, or justice, is entitled to refuse to state a case (cf *Dickson v Valentine*),[5] though he may not refuse to do so on the ground that the matter which it is desired to raise is not relevant, because that is for the High Court to decide.[6] In *McQuarrie v Carmichael*[7] the sheriff declined to state a case but simply wrote a short note asserting (correctly, as the appeal court acknowledged) that the matter desired to be brought under review was not a matter that could be brought under review in a stated case (i e the truthfulness of witnesses). The court, agreeing with the sheriff, said that he could not be compelled to state a case upon a clearly unstateable, i e obviously irrelevant, ground. In *Dickson v Valentine* the sheriff – although not obliged to state a case because of the unspecific character of the matter ('the sheriff erred in law') – in fact stated a case: in the circumstances, the appeal court entertained the appeal, and refused it. It is a matter of degree, but in doubt the sheriff or justice should state a case as fully as he can. An extreme example, in a solemn case,[8] of a refusal by the High Court to accept an inadequately stated ground of appeal is *Mitchell v HM Advocate*[9] where, despite the fact that the appellant had been convicted of murder at a trial in which he pled diminished responsibility, the High

Court, referring to the Practice Note of 29 March 1985, refused to entertain an appeal upon a ground stated as follows: 'The learned trial judge rehearsed incorrectly the crucial evidence of the psychiatric witness and in so doing misdirected the jury.' The court regarded that as entirely lacking in specification and refused the appellant's motion to adjourn the case. In *Anderson v McClory*[10] the court, accepting the Crown's submission, declined to entertain an argument that a police request to a motorist to provide a specimen was not in accordance with section 7(1)(b) of the Road Traffic Act 1988, the only matter raised in his application being whether, as on the facts stated, the sheriff was entitled to convict the accused on charge (2).

What is necessary is that the statement should explain in some detail what it is that the appellant is seeking to bring under review so that the court when stating the case can be in no doubt as to what the particular issue is: *Durant v Lockhart*.[11] Accordingly, if, for example, the point which it is desired to raise is a point as to sufficiency of evidence, it is not enough just to say 'The evidence was insufficient to justify conviction'. The particular alleged weakness must be identified in such a way that the inferior court can state in the findings in full all matters relevant to the point which is to be taken. In *Durant v Lockhart*,[11] the point which it was desired to raise was whether or not it was necessary to adduce certain additional evidence to buttress, and thus to enable the Crown to depend upon, a statutory presumption contained in the Gas Act 1972, i e. that proof of one state of facts 'shall be *prima facie* evidence of' [the facts necessary to establish guilt]. What, therefore, should have been put into the application was some such form of words as: 'The provision as to "*prima facie* evidence" contained in the Gas Act 1972, Schedule 4, paragraph 20(3), did not, without additional evidence, provide sufficient evidence to infer guilt: there was no other sufficient evidence to establish guilt.'

It is equally to be stressed that the point must be stated clearly and unambiguously.[12] It is not possible to spell out any more general rule or statement of what section 176(1)(b) requires: see e g *MacDougall, Petitioner*[13] where, although the ground was misconceived, the court held that the sheriff should have stated a case, and remitted to him to do so. In an exceptional case where the temporary sheriff completely and finally failed to state a case, the court, dealing with the matter by way of bill of suspension, in effect stated a case itself and posed and answered the necessary question.[14] As the considerations which apply in framing 'a full statement of all matters which the appellant desires to bring under review' (section 176(1)(b)) are effectively the same as those that apply to 'a full statement of all the grounds of appeal' (section 110(3)), reference should be made to the treatment of grounds of appeal in solemn cases in chapter 2.[15] The parties should propose the questions which are to be submitted for the opinion of the court. In certain instances, if this is well done, nothing more may be required in order to satisfy the requirement (on the appellant) of making a full statement of the matters he desires to bring under review: see 3.25 below. If an applicant for a stated case lodges an application which the court regards as not falling within the statute, the court's refusal to state a case disposes of the matter. It may still be possible to raise the matter as a devolution issue: cf 5.01 ff below. If the seven-day period has not expired it is competent to submit another application and, if it meets the statutory requirements, the court must state a case.[16] In *Galloway v Hillary*[17] the sheriff allowed a timeous, but insufficient, application to be amended after the expiry of the seven days: this seems a sensible way to proceed, though its competency might be open to question.

1 Criminal Procedure (Scotland) Act 1995, s 182(3).
2 1986 SCCR 482.
3 1989 SCCR 368.
4 Cf 2.03 above.
5 1988 SCCR 325.
6 *McTaggart, Petitioner* 1987 SCCR 638; see also *MacDougall, Petitioner* 1986 SCCR 128; *Crowe, Petitioner* 1994 SCCR 748; *Leonard, Petitioner* 1995 SCCR 39; *Reid, Petitioner* 1996 SCCR 830.
7 1989 SCCR 371.
8 The principle is the same in solemn and summary cases.
9 1991 SCCR 216.
10 1991 SCCR 571.
11 1986 SCCR 23.
12 *Durant v Lockhart* 1986 SCCR 23 at 27.
13 1986 SCCR 128.
14 At 2.26 ff.
15 *Brady v Barbour* 1994 SCCR 890.
16 *Singh, Petitioner* 1986 SCCR 215.
17 1983 SCCR 119.

3.20 Interim regulation if appellant in custody

If a convicted person who is in custody appeals under the Criminal Procedure (Scotland) Act 1995, section 176, the court of first instance may do all or any of the following: (1) grant bail;[1] (2) grant a sist of execution; (3) make any other interim order.[2]

The court before which the appellant has been convicted has a discretion to suspend the orders specified in section 193 (disqualification, forfeiture, destruction etc) pending the determination of the appeal. Section 193A allows the court to suspend the whole or any part of a person's sentence. The Act of Adjournal (Criminal Procedure Rules) 1996, Rule 19.10A specifies that this type of application has to be made in the application for the stated case (or the note of appeal, as the case may be). It should be remembered that the appeal may be determined without ever having been called in court: final refusal of leave to appeal 'determines' the appeal.

1 See Chapter 8 ff below.
2 See Chapter 8 below; Criminal Procedure (Scotland) Act 1995, s 176(1).

3.21 Preparation of the draft stated case

The draft stated case must be prepared within three weeks of 'the final determination of the proceedings' (see 3.16 above; the same considerations apply as to when that period starts to run).[1] The three-week period for preparation of the draft stated case may be extended by the sheriff principal for such period as he considers reasonable if a sheriff or justice against whose judgment an appeal is taken is temporarily absent from duty and the court at which the judgment was pronounced is situated within his sheriffdom.[2] The draft stated case must be issued 'forthwith' to the appellant or his solicitor and a duplicate issued to the respondent or his solicitor.

1 Criminal Procedure (Scotland) Act 1995, s 178(1).
2 CP(S)A 1995, s 194(2); Act of Adjournal (Criminal Procedure Rules) 1996, Rule 19.4 and Form 19.4.

3.22 Form of stated case

The stated case (and the draft) must be, as nearly as may be, in the form of Form 19.2-B. It must 'set forth the particulars of any matters competent for review which the appellant desires to bring under the review of the High Court and of the facts, if any, proved in the case, and any point of law decided, and the grounds of the decision'.[1] Form 19.2-B contains, in italics, clear instructions as to the details that have to be filled in. It is not necessary to repeat those instructions here. It is to be noted, however, that it may be necessary to set out not only '*the facts admitted or proved*' as indicated in the form but also a summary of '*the Crown evidence and inferences drawn*' when there has been an unsuccessful submission of no case to answer. Logically the summary of the Crown evidence etc should be presented first. The italicised instructions in the form do not make this clear. It is not normally necessary to narrate in the stated case all the charges contained in the complaint, as the appeal court judges are each provided with copies of all relevant papers, including the complaint.[2] Unless there is some very good reason for it, charges which resulted in acquittal should not be narrated in full. The narration of wholly unnecessary detail suggests that the narrator has an inadequate grasp of what matters. It is, therefore, preferable (unless there is some good reason to the contrary) for the narrative in the stated case to say something such as: 'The appellant faced five charges: (1) assault upon James Smith, (2) assault upon Janet Brown, (3) breach of the peace at the *locus* of the assault in charge (1), (4) vandalism at the same place, (5) a Bail Act offence, all as set forth in the complaint; the Crown asked me to convict the appellant on charges (1), (3) and (4).' 'Findings in fact . . . ought to be crisp, clear and certain', and not 'a mere recitation of the evidence'.[3] All the facts relevant to conviction must be stated. These include facts established by inferences from primary facts: *Walton v Crowe*[4] And, in a case where an appeal is taken against sentence as well, all facts that bear upon the sentence imposed must also be stated, so that the High Court may understand precisely the basis upon which the sentence rests.[5]

The fullness with which the facts need to be stated depends to some extent upon the terms of the statement of matters lodged by the appellant under the Criminal Procedure (Scotland) Act 1995, section 176(1), including any amendment or addition thereto; but all the relevant facts must be stated. If in the light of the appellant's statement of matters some matters of fact which are germane to the decision(s) are peripheral to the points to be brought under review they should be stated with brevity; but no fact which is material to the result (conviction, acquittal, sentence) can be omitted. All the facts which are important in the light of the matters to be brought under review must be fully stated. 'The findings in fact ought to include all findings of fact made by the sheriff (or justice) and if the court has drawn an inference from the facts, then the inference drawn ought to be recorded as part of the findings in fact.'[6] It is a mistake, therefore, when inferences of fact are made from the primary facts, to confine those inferences to the note, though it is quite appropriate to refer to them there as well: to explain them, for example. They must go into the findings in fact. If the accepted evidence from witnesses A and B is that 'All admirals are sailors', and from C and D that 'X is an admiral', the inference drawn by the court that X is a sailor is as much a matter of fact as any other fact testified to directly by a witness speaking to his own observation. Of course, in a case where the inference is not a necessary or mechanical one (as in the example quoted) the justice or sheriff should (if it is germane to the review matters) explain why he made the inference; but the inference itself, if one is properly made, is always a fact which has its proper place in the findings in fact. A stated case may raise questions which were decided by two different sheriffs, one deciding a preliminary matter of competency and relevancy, the other deciding the case on the basis of the proof.[7]

1   Criminal Procedure (Scotland) Act 1995, s 178(2).
2   *Friel v Initial Contract Services Ltd.* 1993 SCCR 675.
3   *Gordon v Allan* 1987 SLT 400, per LJ-G Emslie.
4   1993 SCCR 885.
5   *Industrial Distributions (Central Scotland) Ltd v Quinn* 1984 SCCR 5.
6   *Mundie v Cardle* 1991 SCCR 118.
7   *Beattie v Tudhope* 1984 SCCR 198.

3.23   The evidence and the facts

The facts are not the evidence. The evidence given on oath may enable the judge to hold facts proved by the evidence; but the facts are effectively a creation or composition of the court, using the material provided by the evidence. Facts may be established in various ways, for example by formal admission or agreement[1] or by inference from other facts or by the effect of a presumption[2] or from judicial knowledge, as well as by the normal method of the court's accepting as a fact that which a reliable witness swears he observed. The Criminal Procedure (Scotland) Act 1995, section 255 (offence allegedly committed in any special capacity – such as the holder of a licence, or as a prostitute) provides an example of a fact being deemed to be admitted if it has been properly averred and has not been challenged by the method specified in the section. Section 258 allows 'uncontroversial evidence' to be treated as conclusively proved if the procedures prescribed by the section are followed.

When constructing or making findings in fact, the decision to hold a particular 'fact' established must be based upon a consideration of the whole evidence bearing upon that 'fact': cf *Jordan v*

Allan[3] in which, although the findings in fact warranted the conviction of failing to stop at a traffic-light controlled junction, the court quashed the conviction because it was not satisfied that the justice had considered all the evidence. In that case, the Lord Justice-General said:[4]

'The difficulty in the case is ... that the justice appears to have made these findings in fact without considering the evidence of the appellant himself, giving an explanation for the manner of, or the timing involved in, the crossing at the junction. The stated case sets out the findings ... and proceeds as follows: "The appellant then gave evidence on his own behalf as follows:" [a summary of the appellant's evidence was then given]. The justice does not say whether he took it into account. He does not say whether he believed the appellant's explanation. He does not say that he disbelieved the appellant's explanation. In that state of play, the findings in fact cannot be treated as the findings in fact made upon the whole evidence, and what we shall do is to answer the question in the case in the negative and quash the conviction'.

White v Allan[5] provides a good example of a wholly *inadequately* stated case. There were no proper findings in fact, merely the narration of some evidence; there were no questions, and the statutory procedures for dealing with proposed adjustments had been ignored. The court allowed the accused's appeal but indicated that such imperfections in the stating of the case would 'normally' have necessitated a remit back to have the case properly stated, as happened in *Ward v Crowe*.[6] Whether a remit would now be the normal course to be followed by the appeal court is doubtful; for the sifting judge has power, under the Act of Adjournal (Criminal Procedure Rules) 1996, Rule 19.18, to remit before deciding whether or not to grant leave to appeal and it should be exercised if the case is wholly inadequately stated. There is, however, no universal rule of law that every relevant piece of evidence must be separately addressed in the judge's note and assessed, weighed and counted.[7] If evidence has been led and it contradicts the evidence on which the finding in fact is based, that evidence should be discussed in the note and the judge should explain why he has chosen the one piece of evidence as reliable and rejected the contradicting evidence. A bald statement of preference may well not be enough. There must be some indication as to the mental process that resulted in the conclusion; there must be stateable and defensible reasons for the choice made.[8] It follows that the findings in fact should not set out the evidence.[9] 'If discussion of evidence is relevant for the purposes of an appeal the place for that discussion is in the note which follows the findings which, upon the evidence, the justice has found himself able to make'.[10] This must be understood subject to section 179(7) (proposed adjustments) – see 3.30 below. Facts bearing upon 'special reasons' for not disqualifying or 'exceptional hardship' which derive from the evidence should go into the findings in fact, if sentence is a subject of review; but all reasoning on such matters belongs in the note.

1 Criminal Procedure (Scotland) Act 1995, s 256.
2 E g as in *Durant v Lockhart* 1986 SCCR 23.
3 1989 SCCR 202.
4 At 203.
5 1985 SCCR 85.
6 1999 SCCR 219.
7 *Mowbray v Guild* 1989 SCCR 535.
8 *Petrovich v Jessop* 1990 SCCR 1; see also *Bowman v Jessop* 1989 SCCR 597 at 598E-F.
9 Cf *Pert v Robinson* 1956 SLT 23, a case under the Summary Jurisdiction (Scotland) Act 1954.
10 *Gordon v Allan* 1987 SLT 400.

3.24 Form of case – when submission of no case to answer

If at the end of the Crown case the defence makes a submission of no case to answer, the submission may be upheld, in which event there will be no evidence led for the defence. Alternatively, it may be rejected and evidence may or may not be led for the defence. If the submission is rejected, a conviction may or may not follow. In *Wingate v McGlennan*[1] the appeal court offered general guidance to inferior courts as to how cases should be stated where submissions have been made in terms of the Criminal Procedure (Scotland) Act 1975, section 345A, now the Criminal Procedure (Scotland Act 1995, section 160 (no case to answer). Three different situations were identified in the opinion of the court and dealt with as follows:

'(1) Where a submission of no case to answer in terms of section 345A [now section 160] has been upheld, and the accused has been acquitted, the Crown may appeal against that decision of the sheriff. In that event the stated case should not contain any findings in fact, but should simply set out the evidence adduced by the prosecution and any inferences drawn[2] therefrom by the sheriff (*Keane v Bathgate* 1983 SCCR 251).

(2) Where a submission of no case to answer in terms of section 345A has been made and has been rejected, the accused may choose to lead no evidence. If the sheriff proceeds to convict the accused in such circumstances, and the accused then appeals against conviction, and the stated

case includes a question asking whether the sheriff was justified in rejecting the submission of no case to answer, the stated case should contain
findings in fact in the usual form. Normally there will be no need for the
sheriff to set out separately the evidence adduced by the prosecution and
the inferences drawn from it because, since no evidence was led by the
defence, his findings in fact must necessarily be based solely upon the
evidence adduced by the prosecution, and must accordingly represent
what the evidence for the prosecution established. The sheriff should,
however, in the note annexed to his findings in fact explain briefly upon
what evidence his findings were based. There may, however, be exceptional cases where questions arise as to whether the evidence led justified
the sheriff in drawing particular inferences and in such cases the sheriff
may require to set out in detail the evidence adduced by the prosecution.
In making the findings in fact, the sheriff may not have accepted all the
Crown evidence, but the court will usually be able to ascertain the evidence adduced by the prosecution from the findings in fact and from
what the sheriff says about the evidence in the note annexed to the findings in fact. If the sheriff has not accepted certain evidence in making the
findings in fact, the accused who is contending that there was no case to
answer cannot be prejudiced if no reference is made in the case to such
evidence. In a case where the accused had led no evidence, the issue
which is raised by the question whether the sheriff was justified in rejecting the submission of no case to answer is virtually the same as that
raised by the question whether the sheriff on the facts stated was entitled
to convict.

(3) Where a submission of no case to answer in terms of section 345A
has been made and has been rejected, and the accused has proceeded to
lead evidence and has thereafter been convicted, he may appeal against
his conviction. If the stated case contains a question as to whether the
sheriff was justified in rejecting the submission of no case to answer, the
stated case will require, first, to set out the evidence adduced by the prosecution and any inferences drawn therefrom and secondly, to set out the
findings in fact which, of course, must be made on the whole evidence
that has been led before the sheriff.[3] As was observed in *Keane v Bathgate*
if the defence has led evidence, findings in fact can be made only by considering the evidence led by the prosecution against any evidence which
the defence has thereafter adduced. In a case where the accused has led
evidence, the question whether the sheriff was justified in rejecting the
submission of no case to answer raises a different issue from that raised
by the question whether the sheriff on the facts stated was entitled to
convict.

Categories (2) and (3) represent exceptions to the general rule that
where a stated case contains findings in fact, it should not set forth the
evidence upon which the findings are based unless there is a question

asking whether there was sufficient evidence to entitle the sheriff or justice to make a specific finding.'

The submissions of both parties on the 'no case to answer' submission should be narrated by the judge and he should indicate his view in relation to them. So in a case[4] where one of the sheriff's questions was 'Was I correct in upholding the defence submission of no case to answer . . . ?' the High Court was unable to answer that question because the sheriff had not stated what those submissions were. A better form of question would be: 'On the evidence narrated did I err in rejecting the submission made in terms of section 160 [in respect of Charge N]?' Form 19.2-B (Form of stated case) has now replaced the form that was in use in 1991. The new form specifically instructs that the Crown evidence must be summarised where there is an appeal against a decision on a submission of no case to answer. It is now easier to see that the instructions in Category 2 are unsatisfactory. It is asserted there that if the sheriff convicts on the basis of the Crown evidence (the accused having adduced no evidence) 'his findings in fact must necessarily be based solely upon the evidence adduced by the prosecution, and must accordingly represent what the prosecution established'. The opinion goes on to say that the sheriff should 'explain briefly' upon what evidence his findings were based. This method of stating the case could make it difficult for the defence – or even the prosecution – to argue properly issues of corroboration and sufficiency of evidence, which usually lie at the root of a no case to answer submission. The better practice now would be to follow the instructions set forth in Form 19.2-B and to 'summarise the Crown evidence and the inferences drawn'. In *Wingate v McGlennan*, the appeal court dealt with three situations. There is a fourth; because the judge may repel the submission, hear evidence from the defence and acquit. In that event, the Crown might wish to appeal.[5] The most appropriate form of appeal is still by way of stated case. The Crown, of course, will have no appeal against the ruling on the 'no case to answer' submission but the defence may decide to raise this issue, and would be entitled to do so. In that event, the judge should state the case as if it fell under head (3) in *Wingate v McGlennan*, *mutatis mutandis*. If the submission of no case to answer, under section 160, is made on more than one ground and the presiding judge upholds the submission on one of the grounds, he must still reach and express his decision on all the grounds. If he does not, there may be a remit to him to do so[6].

1   1991 SCCR 133.
2   It respectfully appears to be premature to *draw* inferences at this stage: it would be better simply to indicate what inferences of fact pointing to guilt would appear to be able to be drawn on the evidence adduced.
3   *Bowman v Jessop* 1989 SCCR 597.
4   *Cardle v Wilkinson* 1982 SCCR 33.
5   On a point of law: Criminal Procedure (Scotland) Act 1995, s 175(3).
6   *Lockhart v Milne* 1992 SCCR 864; *Walkingshaw v Robison and Davidson Ltd* 1988 SCCR 318.

3.25   Form of questions in stated cases

Neither the Criminal Procedure (Scotland) Act 1995 nor Form 19.2-B of the Act of Adjournal (Criminal Procedure Rules) 1996 prescribes the form of questions which are to be added at the end of the stated case, although Form 19.2-B instructs that the questions are to be stated in numbered paragraphs. There are, however, many reported cases containing comments upon questions that have been submitted, approving or disapproving the form of questions asked. As a matter of general principle, each question should be as succinct and pointed as the circumstances allow. Simplicity is the paramount virtue in such matters. If the questions are couched in terms of impenetrable obscurity, it may be easier for the appellant to persuade the appeal court that the judge in the inferior court has failed to understand the point. Each question should raise a different point from each other question in the same case. If there is, as there usually is, a logical sequence to the questions, such that question 2 cannot be answered except in the light of the answer to question 1, that logical order should be observed in the presentation of the questions. The questions should be closely related to the statement of matters which the appellant desires to bring under review.[1] Whatever questions are asked, they may simply be superseded, if they are not considered to be appropriately worded, as in *Robertson v Aitchison*[2] (a fundamental nullity case), or ignored, as in *Marshall v Smith*[3] or reformulated by the appeal court. If the question in the stated case contains an obvious error the court may simply amend the error and answer the amended question.[4] In *Waddell v MacPhail*[5] the appellants had been convicted of the common law crime of attempting to pervert the course of justice, in respect that, when asked by the police, who were then exercising a statutory power to require information from the appellants as to the identity of the driver of a car, they gave false replies. The court rewrote the justices' question[6] so that it read, 'Was I entitled to allow the evidence of the replies to a statutory requirement to support a common law charge when there was a statutory charge available?', and disposed of the case by answering that question. In *Conner v Lockhart*[7] there was no question directed to the question of conviction at all but the court, having formed the view that the sheriff had erred in law by permitting cross-examination of the appellant about his previous convictions when he should not have done so, held that a miscarriage of justice had occurred and that the conviction should be quashed even in the absence of an appropriate question.

1   Criminal Procedure (Scotland) Act 1995, s 176.
2   1981 SCCR 149.
3   1983 SCCR 156.
4   *McCuaig v Annan* 1986 SCCR 535.
5   1986 SCCR 593.
6   Cf 1986 SCCR at 595.
7   1986 SCCR 360.

3.26 Standard questions

In all cases in which there has been a conviction there ought to be a standard question:

'On the facts stated, was I entitled to convict the appellant (on Charge 2)?'

Similarly, where, on the basis of the facts established at trial, the judge has acquitted, the standard question will be:

'On the facts stated, was I entitled to acquit the respondent?'

Whenever, by way of stated case, the appellant challenges both conviction and sentence, the standard question on sentence will be:

'Was the sentence I imposed excessive?'

or, if there were several convictions, each resulting in its own distinct penalty, there may be several questions:

'Was the sentence I imposed on charge X/charge Y excessive?'

3.27 Questions related to evidence

In a number of cases the real issues have related to the evidence. The following examples are worth studying. In *Peebles v MacPhail*[1] the real issue was whether or not the sheriff was entitled to infer *mens rea* in a case where the appellant had become angry, slapped her two-year-old child on the face with moderate force, knocking him off balance and leaving a red mark on his face. Having set out the facts and his reasoning the sheriff asked 'On the facts admitted or proved, was I entitled to find that the appellant possessed the necessary *mens rea* to commit the offence of assault?[2] On the facts stated was I entitled to convict the appellant?' The court found these questions satisfactory and answered them.

In *Girdwood v Houston*,[2] a case well worth studying as a model, the charge was one of reset. The evidence enabled the sheriff to make findings in fact including '13. The appellant reset the four fishing rods, the rod bag, the three fishing reels and the gun-clearing rod'. The questions were in the following terms: '1. Did I err in law in repelling the submission made on behalf of the appellant in terms of section 345A of the Criminal Procedure (Scotland) Act 1975? [The reference now would be to section 160 of the 1995 Act]. 2. Was there sufficient evidence in law to entitle me to make finding 13? 3. On the facts stated was I entitled to convict the appellant? 4. Was the sentence imposed excessive?' The case serves as a model of how to draft clear findings in fact and reasons in support of the court's conclusion, as well as clear questions.

In *Watt v Annan*[3] the vital issue of fact was whether or not a Stihl saw found in the appellant's possession was the same saw as one proved to have been stolen about six months earlier. The sheriff's conclusion that it was (that conclusion being an inference from the other evidence) was stated in the findings in fact as: '7. The Stihl saw stolen as narrated in finding 3 and the Stihl saw found in the appellant's house are one and the same.' There followed two questions: '1. On the evidence, was I entitled to make finding in fact 7? 2. On the facts stated, was I entitled to convict?' The court was able to answer the first question in the affirmative; but answered the second question in the negative on the basis that the conviction referred to therein was one of theft and should properly have been one of reset. However, the court went on to find that on the facts stated the sheriff was entitled to convict the appellant of reset and should have done so. The result was to substitute a conviction of reset for one of theft and the penalty was reduced. In any case in which the findings in fact contain a vital finding which is clearly an inference from the other findings the case should always include a question directed as to whether or not the vital finding was one that the court was entitled to make in the light of the other findings in fact based upon the evidence.[4] In *Kincaid v Tudhope*[5] the only issue at the trial was whether the appellant had demonstrated that he had had a reasonable excuse for having an offensive weapon in his possession at the time and place alleged in the complaint. The justice was not satisfied that the appellant had discharged the onus upon him of demonstrating that he had a reasonable excuse for such possession. It was said by the appeal court that the question should properly have been: 'Was there material in the case upon which I was entitled not to be satisfied that there was reasonable excuse for the possession [by the appellant] of the offensive weapon at 4 o'clock in the morning in Walnut Street in Glasgow on 28 March 1982?' If the issue is whether or not upon evidence (which is narrated in the case) the judge was entitled to make a particular finding there should be a question such as 'Was I, upon the evidence narrated, entitled to make finding N?'.

1   1989 SCCR 410.
2   1989 SCCR 578.
3   1990 SCCR 55.
4   *Argo v Carmichael* 1990 SCCR 64.
5   1983 SCCR 389.

3.28   Mixed questions

It may be necessary to ask a question which is effectively a mixed question of fact and law.

In *Coull v Guild*[1] the issue was whether or not the appellant, by possessing a sheath knife in the grounds of a hospital, was guilty of an offence under section 1(1) of the Prevention of Crime Act 1953. Two questions were asked: '(1) Was I entitled to hold it proved that the ground of Victoria Hospital, Kirkcaldy was a public place in terms of the Prevention of Crime Act 1953? (2) Was I entitled to hold that the knife, label production No. 1, was *per se* an offensive weapon?' The Lord Justice-Clerk stated: 'Somewhat surprisingly there was no question in the form, "On the facts set forth was I entitled to find the appellant guilty as libelled?".' This reflects the rule that there should *always* be such a question when the appellant challenges a finding of guilt. The two questions put were satisfactorily framed. In the event, the court answered question No 2 in the negative and quashed the conviction. In *Valentine v McPhail*[2] the issue was whether or not the sheriff (who had sustained a 'no case to answer' submission) was entitled to hold that it could not be established, on the basis of the material before him, that the Camic breathalyser was an approved device within the meaning of section 8(1) of the Road Traffic Act 1972. The questions in the case were in the following terms: '(1) Was I correct in holding that it was necessary for the Crown to prove the device in question was an "approved device"? (2) Was I entitled to sustain the defence submission under section 345A of the Criminal Procedure (Scotland) Act 1975 that there was no case to answer?' The court (and both parties) considered that these questions were not in the proper form and substituted therefor one question: 'Was it essential, in order to prove that the device was of an approved type, to produce and prove the Breath Analysis Devices (Approval) Order 1983?' This was selected as the correct question because it was plain from the stated case itself that had the Crown produced and proved the said 1983 order the sheriff would have been satisfied that the device was 'approved'. The court held that, having regard to judicial knowledge, the proper inference to be drawn from the facts was that the device was of a type approved by the Secretary of State. The court accordingly answered the amended question in the negative and remitted the case to the sheriff to proceed as accords.

In *Robertson v Gateway Food Markets Ltd*[3] the sheriff had sustained a 'no case to answer' submission on the basis that a quantity of steak taken from a packet sold by a shop to a customer and tested by analysis was a 'sample' within the meaning of a statutory provision. The Crown appealed on the ground that the material was not a 'sample'. In these circumstances the appropriate questions were: '(1) Was I entitled to hold that the environmental health officers dealt with a sample in relation to the packet of steak delivered to them by Mrs McDowell [the purchasing customer]? (2) Was I correct in holding that the respondents have no case to answer?' A better formulation of question (2) would be: 'Was I *entitled to hold* that the respondents *had* no case to answer?'

1   1985 SCCR 421.
2   1986 SCCR 321.
3   1989 SCCR 305.

3.29   Procedural questions

In *Brown v McLeod*[1] the question was whether or not the sheriff was entitled in the circumstances of the case to grant the prosecutor's motion to amend the complaint's description of the *locus* where a driving offence was alleged to have occurred. The question that the court was content to entertain said simply: 'Did I err in permitting the Crown to amend the complaint?' This is a good example of the virtue of simplicity.

In *Turnbull v Allan*[2] the only issue was whether the sheriff's refusal to grant an adjournment to the appellant was oppressive and resulted in a miscarriage of justice in respect that the appellant was unable properly to present his case. Nonetheless, quite properly, the sheriff stated the facts upon which the conviction was based and asked the following questions: '(1) On the facts stated, was I entitled to find the appellant guilty as libelled? (2) Did I act oppressively in refusing to grant an adjournment at the trial? (3) Did my refusal to grant an adjournment at the trial cause a miscarriage of justice?' All these questions were regarded as satisfactory and were answered by the court.

In general, it may be said that, if a particular legal issue has been raised by the appellant in the application, a question of law must be framed to put that issue clearly before the court and in a way that separates it from all other issues. Although from time to time the High Court may allow an argument to be presented that is not properly encapsulated in one of the questions, it is impossible to approach the framing either of the application or of the stated case upon the assumption that the court might be indulgent. There are ample opportunities to put the issue properly into the case, and there are serious disadvantages for the administration of justice if that is not properly done. Accordingly, such indulgence is sometimes not granted.

The case of *Thomson v Allan*[3] provides a model for a stated case in relation not only to the findings in fact but also to the whole structure, content, character and quality of the note. It also contains three model questions for a case in which the sheriff has rejected a submission in terms of the Criminal Procedure (Scotland) Act 1995, section 160 (no case to answer) and proceeded to convict: '(1) Did I err in rejecting the appellant's submission of no case to answer? (2) Was the police officer entitled to make a second requirement of the appellant to provide two specimens of breath for analysis after the appellant had failed to provide two specimens of breath following upon the first requirement? (3) On the facts stated, was I entitled to convict the appellant?' The aim when framing the questions must always be to keep them short, simple, clear and exhaustive of the issues placed before the appeal court.

1   1986 SCCR 615.
2   1989 SCCR 215.
3   1989 SCCR 327.

3.30   Adjustment of case: section 179

Within three weeks of the issue of the draft stated case each party must cause to be transmitted to the court and to the other parties or their solicitors a note of any adjustments he proposes should be made to the draft case; alternatively, he must intimate that he has no adjustments to propose.[1] The adjustments must relate to evidence heard, or purported to have been heard, at the trial. They must not relate to evidence which was not heard at the original proceedings but which it is proposed to present in support of a ground of appeal founded upon the provision contained in the Criminal Procedure (Scotland) Act 1995, section 175(5). Such a ground of appeal should, if possible, appear in the application for a stated case or in an amendment or addition thereto as permitted by section 176(3). However, it is quite likely that the new, unheard, evidence is not discovered – or it may not have come into existence – until later. In that event, leave to appeal in respect of the new proposed ground will not have been obtained; and special leave should be sought timeously (i e not later than seven days before the date fixed for the hearing of the appeal) in terms of section 180(8) and (9), as was done in *Ward v Crowe*.[2] If the unheard evidence comes to light too late to enable the appellant to give the 7 days' notice required by section 180(9) the appeal court should be invited to allow the new ground to be argued. Under the influence of the case law of the European Court of Human Rights, the appeal court is likely to entertain such a request, responsibly made, even if the hearing might have to be postponed, as it almost certainly would. If the appellant does not lodge adjustments and does not intimate that he has no adjustments to propose, he is deemed to have abandoned his appeal.[3] If he is deemed to have abandoned his appeal and has previously been granted bail the inferior court has power to grant warrant to apprehend and imprison him for such period of his sentence as at the date of his bail remained unexpired, such period to run from the date of his imprisonment under such warrant.[4] Section 181 empowers the High Court to direct that an applicant who has failed to comply with the statutory requirement within the three weeks specified in section 179(1) may be afforded further time to comply with that requirement. An application for a direction from the High Court that the appellant/applicant be afforded further time has to be made in writing to the Clerk of Justiciary, stating the grounds for the application.[5]

The High Court has the usual power to dispose of such an application in like manner to the disposal of bail appeals, coupled with power to dispense with a hearing or to make further inquiry. In practice such applications are dealt with in chambers without a hearing. The Clerk of Justiciary informs the clerk of the inferior court of the result of the High Court's decision. If adjustments are proposed within the three weeks (or any extended period) or if the judge desires to make any alterations to the draft case there must, within one week of the expiry of the period allowed for adjustment, be a hearing (unless the appeal has been abandoned or has been deemed to be abandoned). The hearing is for the purposes of considering such adjustments or alterations.[6] Even if a party is not represented at the hearing, the hearing proceeds. At the hearing, where any adjustment proposed by a party and not withdrawn is rejected by the judge, or any alteration proposed by the judge is not accepted by all the parties, that fact must be recorded in the minute of the hearing. The Act of Adjournal (Criminal Procedure Rules) 1996, Form 19.2-C provides the style for the minutes of procedure in an appeal by stated case and includes clear references to adjustments and alterations.

Within two weeks of the date of the hearing or, if there is no hearing, then within two weeks of the expiry of the adjustment period, the judge (except in the case of abandonment) must state and sign the case. He must append to the case any proposed adjustment rejected by him, a note of any evidence rejected by him which is alleged to support that adjustment and the reasons for his rejection of that adjustment and evidence. He must also append a note of the evidence upon which he bases any finding of fact that is challenged on the basis that it is unsupported by the evidence, such challenge having been advanced by a party attending an adjustment hearing. *Wilson v Carmichael*[7] provides a good example of this process at work in a case where the appellant proposed radical adjustments to the vital findings in fact, and the appeal court took some account of material rejected by the sheriff. The court that receives adjustments or representations at a hearing must take care to deal fairly with the representations and must give adequate and defensible reasons for rejecting significant adjustments. Thus in *Ballantyne v MacKinnon*,[8] when the sheriff had rejected a proposed adjustment of importance for a wholly improper reason, the court found that the sheriff's treatment of the adjustments was so unsatisfactory that the conviction could not be allowed to stand. . The court effectively accepted the rejected adjustments in concluding that the conviction fell to be quashed. In *O'Hara v Tudhope*[9] the sheriff rejected a proposed adjustment whereby a question relating to corroboration would have been added to the stated case: the appeal court allowed the appellant to argue the corroboration point and did not find it necessary to remit the case to the sheriff with a direction to add the necessary question. If the sheriff does not give satisfactory reasons for rejecting proposed adjustments the case may be remitted back to him: *Owens v Crowe*.[10] *McLeod v Campbell*[11] is a good example of the importance of raising during the period of adjustment any important issue that is not in the draft stated case or that arises out of the draft stated case. There the court held that the respondent in a Crown appeal, not having taken the opportunity to raise a material issue during the period of adjustment, was not to be allowed to raise it at the hearing of the appeal. The period of one week during which the hearing must take place or the two weeks allowed by section 179(7) for final statement and signature of the case may be extended by the sheriff principal exercising powers under section 194(2). Any period of time prescribed under section 179 is automatically extended by section 194(1) if the prescribed period expires on the Saturday, Sunday or court holiday prescribed for the relevant court. The extension is into the next day that is *not* a Saturday, Sunday or such court holiday.

1 Criminal Procedure (Scotland) Act 1995, s 179(1).
2 1999 SCCR 219.
3 CP(S)A 1995, s 179(3).
4 CP(S)A 1995, s 177(5).
5 CP(S)A 1995, s 181(2).
6 CP(S)A 1995, s 179(4).
7 1982 SCCR 528.
8 1983 SCCR 97; see also *McDonald v Scott* 1993 SCCR 78.
9 1986 SCCR 283.
10 1994 SCCR 310.
11 1986 SCCR 132.

3.31   Signature and transmission of stated case: section 179

Once the case has been signed the clerk of court must send the case to the appellant or his solicitor and a duplicate of the case to the respondent or his solicitor and transmit the complaint, productions and any other proceedings in the cause to the Clerk of Justiciary.[1] Within one week of receiving the case (unless that period is extended by the High Court under the procedure contained in section 181) the appellant or his solicitor as the case may be must cause it to be lodged with the Clerk of Justiciary.[2] The clerk of court retains label productions unless the Clerk of Justiciary asks for them to be sent to him. If the appellant or his solicitor fails to lodge the case timeously with the Clerk of Justiciary he is deemed to have abandoned his appeal (see also 3.32 below).

1   Criminal Procedure (Scotland) Act 1995, s 179(8).
2   CP(S)A 1995, s 179(9).

3.32   Abandoning the appeal

An appellant who proceeds by stated case may, at any time prior to
lodging the case with the Clerk of Justiciary, expressly abandon the
appeal by minute signed by himself or his solicitor written on the
complaint or lodged with the clerk of the inferior court, and intimated to the respondent or the respondent's solicitor.[1] The Clerk of
Justiciary or clerk of the inferior court, as the case may be, has then
to notify the other interested parties as prescribed by the Act of
Adjournal (Criminal Procedure Rules) 1996, Rule 19.8. Such
abandonment is without prejudice to any other competent mode of
appeal, review, advocation or suspension.[2] The Criminal Procedure
(Scotland) Act 1995, section 184(2) provides: '*Subject to section 191
of this Act*, on the case being lodged with the Clerk of Justiciary, the
appellant shall be held to have abandoned any other mode of
appeal which might otherwise have been open to him.' Failure to
appear when the case calls in the High Court normally results in
the case being treated as abandoned, even if an excuse for the failure later emerges.[3] There may be room for a relaxation of this practice in the light of the Human Rights Act 1998.

Section 191 preserves the right of appeal by bill of suspension
against a conviction (or by advocation against an acquittal) on the
ground of an alleged miscarriage of justice. The bill requires leave
to proceed from the High Court if the same ground of appeal is
referred to in the application for a stated case and if the appeal by
way of stated case has not yet been finally disposed of or abandoned. Failure to lodge the stated case timeously has the effect
that the appellant is deemed to have abandoned the appeal, and
such deemed abandonment brings section 177 into operation,
allowing the inferior court to grant warrant to apprehend and
imprison in the circumstances there specified.[4] But the High
Court has power retrospectively to allow late lodging.[5] In practice,
up until the actual calling of the case in court for oral hearing, an
appellant is allowed to abandon by this minute procedure. If the
case is actually called, the appellant, if he then wishes to abandon,
should seek leave of the court to abandon at the bar of the court.
A motion made at the bar, before any submissions are made, is in
practice usually granted. After submissions have started, the court
may refuse leave to abandon and, if the appeal has been taken
against both conviction and sentence, may exercise its power to
increase the sentence.[6]

1   CP(S)A 1995, s184.
2   CP(S)A 1995, s 184(1).
3   *McMahon v MacPhail* 1991 SCCR 470 (no funds to travel to Edinburgh);
    Pratt v Normand 1994 SCCR 881 (address changed from domicile of citation).
4   CP(S)A 1995, s 177(5).
5   CP(S)A 1995, s 181.
6   CP(S)A 1995, ss 183(3) and 189(1).

3.33   Record of procedure in appeal

When an appeal is taken by way of stated case the clerk of the inferior court must provide a record of the procedure in that court in the form prescribed by the Act of Adjournal (Criminal Procedure Rules) 1996, Rule 19.2(3), namely Form 19.2-C, which covers all eventualities.[1]

1   Criminal Procedure (Scotland) Act 1995, s 176(5).

3.34   Duties of solicitors: lodging, printing etc

The Act of Adjournal (Criminal Procedure Rules) 1996, Rule 19.11 sets forth the duties incumbent upon solicitors who are acting in relation to appeals once they have reached the Clerk of Justiciary. These duties may be carried out by a solicitor who practises in Edinburgh but it is not mandatory to appoint an Edinburgh solicitor. The appellant's solicitor is required to enter appearance and comply with the provisions of the Criminal Procedure (Scotland) Act 1995, section 179(9) by lodging the case within one week, or within any extended period obtained under section 181. In practice, what happens if an Edinburgh solicitor has been appointed, is that the appellant's local solicitor, when marking the appeal, informs the clerk of court who his Edinburgh solicitor is to be. The clerk of court informs the Clerk of Justiciary who then gives whatever information or notification is necessary to the Edinburgh solicitor. The appellant's solicitor (or the appellant himself, if unrepresented) must have the complaint, the minutes of proceedings and the stated case printed. He must return the process to the Clerk of Justiciary not later than seven days before the hearing and provide copies of the print to the Clerk of Justiciary (four copies) and the respondent or his solicitor (three copies). If the appellant or his solicitor cannot do all of these things he must inform the Clerk of Justiciary, *in writing,* not later than seven days before the hearing. The Clerk of Justiciary has a discretion to postpone the hearing by dropping the case from the Justiciary Roll, though he will usually consult the chairman of the court before doing so. The reason has to be substantial, e g illness, or awaiting the outcome of a legal aid application. The unavailability of a particular counsel is not normally considered a good reason for withdrawing a case from the roll. If the Clerk of Justiciary does not drop the appeal from the roll, the court may, at the hearing, allow the appeal to be dropped from the roll. Often a continuation is granted on the express understanding that, even if the problem is still unresolved when the appeal is next put out on the roll, the hearing must then proceed. The court may dismiss the appeal after hearing from the appellant or his representative, if any such person is present. If no one appears, it is usual for the court to dismiss the appeal for want of insistence and to grant any warrants that may be appropriate. The Clerk of Justiciary will have issued a list of appeals with the respective dates of hearing in the Justiciary Roll, giving the solicitors representing all parties at least 14 days' notice that their appeal has been listed for hearing.[1] Party appellants are sometimes excused failure to comply with the detailed rules as to what has to be lodged if the court (and the Crown) can deal with the appeal on the basis of what is available.

1 Act of Adjournal (Criminal Procedure Rules) 1996, SI 1996/513, Rule 19.14.

3.35 Time limits – and possible extensions

The various periods allowed by the Act for the taking of any necessary procedural steps have been noted in the text describing those steps, and it has also been noted that the periods may in some cases be extended. In brief, the position is as follows:

The limits
(a) lodging of application for stated case and sending copy to the other party – within one week of final determination;[1]
(b) issuing of draft case - within three weeks of final determination;[2]
(c) intimating adjustments, or that none are proposed – within three weeks of the issue of the draft stated case;[3]
(d) alteration of the application and intimation to the other party – within the same three week period mentioned in (c);[4]
(e) the adjustment hearing (if necessary) – within one week of the end of the period in (c);[5]
(f) signing of the case – within two weeks of the adjustment hearing (if any) or, if no such hearing, within two weeks of the end of the period in (c);[6]

(g)   sending of case, by the clerk of court, to appellant (duplicate to other party) – as soon as the case has been signed;[7]

(h)   transmitting complaint, productions and any other proceedings in the cause to Clerk of Justiciary – as soon as the case has been signed;[8]

(i)   lodging of signed case with Clerk of Justiciary - within one week of the appellant (or his solicitor) receiving the signed case;[9]

(j)   abandonment by minute – at any time before lodging case; in practice, abandoning by minute is allowed up to the calling of the case[10] (see 3.32 above);

(k)   returning the process to the Clerk of Justiciary[11] – not later than seven days before the High Court hearing;[12]

(l)   providing copies of prints to the Clerk of Justiciary and the other side - at the same time as (k);[13]

(m) issuing list of appeals – 14 days' notice (given by Clerk of Justiciary) of the date of the hearing.[14]

Extension of foregoing limits

(1)   All the foregoing periods of time [except those mentioned in (k), (l) and (m)] are automatically extended by a period (of up to four days) if section 194(1) applies:

> 'If any period of time specified in any provision of this Part of this Act relating to appeals expires on a Saturday, Sunday or court holiday prescribed for the relevant court, the period shall be extended to expire on the next day which is not a Saturday, Sunday or such court holiday'.

(2)   The power of the sheriff principal to extend, for such period as he considers reasonable certain prescribed time limits on account of the temporary absence of a judge in his sheriffdom may be exercised retrospectively;[15] it extends to (b), (e) and (f) above, and, as a result, delays the dates in (g), (h) and (i).

(3)   The powers of the High Court to direct that a further period of time be afforded to the applicant for the procedural steps in a stated case[16] extend to (a) above and to (c), (d) and (i) above respectively. These powers are exercised *after* a failure to comply with a prescribed timetable; they are not available to grant an extension before the period has expired. When the High Court grants an extension of the period in section 176(1) the effect in practice, unless it is otherwise stated, is that the date of granting the extension is treated as if it were the date of final determination. Equally, any other extension has the effect of postponing any dependent deadlines to the end of the extended period allowed.

Use of nobile officium to excuse procedural failure
Extensions of time are not obtainable by petition to the *nobile officium* if the circumstances narrated in the petition are such that
they disclose that a statutory procedure could have been, but was
not, used.[17] However, the *nobile officium* is there to fill all gaps and,
if one should appear, this power may be invoked – as in *Rae,
Petitioner*[18] in which a judge neglected to consider a statutory
application at all on its merits. The High Court, when considering
an application for extension of time under these provisions of the
Act, has a duty to exercise its discretion under reference to all the
known, relevant circumstances drawn to its attention.[19]

1 Criminal Procedure (Scotland) Act 1995, s 176(1)(a).
2 CP(S)A 1995, s 178(1).
3 CP(S)A 1995, s 179(1).
4 CP(S)A 1995, s 176(3).
5 CP(S)A 1995, s 179(4).
6 CP(S)A 1995, s 179(7).
7 CP(S)A 1995, s 179(8).
8 CP(S)A 1995, s 179(8).
9 CP(S)A 1995, s 179(9) and Act of Adjournal (Criminal Procedure Rules)
   1996 SI 1996/513, rule 19.11(3).
10 CP(S)A 1995, s 184 and Criminal Procedure Rules 1996, rule 19.8.
11 Criminal Procedure Rules 1996, rule 19.12(1)(b).
12 See 3.22 above.
13 Criminal Procedure Rules 1996, rule 19.12(1)(c).
14 Criminal Procedure Rules 1996, rule 19.14.
15 CP(S)A 1995, s 194(2); *Burns v Lees* 1992 SCCR 244.
16 CP(S)A 1995, s 181(1).
17 *Berry, Petitioner* 1985 SCCR 106.
18 1981 SCCR 356.
19 *Berry, Petitioner* 1985 SCCR 106 at 109, per the report of Lord Wheatley.

3.36 Fresh evidence

An appellant whose appeal is against conviction or sentence or
both, and who appeals under the Criminal Procedures (Scotland)
Act 1995, section 175, may bring under review of the High Court
any alleged miscarriage of justice in the proceedings on the basis of
the existence and significance of evidence which was not heard at
the original proceedings[1]. (The Crown cannot appeal on this basis.)
Such evidence may form the basis of an appeal at the instance of an
appellant if, but only if, there is a reasonable explanation of why it
was not heard at those proceedings. The provisions governing the
conditions that have to be met before any such evidence can be
allowed to be introduced in support of the appeal are contained in
section 175(5), (5A), (5B), (5C) and (5D) of the 1995 Act. They

were introduced into that Act by section 23 of the Crime and Punishment (Scotland) Act 1997, and amended by the Crime and Disorder Act 1998, Schedule 8, paragraph 123. The wording of the provisions is the same in summary as in solemn appeals:[2] the legal considerations are the same.[3] These considerations are discussed in chapter 7. In *Marshall v Smith*[4] the appellant, proceeding by way of stated case, and founding on the differently worded provisions contained in the Criminal Procedure (Scotland) Act 1975, as amended, brought under review upon an alleged 'miscarriage of justice in respect of additional, significant evidence which was not heard at the trial'. In fact, no new evidence was led, as the Crown conceded at the appeal court hearing that an examination of the police record showed that material police evidence, which the sheriff had believed, was untrue. The court, without hearing evidence quashed the conviction. However, the new evidence provisions are contained in section 175, which provides for an appeal *with leave* granted in accordance with section 180. Section 175 is 'without prejudice to any right of appeal under section 191'. Section 191 preserves a right of appeal by bill of suspension 'where an appeal under section 175 would be incompetent or inappropriate; but it introduces neither the 'leave' provisions in section 180 or 187, nor the provisions in section 175 relating to evidence not heard at the trial. Although section 182(5) also allows the court inter alia to 'hear any evidence relevant to any alleged miscarriage of justice', this provision pre-dated the introduction of the various provisions that allowed the court to hear additional, new or unheard evidence. In these circumstances, it appears that the ground of appeal contained in section 175(5)-(5D), relating to evidence 'not heard' at the original proceedings, may not be advanced in an appeal by way of bill of suspension.

1   Criminal Procedure (Scotland) Act 1995, s 175(5).
2   CP(S)A 1995, s 106.
3   The new provisions were invoked in a stated case: *Ward v Crowe* 1999 SCCR 219.
4   1983 SCCR 156.

3.37   Abandoning appeal against conviction; continuing with appeal against sentence

A person who has appealed against both conviction and sentence may abandon the appeal in so far as it is against conviction but proceed with the appeal against sentence alone.[1] The procedure is governed by the Act of Adjournal (Criminal Procedure Rules)

1996, Rule 19.6. The appellant must make an application by minute (using Form 19.6) signed by him or his solicitor and intimated by him to the respondent. He has to lodge the minute with the clerk of the court which imposed the sentence being appealed against – or with the Clerk of Justiciary if the stated case has already been lodged; in that event, the Clerk of Justiciary sends a copy of the minute to the clerk of the court which imposed sentence. If, before the minute has been lodged, copies of the stated case and relative proceedings have been lodged with the Clerk of Justiciary those copies are used for the High Court appeal hearing. Once the minute has been lodged the procedure is regulated by the Criminal Procedure (Scotland) Act 1995, section 186(3)-(9) as if the minute were a note of appeal against sentence lodged in terms of section 186: see 3.39 below.

1   Criminal Procedure (Scotland) Act 1995, s 175(8).

3.38   Appeals by accused against hospital orders etc

In terms of the Criminal Procedure (Scotland) Act 1995, section 60, if a hospital order,[1] interim hospital order[2] (but not a renewal thereof), guardianship order[3], a restriction order[4] or a hospital direction[5] has been made by a court in respect of a person charged or brought before it, he may, without prejudice to any other form of appeal under any rule of law (or, when an interim hospital order has been made, to any right of appeal against any other order or sentence which may be imposed), appeal against that order or, as the case may be, direction in the same manner as against sentence, i e by note of appeal on Form 19.3-A.

1   Criminal Procedure (Scotland) Act 1995, s 58(4).
2   CP(S)A 1995, s 53(1).
3   CP(S)A 1995, s 58(6).
4   CP(S)A 1995, s 59(2).
5   CP(S)A 1995, s 59A(1).

3.39   Appeals by accused in cases involving insanity

Under the Criminal Procedure (Scotland) Act 1995, section 54(1) a court of first instance may make a finding that a person is insane, so that his trial cannot proceed. That finding may be appealed under section 62(1)(a). Under section 55(2) a court of first instance may make a finding, following an examination of facts ordered under section 54(1)(b), that the accused did the act or made the omission constituting the offence which has brought him before the court. That finding may be appealed under section 62(1)(b). If a person is acquitted in a court of first instance on the ground of his insanity at the time of the act or omission constituting the offence, or there is a finding under section 55(2) then, in either case, the court may make an order under section 57(2) – equivalent to a hospital order, a restriction order or a guardianship order. The accused may appeal against any such finding or order by following the procedure contained in section 62. The appeal must be in writing and lodged within the periods respectively prescribed in subsection (2): seven days for a section 54(1) finding; 28 days for a finding under section 55(2); 14 days for an appeal against an order made under section 57(2) of an order under section 55(2). These provisions are without prejudice to any appeal rights available in connection with preliminary diet procedure. Section 62(5) permits the appellant to attend his appeal unless the High Court determines otherwise.[1] The powers of the High Court are to affirm the decision of the court of first instance, to make a different finding, order or disposal, or to remit the case with directions.[2] If a person has a right of appeal under section 62(1)(c) – against an order made under section 57(2) – he has no right of appeal under section 60.[3]

1 Criminal Procedure (Scotland) Act 1995, s 62(5).
2 CP(S)A 1995, s 62(6).
3 CP(S)A 1995, s 62(7).

APPEALS AGAINST SENTENCE

3.40 Appeal against sentence alone

The Criminal Procedure (Scotland) Act 1995, section 175(2) gives to a person convicted, or found to have committed an offence, in summary proceedings the right – but only with leave granted under section 187 – to appeal against the sentence or various other disposals. He may appeal against the sentence passed on conviction or against his absolute discharge or admonition or any probation order or any community service order or any order deferring sentence. A supervised attendance order is not a sentence within the meaning of this section and may be appealed by petition to the *nobile officium*.[1] However, a supervised attendance order made under section 236 in respect of 16- or 17-year-olds is a sentence for this purpose.[2] Section 191 (appeal by bill of suspension or advocation on ground of miscarriage of justice) applies expressly only to appeals against conviction or acquittal; but does so without prejudice to any rule of law relating to bills of suspension or advocation in so far as such rule of law is not inconsistent with the section. Accordingly, a person who desires to appeal against sentence alone, or against his absolute discharge, an admonition, or any order specified in section 175(2)(c), should pursue the appeal by note of appeal.[3] But, as sections 175(1) and 191(4) save the common law right to proceed by way of a bill of suspension in respect of any alleged fundamental irregularity relating to the imposition of the sentence, an appeal by bill of suspension may be competent. Section 175(10) re-enacts the provision in the Criminal Procedure (Scotland) Act 1975[4] to the effect that, where a statute provides for an appeal from summary proceedings to be taken under any public general[5] or local enactment, the appeal is to be taken under Part X of the 1995 Act. In addition to the more common and familiar sentences there are other less common orders which are also appealable by note of appeal in the same manner as ordinary sentences: see 2.23 above.

1 *McGregor, Petitioner* 1999 SCCR 225.
2 Criminal Procedure (Scotland) Act 1995, s 236(8).
3 CP(S)A 1995, ss 175(9) and 186(1).
4 Criminal Procedure (Scotland) Act 1975, s 283(2).
5 E g the Civic Government Act 1982, s 7(8).

3.41 Note of appeal against sentence alone or other disposal

When there is to be no appeal against conviction, the appeal, whether against sentence alone or against absolute discharge, admonition or other order specified in the Criminal Procedure (Scotland) Act 1995, section 175(2)(c), has to be by note of appeal.[1] The form to be used is that prescribed by the Act of Adjournal (Criminal Procedure Rules) 1996, Rule 19.3(1), namely Form 19.3-A. It has to be lodged with the clerk of the court from which the appeal is to be taken.[2] This must be done within one week of the passing of the sentence or other disposal, or deferral, of the case. If the appellant fails to comply with the requirement to lodge his note of appeal within the week he may thereafter apply to the High Court for a direction that further time be afforded him to enable him to lodge his note of appeal out of time.[3] The procedure for dealing with such an application is the same as that prescribed in respect of a failure by an appellant to apply for a stated case within the one week allowed in section

176(1).[4] If the High Court extends the period for lodging the note of appeal, the periods of one week[5] and two weeks[6] are deemed to run from the date which is two days after the date on which the High Court makes the order extending the period, not from the date when sentence was passed.[7]

1   Criminal Procedure (Scotland) Act 1995, s 186(1).
2   CP(S)A 1995, s 186(2).
3   CP(S)A 1995, ss 186(8) and s 181.
4   CP(S)A 1995, ss 181(1) and (2); s 186(8).
5   CP(S)A 1995, s 186(2)(a).
6   CP(S)A 1995, s 186(4).
7   Act of Adjournal (Criminal Procedure Rules) 1996, SI 1996/513, rule 19.4(2).

3.42   Grounds of appeal

The only statutory ground of appeal is 'any alleged miscarriage of justice' (including a miscarriage based on fresh evidence).[1] In appeals against sentence the test is no longer (as before 1980) whether the sentence was harsh and oppressive but whether it was excessive.[2] Thus the considerations which are discussed in relation to grounds of appeal generally in solemn cases are applicable in summary cases: see 2.26 ff. Clearly, most circumstances that would have led to a sentence being characterised as 'harsh and oppressive' in the past would be likely to be regarded now as indicative that the sentence was excessive and that accordingly a miscarriage of justice had occurred. And, although 'excessiveness' is the primary criterion, the appeal court has been known to look at other matters, including 'comparative justice', or the public interest, or new material not properly before the inferior court, in arriving at the conclusion that a sentence which would not normally be regarded as excessive should be quashed in the special circumstances, perhaps as 'inappropriate'.

1   Criminal Procedure (Scotland) Act 1995, s 175(5).
2   *Addison v MacKinnon* 1983 SCCR 52; *Donaldson v HM Advocate* 1983 SCCR 216 (a solemn case).

3.43   Interim regulation if appellant in custody

The Criminal Procedure (Scotland) Act 1995, section 177 is applied to appeals against sentence or other sentence-type disposal by section 186(1). Reference should therefore be made to chapter 8.

3.44   Procedure following lodging of note of appeal

On receiving the note, the clerk of the court from which the appeal is to be taken must send a copy to the respondent or his solicitor and obtain a report from the judge who imposed the sentence, or otherwise disposed of the case, including making a a remit under section 49 of the Criminal Procedure (Scotland) Act 1995 to the children's Principal Reporter.[1] The judge's report should be provided without delay, i e within one week. It is unnecessary for each of several justices who have constituted the bench to prepare a separate report: only one is required.[2] Within two weeks of the passing of the sentence, or other sentence-type disposal, the clerk of the sentencing court sends the Clerk of Justiciary the note of appeal, together with the report of the sentencing judge, a certified copy of the complaint, the minute of proceedings and any other relevant documents and also sends copies of the judge's report to the respective parties or their solicitors.[3] The two-week period may be extended by the sheriff principal if the sheriff or justice concerned is temporarily absent from duty. In relation to the contents of the judge's report, nothing need be added to what is said in relation to the judge's report in solemn appeals, notably at 2.40 ff. If the judge's report is not furnished timeously the High Court may extend the period for it to be made available, may expressly instruct the judge to furnish the report, or, in exceptional circumstances, may hear and determine the appeal without the report. However, the sentencing judge may be directed to produce a report even when the ground contained in the note of appeal is inadequate: this is clear from *Henry v Docherty*[4] where the sheriff, faced with wholly inadequate grounds, wrote a brief report stating that he was of opinion that there was no other appropriate method of dealing with either appellant otherwise than by a sentence of six months' detention. The court, however, stated that the sentencing judge should be able to produce a report describing the circumstances of the offence,[5] the circumstances of the appellant, the reasons he had for imposing the sentence under appeal and any other information which he considers relevant. This certainly includes the terms of any plea in mitigation and the effect given to it by the sentencing judge. The appeals in *Henry v Docherty* were remitted to the sheriff in order that he could provide to the court 'a supplementary report containing the minimum information outlined in the opinion of the court of even date and any other information he considers is relevant to the appeal'.

1 Criminal Procedure (Scotland) Act 1995, s 186(3).
2 *Mullins v Walkingshaw* 1996 G.W.D. 27-159.
3 CP(S) A 1995, s 186(4).
4 1989 SCCR 426.
5 Cf *Steele v MacKinnon* 1982 SCCR 19 as to the importance of narrating the circumstances.

3.45 Abandonment of appeal against sentence etc

An appellant may abandon his appeal by minute (Act of Adjournal (Criminal Procedure Rules) 1996, Form 19.7) signed by himself or his solicitor lodged. If the note of appeal has not yet been sent to the Clerk of Justiciary, the minute has to be lodged with the clerk of the sentencing court. In any other case, the minute has to be lodged with the Clerk of Justiciary. In either event, intimation must be made to the respondent.[1] The Clerk of Justiciary or the clerk of the sentencing court, as the case may be, on the lodging with him of the minute abandoning the appeal, must notify the Crown Agent or prosecutor, as the case may be, of the lodging of the minute; and the Clerk of Justiciary, where the minute is lodged with him, notifies the clerk of the sentencing court immediately.[2]

1 Criminal Procedure (Scotland) Act 1995, s 186(9).
2 Act of Adjournal (Criminal Procedure Rules) 1996, SI 1996/513, rule 19.8.

3.46 Record of procedure in appeal

The clerk of the sentencing court must send to the Clerk of Justiciary the minute of proceedings showing the different steps of procedure in the appeal, and such record is evidence of the dates on which the various steps of procedure took place: Act of Adjournal (Criminal Procedure Rules) 1996, Form 19.3-B is the prescribed form. However, the order or interlocutor pronounced in open court is what is important; it overrides an incorrect written record of the court's order: *Heywood, petitioner.*[1]

1 1998 SCCR 335.

3.47 The hearing: duties of solicitors etc

The High Court fixes the date for the hearing. The Clerk of Justiciary, after consultation with the Lord Justice-General or the Lord Justice-Clerk, issues a list of appeals with the respective dates of hearing on the Justiciary Roll. A copy is sent to the solicitors for the parties (and the appellant himself if he is unrepresented) at least 14 days prior to the hearing.[1] Intimation to the appellant is made by recorded delivery and first class post at the address given in any bail order, if he is on bail, or to the address he has given in his note of appeal. It follows that if an appellant has changed his address without informing the Clerk of Justiciary he will not receive intimation of his appeal and may be held not to be insisting in his appeal. The appeal is therefore liable to be refused for want of insistence and, if appropriate, a warrant will be issued for his arrest. Where an appellant has been granted bail, he must appear personally in court at the diet appointed for the hearing of the appeal. If he does not appear, the appeal court, in the absence of any explanation, usually drops the case down the roll to allow further opportunity for the appellant to appear, or for an explanation of his absence to be furnished. If he later appears, his appeal may be allowed to proceed. If he does not appear at all and no satisfactory explanation is forthcoming the court may, on cause shown, permit the appeal to be heard in his absence[2] or drop the case from the roll. It is usual to treat the case as abandoned; in that case the High Court will, if the Crown so moves, grant a warrant for the apprehension and imprisonment of the appellant. As the Criminal Procedure (Scotland) Act 1995, section 177 is applied (by section 186(10) to appeals against sentence etc, the provisions of section 176(6) apply as well as those of section 177(5). Section 176(6) permits the court to order that a bailed appellant who abandons his appeal, but does so at a time when he is in custody or serving a term of imprisonment imposed *subsequently* to the sentence appealed against, should start to serve the unexpired portion of the sentence in respect of which he had been bailed from the date of the expiry of the term of imprisonment subsequently imposed. In *Proudfoot v Wither*[3] (in an appeal by bill of suspension) it was held that it was contrary to natural justice for the court to make such an order without first giving that appellant an opportunity to make representations to the court on the matter. Section 177(7) now prevents the court from making such an order without first notifying the appellant of its intention to do so and considering any representations made by him or on his behalf. Otherwise the court must make the sentences run concurrently.

---

1   Act of Adjournal (Criminal Procedure Rules) 1996, SI 1996/513, rule 19.14.
2   Criminal Procedure (Scotland) Act 1995, s 192(2)(b).
3   1990 SCCR 96.

3.48 Conviction not to be quashed on certain grounds

The Criminal Procedure (Scotland) Act 1995, section 192(3) provides as follows:

'No conviction, sentence, judgement, order of court or other proceeding whatsoever in or for the purposes of summary proceedings under this Act—

(a) shall be quashed for want of form; or

(b) where the accused had legal assistance in his defence, shall be suspended or set aside in respect of any objections to—

   (i) the relevancy of the complaint, or to the want of specification therein; or

   (ii) the competency or admission or rejection of evidence at the trial in the inferior court,

unless such objections were timeously stated.'

The problem may be to distinguish between what is mere want of form and what is error of substance.[1] The same underlying principles and reasoning as to the timeous taking of points of admissibility, relevancy, competency and procedural irregularities apply also where there has been an acquittal rather than a conviction.[2] However, defective proceedings which may materially prejudice the accused cannot be regarded as affected by want of form only.[3]

1 See, for example *Ogilvy v Mitchell* (1903) 4 Adam 237; *Smith v Sempill* (1910) 6 Adam 348; *Dunsire v Bell* (1908) 5 Adam 625.
2 *Skeen v Murphy* 1978 SLT (Notes) 2.
3 *Cameron v Waugh* 1937 JC 5; *Ogilvy v Mitchell* (1903) 4 Adam 237: *Johannesson v Robertson* 1945 JC 146; *Beattie v McKinnon* 1977 JC 64; *Scott v Annan* 1981 SCCR 172.

4. Appeals by the Crown

4.01 Right of appeal: general

The Crown's rights of appeal are more limited than those of an accused. However, unlike a person convicted or sentenced, the Crown does not need leave to appeal, as required by the accused under the Criminal Procedure (Scotland) Act 1995, sections 106(1) and 175(2). In certain limited circumstances, the Crown may have to obtain leave under other statutory provisions. The Crown[1] may, with the leave of the court of first instance, appeal to the High Court against a decision at a first diet or a preliminary diet under section 76A but has no right of appeal against acquittal in solemn proceedings. There is a right of appeal in respect of sentences that the Lord Advocate considers are unduly lenient – see 4.17 below. During the proceedings, or after they have been effectively dismissed without evidence being led, the Crown has a limited right to seek review by the process of advocation.

Advocation may be used to appeal, without leave, against a decision at a preliminary diet: see 4.06 below. And after an acquittal, though without challenge to the acquittal itself, the Lord Advocate may take a 'Reference' to the appeal court on a question of law: see 4.04 below. In summary proceedings, the prosecutor may appeal,[2] but only on a point of law, against an acquittal,[3] or a sentence passed, in such proceedings. By such an appeal the Crown may bring under review any alleged miscarriage of justice in the proceedings. The Crown cannot, however, submit that an acquittal or a sentence should be reviewed on the basis of fresh evidence. Advocation is also available to the Crown in summary proceedings. The Crown may competently apply by petition to the *nobile officium* in appropriate circumstances.[4] The prosecutor has a right in summary proceedings to consent to set aside a conviction.[5] The Crown has the right to appear at the hearing of any criminal appeal, although Crown counsel who appear there instructed by the Crown Agent are not called upon to address the court on matters of sentence, except where the point at issue is one of competency or the appeal has raised some question of fact upon which the Crown might be able to shed some light. However, where the Crown appeals against sentence on the ground that it is unduly lenient or inappropriate (see 4.17 below) Crown counsel, of course, address the court. In both solemn[6] and summary[7] proceedings the Crown may appeal against the refusal of any application to extend the maximum periods prescribed to prevent delay in criminal proceedings.

---

1 A private prosecutor enjoys similar rights of appeal as the Crown, but no right under the Criminal Procedure (Scotland) Act 1995, s 123 (Lord Advocate's Reference), or in respect of sentence.

2   CP(S)A 1995, s 175(3).
3   See 4.07 below.
4   Cf chapter 6.
5   CP(S)A 1995, s 188 (1); see 4.15 below.
6   CP(S)A 1995, s 65(8).
7   CP(S)A 1995, s 147(3).

4.02   Appeals from preliminary diets

The Criminal Procedure (Scotland) Act 1995, section 72 provides for a preliminary diet to be held to allow the court before which the trial is to take place to deal with certain issues before the trial, being matters of which notice has been given before the first diet in terms of section 71(2) or under section 72 (preliminary diet): see 2.03 ff above. The Crown is a 'party' within the meaning of the section and may give written notice of an intention to raise a preliminary matter, namely some point that in the opinion of the prosecutor could be resolved with advantage before the trial. Thus in *McDonald v HM Advocate*; *Valentine v McDonald*[1] the accused had lodged what purported to be a notice of special defence under section 82(1) of the Criminal Procedure (Scotland) Act 1975 (effectively asserting a conspiracy against him by various criminal authorities). The Crown lodged a notice under section 76(1)(c) (now section 72) both challenging the competency and relevancy of the special defence and also asking the court to hold that certain witnesses cited by the defence should be excused from complying with their citations; the sheriff's decisions were appealed to the High Court and the Crown's submissions were upheld. The Crown's statutory right to appeal is governed by section 74 of the 1995 Act.

1   1989 SCCR 165.

4.03   Preliminary diet appeal procedure

As with appeals by accused persons, the Crown's right of appeal is governed by the Criminal Procedure (Scotland) Act 1995, section 74 and the Act of Adjournal (Criminal Procedure Rules) 1996, SI 1996/513, rules 9.11 to 9.17; leave of the court of first instance is required. The application for leave to appeal must be made by motion to the judge at the diet; it must be made immediately following the making of the decision, and the application must be granted or refused there and then. The appeal is by note of appeal. The appeal may be abandoned in accordance with Rule

9.17. The procedure in Crown appeals is for all practical purposes the same as that governing appeals by accused persons: reference should be made to 2.04 above.

4.04 Lord Advocate's Reference

Where a person tried on indictment is acquitted or convicted of a charge, the Lord Advocate may refer to the High Court for its opinion a point of law which has arisen in relation to that charge.[1] The words 'or convicted' were inserted into this section by the Criminal Justice (Scotland) Act 1995, Schedule 6, paragraph 91, to allow the Crown to seek authoritative rulings on points that have arisen in a trial and have been decided against the Crown, though not resulting in an acquittal. The Clerk of Justiciary must send to the person tried and to any solicitor who acted for him at the trial a copy of the Reference and intimation of the date fixed by the appeal court for a hearing. The person tried has a right to participate in the Reference proceedings. In pursuance of that right, he may, not later than seven days before the date fixed for the hearing, intimate in writing to the Clerk of Justiciary and to the Lord Advocate (per the Crown Agent) either (a) that he elects to appear personally at the hearing, or (b) that he elects to be represented there by counsel.[2] Except by leave of the court on cause shown, he cannot participate personally or through counsel in the hearing proceedings if he has not intimated his election in writing as permitted by section 123(2)(b); this rule is without prejudice to 'his right to attend'. His right to attend presents no problem if he is at liberty; but if he is in custody on another matter he has no statutory 'right' to be brought from custody to attend a Reference hearing in respect of which he has made no written election under section 123(2)(b). Where there is no intimation by that person that he elects to be represented at the hearing by counsel, the High Court appoints counsel to act at the hearing as *amicus curiae*[3] to try to ensure that the issue is fully debated. The Lord Advocate meets the taxed costs of the representation.[4] The opinion of the High Court on the point of law referred by the Lord Advocate has no effect upon the acquittal.

1   Criminal Procedure (Scotland) Act 1995, s 123(1).
2   CP(S)A 1995, s 123 (2)(b).
3   CP(S)A 1995, s 123(3).
4   CP(S)A 1995, s 123(4).

4.05   Lord Advocate's Reference – points of law

The Lord Advocate's Reference procedure has not often been used. The first example of its use was *Lord Advocate's Reference (No 1 of 1983).*[1] The reference was presented in the form of a petition, the terms of which are set forth on pages 64-65 of the 1984 SCCR report. It narrated the material circumstances with commendable brevity and the court was supplied with transcripts of the material parts of the proceedings. Two questions of law were specified and 'referred' in the petition. The acquitted person did not elect to be represented by counsel, and senior counsel was appointed as *amicus curiae* by the court in terms of the Criminal Procedure (Scotland) Act 1975, section 263A(3), now section 123(3) of the 1995 Act; he received his instructions from the Clerk of Justiciary. The same procedure was followed in *Lord Advocate's Reference (No 1 of 1985);*[2] the acquitted person was represented at the hearing by senior counsel. As Sheriff Gordon's editorial commentary in the latter case makes clear,[3] the same trial had led to certain convictions and closely related points of law were considered by a differently constituted High Court on appeal. There seems to be no good reason why a Lord Advocate's Reference should not be put out for hearing at the same time and before the same court as an appeal arising from the same proceedings. Other Lord Advocate's References are reported in 1992 SCCR 724 (proof of documents); 1992 SCCR 960 (crime committed as a joke); 1995 SCCR 177 (causation in culpable homicide, where death followed supplying of controlled drug); 1996 SCCR 516 (method of proving bank statements).

1   1984 JC 52; 1984 SCCR 62.
2   1986 SCCR 329.
3   1986 SCCR 329 at 338-339.

4.06   Advocation in solemn proceedings

The Criminal Procedure (Scotland) Act 1995, section 131(1) provides:

'Without prejudice to section 74 of this Act, the prosecutor's right to bring a decision under review of the High Court by way of bill of advocation in accordance with existing law and practice shall extend to the review of a decision of any court of solemn jurisdiction'.

This provision was originally inserted into the Criminal Procedure (Scotland) Act 1975 by the Criminal Justice

(Scotland) Act 1980. The 'existing law and practice' there referred to was built up in relation to bills of advocation for sheriff and jury proceedings; but there were few examples of the use of this procedure and 'the existing law and practice' is somewhat ill-defined. The procedure was used in *HM Advocate v McCann*[1] to bring under review a sheriff's decision on a matter of competency and to seek the recall of his order declaring the accused (respondent) forever free from all questions or process for the crime for which he was charged. The sheriff had erroneously sustained a plea to the competency based on a misreading of the 110-day rule[2] (as it was then worded). The court passed the bill and recalled the order. There was no issue raised as to the competency of the procedure. Proceeding by bill of advocation was not abolished when preliminary diet procedure was introduced[3] and may be used even in circumstances in which preliminary diet procedure would be available or where the judge at the preliminary diet has refused the Crown leave to appeal.[4] It is also clear that the Crown may proceed by bill of advocation even if leave to appeal has been granted at the preliminary diet and the Crown has not exercised that right of appeal with leave.[5] The use of advocation procedure increased in recent years but the court has sometimes taken a restrictive view of its competency in solemn proceedings: see Chapter 3; 3.2, 13.13. A bill of advocation was used in *HM Advocate v McDonald*[6] to bring under review a decision by the trial judge (with two consulted judges) upholding a plea to the competency of an indictment: the plea had been taken when the diet of trial was called in the High Court and it was successfully argued at that stage that the proceedings were vitiated by a fundamental nullity. The accused lodged answers to the Lord Advocate's bill of advocation. A court of five judges upheld the Crown's submissions, passed the bill and recalled the decision of the trial judge. In *HM Advocate v McKenzie*[7] the trial judge, after the accused had pled guilty to serious assaults upon a woman, continued the case on the matter of sentence and required the Crown to contact the woman to ask her (but only if she was willing to assist the court) if she was prepared to say what she felt in relation to the disposal of the case. The Crown, by bill of advocation, asked the appeal court to hold that the judge's requirement was incompetent, erroneous and contrary to law and should be set aside. The appeal court agreed, passed the bill, relieved the Crown of the 'requirement' and directed the judge to proceed as accords (i e to deal with sentence in the ordinary way). The court considered the question of competency and concluded that 'there are present here such special and peculiar circumstances ... that it is right for us to entertain this bill'. In *Carmichael v Sexton*[8] the Crown successfully appealed against a refusal by a sheriff of an order under the Bankers' Books Evidence Act 1879 at the stage in proceedings at which persons had been fully committed on petition but no indictment had been served. In *Carmichael v JB*[9] the procurator fiscal successfully appealed to the High Court by bill of advocation against that part of the sheriff's interlocutor which allowed a witness's solicitor to be present when the witness was to be precognosed on oath in relation to a possible offence of rape, at a time when no person had appeared in court in respect of the alleged rape. Accordingly, in solemn proceedings, and in addition to the right of appeal contained in section 74 of the 1995 Act (preliminary diet), it may be competent for the Crown to appeal by way of bill of advocation before the indictment is served, after the case has been effectively dismissed as flawed by fundamental nullity, and even, in special circumstances, after conviction. The essential requirement is that in the course of criminal proceedings a court has made an improper order (or improperly neglected or declined to make an order), resulting in depriving the Crown of some right or privilege which the public prosecutor was entitled to exercise, or imposing upon the Crown some duty or responsibility which should not have been imposed, with the result that the due administration of criminal justice has been put at material risk. In solemn proceedings, the Crown cannot appeal during the trial by bill of advocation against an adverse decision on the admissibility of evidence.[10] However, in *HM Advocate v Khan*[11] it was held that the Crown could advocate a sheriff's decision to refuse to adjourn a long trial in order to allow a juror to recover from a temporary illness: the circumstances were very special.

---

1 1977 JC 1.
2 Criminal Procedure (Scotland) Act 1995, s 65(4).
3 See opening words of the Criminal Procedure (Scotland) Act 1975, s 76A.
4 See *Walkingshaw v Robison and Davidson Ltd* 1989 SCCR 359, a summary case, and *HM Advocate v Mechan* 1991 SCCR 812 at 820, note 3 by the editor of SCCR.
5 *HM Advocate v Sorrie* 1996 SCCR 778; *HM Advocate v Shepherd* 1997 SCCR 246.
6 1984 SCCR 229.
7 1989 SCCR 587.
8 1985 SCCR 333.
9 1991 SCCR 715.
10 *HM Advocate v Thomson* 1994 SCCR 40.
11 1997 SCCR 100.

4.07 Advocation against acquittal in summary proceedings

Although the usual method of appealing against an acquittal on a point of law is by stated case[1] the prosecutor's right to appeal by advocation against an acquittal in a summary prosecution on the ground of an alleged miscarriage of justice in the proceedings is expressly recognised in the Criminal Procedure (Scotland) Act 1995, section 191. Section 191(1), however (which also applies *mutatis mutandis* to proceedings by bill of suspension),[2] enacts that if the prosecutor has already applied for a stated case against the acquittal,[3] and in that application (or in any duly made amendment to it)[4] the same alleged miscarriage of justice is referred to, the appeal by bill of advocation cannot proceed without the leave of the High Court until the appeal by way of application for a stated case has been finally disposed of or abandoned. Reference should also be made to section 184 which provides that on a stated case being lodged with the Clerk of Justiciary the appellant shall be held to have abandoned any other mode of appeal which might otherwise have been open to him; but this deemed abandonment is subject to section 191. Thus, even although the prosecutor has a 'live' application for a stated case or has lodged a stated case, he may, in an exceptional case and with the leave of the High Court, proceed by bill of advocation in respect of an acquittal.

1 See 4.10 below.
2 See 3.06 ff.
3 Under the Criminal Procedure (Scotland) Act 1995, s 176(1).
4 Cf CP(S)A 1995, s 176(3).

4.08 Choice of procedure: advocation or stated case

The considerations that are relevant to the choice to be made between appealing in summary proceedings by stated case or by bill of suspension are similar to those discussed at 3.05 to 3.14 above. In summary, the position is as follows:

(1) In all but the most exceptional cases, any appeal by a prosecutor against an acquittal, in summary proceedings, on the ground of a miscarriage of justice related to the merits should be taken by stated case, not by bill of advocation, so that the considered views of the trial judge will be properly and fully placed before the appeal court.

(2) Appeal by stated case against such an acquittal is always competent, provided that the trial judge is able to sign the stated case and there are proper grounds of appeal.

However, the right to appeal may be lost by a failure to take an essential procedural step timeously; but appeal by bill of advocation against an acquittal is not always competent and will usually be inappropriate if appeal by stated case is available.

(3) If the right to appeal by stated case has been lost, so that the prosecutor can no longer competently appeal by stated case, a right to appeal by bill of advocation may survive.

(4) Unless he obtains the leave of the High Court, the prosecutor cannot, at the one time, found upon the same alleged miscarriage of justice in a stated case (including an application for one) and also in a bill of advocation.

(5) If both methods of appeal are open to the prosecutor, he must consider if unusual circumstances exist so that proceeding by bill of advocation might be more appropriate, having regard to the nature of the alleged miscarriage of justice, the necessity for and the value of placing the trial judge's considered views before the appeal court, and the savings that may be achieved in speed, in time and in effort by proceeding by way of advocation when the point at issue is crisp and clear and does not depend upon some considered assessment by and judgment of the trial judge.

(6) The powers of the court in the Criminal Procedure (Scotland) Act 1995, sections 182(5)(a) to 182(5)(e), 183(1)(d), 185 (authorising a new prosecution) and 183(4) (quashing and substituting sentences) are available, if appropriate, whether the appeal is by stated case or by bill of advocation.

1 Criminal Procedure (Scotland) Act 1995, s 191(3).

4.09 Advocation: other uses

As in the case of solemn proceedings,[1] advocation is the normal procedure used by the prosecutor to bring under review any improper order made by an inferior court, any neglect or refusal by such a court to make an order that it would be appropriate to make, or any other step, proceeding or neglect, the effect of which is to deprive the prosecutor of some right or privilege or procedural step or device to which he is properly entitled in the exercise of his public responsibility in the conduct of criminal proceedings. In *Walkingshaw v Robison and Davidson Ltd*[2] a bill of advocation was successfully used to invite the High Court to direct a sheriff to hear the pleas of parties on questions of competency and relevancy, the sheriff having dismissed the complaint upon wholly erroneous grounds. In *MacKinnon v Craig*,[3] where the sheriff refused to deal with a number of cases because the procurator fiscal depute was not in court when the sheriff was on the bench, ready to deal with them, the Crown obtained an order upon the sheriff to proceed as accords, i e to deal with the complaints in the ordinary way. An improper refusal of a search warrant, which the procurator fiscal had sought by petition, was successfully advocated in *MacNeill*[4] prior to the taking of proceedings against any person.[5] In *Tudhope v Mitchell*[6] a sheriff's unjustified refusal to grant the Crown an adjournment and his decision to desert the diet *simpliciter* were successfully appealed by bill of advocation. In that case, the accused lodged answers to the bill and appeared at the appeal court hearing to oppose the bill; it is not necessary, however, to lodge answers. See also *Carmichael v Monaghan*[7] where the sheriff unwarrantably deserted a diet in the course of the Crown evidence because a witness volunteered information revealing that the accused had a previous conviction. The procedure was successfully used in *Wilson v Caldwell*[8] to challenge an order by the sheriff upon the procurator fiscal to produce at a future adjourned diet copies of photographs of a road accident *locus*; the appeal court agreed with the procurator fiscal that it was not necessary for the sheriff to have such copies for the proper conduct of the case. In *Carmichael v JB*,[9] discussed in 4.06, the procedure was used to challenge part of a sheriff's interlocutor directing that a witness's precognition be taken on oath, in the presence of her solicitor.

1   See 4.06 above.
2   1989 SCCR 359.
3   1983 SCCR 285.
4   1983 SCCR 450.
5   See also *Carmichael v Sexton* 1985 SCCR 333 and *Lees v Weston* 1989 SCCR 177, a petition case (warrant to take fingerprints).
6   1986 SCCR 45.
7   1986 SCCR 598.
8   1989 SCCR 273.
9   1991 SCCR 715.

4.10   Appeal by stated case

The prosecutor in summary proceedings may appeal to the High Court on a point of law under the Criminal Procedure (Scotland) Act 1995, section 175(3) against an acquittal or a sentence. The prosecutor's right of appeal under section 175(3) is more limited than that of an accused person; his right is limited to an appeal on a point of law; but leave to appeal is not necessary. If the judge has neglected to impose a sentence which he was obliged to impose on the basis of the facts, the Crown may appeal; as in *Copeland v Pollock*[1] where the sheriff, though obliged by statute to disqualify a driver who had pled guilty to a statutory charge of driving with excess alcohol in his blood, decided against doing so upon the basis that the circumstances were exceptional and that to disqualify the driver, who was disabled, would be to punish him unduly: the question at issue was a point of law as to the meaning of 'special reasons' in the statute. The ground of appeal against acquittal must be alleged miscarriage of justice.[2] The Crown cannot, however, found upon the existence of additional evidence not heard at the trial to support its assertion that a miscarriage of justice has occurred. Thus, even although the criminal authorities may have discovered vital new evidence pointing overwhelmingly to the guilt of a person who has been acquitted, the Crown cannot appeal against his acquittal on the basis of such evidence. As the appeal must be on a point of law, it follows that if the prosecutor argues for a conviction upon the basis of the facts stated he must usually go so far as to say that, on the facts stated, no reasonable judge could have acquitted. The appropriate question in the stated case would therefore be 'On the facts stated, was I entitled to acquit the respondent?'.

1   (1976) SCCR Supp 111.
2   Criminal Procedure (Scotland) Act 1995, s 175(5E).

4.11   Stated case procedure

The sections of the Criminal Procedure (Scotland) Act 1995 governing the procedure are listed here:

s 175(3): right of appeal on a point of law against acquittal or sentence;

s 174(4) and (4A): right of appeal on a point of law in respect of the disposals listed; and, if the Scottish Ministers (formerly the Secretary of State)[1] make the appropriate order, right of appeal against disposals etc on the ground of undue leniency or inappropriateness. It appears that such an order is in course of preparation. The Secretary of State made an order, coming into force from 1 November 1996, specifying the classes of case in which the prosecutor might appeal against the disposal in summary proceedings: see 4.17 below;

s 175(7): applies the ordinary provisions as to procedure by stated case contained in sections 176–179, 181 to 185, 188, 190 and 192(1) and (2);

s 175(9): requires the prosecutor who appeals by virtue of section 175(4) to proceed by note of appeal in accordance with sections 186, 189(1)–(6), 190 and 192(1) and (2). Stated case procedure is also governed by rules in Chapter 19 of the Act of Adjournal (Criminal Procedure Rules) 1996. The procedure described in chapter 3 of this book (3.15 ff above) applies to appeals by the Crown; the same timetable constraints apply (see 3.33 above) and the same forms are used, with appropriate terminology to reflect the fact that the appeal is by the prosecutor. The prosecutor's right to consent to set aside a conviction (including conviction and sentence) is discussed at 4.15 below. Where an appeal against acquittal is sustained, the High Court may (a) convict and sentence the respondent[2] (but may not impose a sentence greater than the maximum which could have been passed in the inferior court);[3] or (b) remit the case to the inferior court with instructions to convict and sentence the respondent; or (c) simply remit to the inferior court with their opinion on the case. Section 183(3) now permits the High Court to exercise its power under section 189(1) by proceeding to sentence.[4]

1 Scotland Act 1998, ss 53(1)(c) and 117.
2 Criminal Procedure (Scotland) Act 1995, s 183(6).
3 CP(S)A 1995, s 183(7).
4 Effectively overruling *Lockhart v Black* 1993 SCCR 75.

4.12 Bail and other incidental applications

The Crown receives notice of all applications by a convicted person incidental to the appeal, including bail and applications for interim regulation, and is represented at any hearing into such matters. In all bail appeals and incidental applications (other than interim liberation applications and appeals under the Criminal Procedure (Scotland) Act 1995, section 201(4))[1] the Crown intimates to the bail judge whether or not an accused's appeal is opposed. The Crown should be prepared to assist the bail judge if invited to do so. In a Crown appeal the Advocate Depute will address the bail judge first, unless the accused opens by conceding the Crown appeal.

1 Remand in custody for reports.

4.13 Appeals against hospital orders

Reference is made to 3.38 above. The Crown will, as in the case of an ordinary appeal against sentence, take no part in the appeal court hearing regarding hospital orders, guardianship orders or orders restricting discharge, except at the invitation of the court, or, with leave of the court, if it has information that ought properly to be laid before the court.

4.14 Lodging answers to bills

It is usual, but not strictly necessary, for the Crown to lodge answers to bills of suspension or bills of advocation brought by convicted persons and intimated to the Crown. The answers will respond, as far as possible, to all the matters contained in the averments in the bill, at least so far as within the knowledge and sphere of responsibility of the Crown. Pleas in law are usually added to the Crown's answers to make clear what attitude the Crown is to take when the case calls before the appeal court for hearing. An example may be studied in *Durant v Lockhart*[1] where, before conviction, an accused sought to appeal by bill of suspension against a decision by a sheriff to adjourn a diet of trial. The Crown lodged answers containing two pleas in law:

'(1) The bill being premature and thereby incompetent should be dismissed.

(2) In any event, there having been no miscarriage of justice or oppression the bill should be refused.'

Bills of suspension are not appropriate when there is an issue on the facts: *O'Hara v Mill*.[2] However, if in the answers lodged by the Crown matters of fact averred by the complainer (i e the appellant/accused who brings the bill) are disputed by the Crown, the appeal court has hitherto proceeded upon the Crown's assertions of fact.[3] It is arguable that the court may not be able to continue to do so once the European Convention on Human Rights comes to be applied fully, through the mechanism of the Human Rights Act 1998 or of the Scotland Act 1998: in that situation it may be argued that if the court were to proceed upon the contradicted assertions of the prosecutor, the accused person's right to a fair trial (which extends to the appeal hearing) would be violated.[4] The court has power to remit to any fit person, such as the sheriff principal, to inquire and report in regard to any matter or circumstance affecting the appeal.[5] In a case in which the Crown has no real interest or information, answers may not be lodged and the

Clerk of Justiciary, on the instructions of the appeal court, may seek a report from the judge in the inferior court: as in *Craig v Smith*[6] where the matter raised in the bill was the competency of imposing imprisonment in the event of future default (as allowed under section 407(1)(a)) after a section 398[7] inquiry. However, as the issue was a pure legal question of competency, the Crown made submissions to the court supporting the sheriff's reasoning.

1   1985 SCCR 72.
2   1938 JC 4.
3   Cf *O'Hara v Mill* 1938 JC 4.
4   In this context, the reasoning of the court in *Burn, Petitioner* 2000 SCCR 384 – an art 5 case – may be relevant to the application of art 6.
5   Cf Criminal Procedure (Scotland) Act 1995, ss 182(5) and 191(3).
6   1990 SCCR 328.
7   Both sections of the Criminal Procedure (Scotland) Act 1975.

4.15   Consent by prosecutor to set aside conviction

Once a person has been convicted in criminal proceedings, the conviction cannot be altered, or quashed or set aside in whole or in part, except by the High Court.[1] The prosecutor can, however, make it clear to the court that he does not support a conviction or some part of it or that there is some flaw which undermines the sentence in whole or in part; or the prosecutor may concede that the court below erred in some specified way. If the prosecutor intimates to the court that there is some such flaw, the court will usually accept that a conviction or sentence which depends on the matter that the prosecutor no longer supports should be quashed or set aside accordingly, or, at least, that the concession was well founded and properly given.[2] If the prosecutor consents to set aside the judgment appealed against, he must explain why. The matter can be dealt with by a single judge who may choose to refer it to the High Court.[3] The court retains the right to decide the matter for itself and the appeal court may deliver an opinion of the court to explain precisely what is wrong with the conviction which is being quashed or why the sentence is being altered. Thus, for example, in *Jones v HM Advocate*[4] the court held that an important concession by the Crown was well founded, but went on to hold, contrary to the Crown's next and related submission, that a miscarriage of justice had resulted.

1   *O'Brien v Adair* 1947 JC 180 and *Boyle v HM Advocate* 1976 JC 32.
2   See, for example, *Brannon v Carmichael* 1991 SCCR 383.
3   *Macrae v Hingston* 1992 SCCR 911.
4   1991 SCCR 290.

4.16 Minute of consent to set aside

The Criminal Procedure (Scotland) Act 1995, section 188(1), an amended version of section 73 of the Summary Jurisdiction (Scotland) Act 1908, empowers the prosecutor in summary proceedings, if he is not prepared to maintain the judgment appealed against, to prepare a minute stating that he consents to the conviction and sentence being set aside, either in whole or in part.[1] This right arises once an appeal has been taken, whether under section 175(2) or by suspension or otherwise, and intimated to the prosecutor. It may, and should, if possible, be exercised at once. It is exercisable without prejudice to the prosecutor's right of appeal under section 175(3) or (4). It may be exercised even if the convicted person has taken no appeal, provided that the prosecutor, at any time, decides that he is not prepared to maintain the judgment on which the conviction is founded or a sentence imposed; he can apply by a relevant minute to set aside the conviction and/or sentence. Section 188 envisages that the accelerated special procedure which it authorises should be initiated immediately upon the taking of an appeal, i e as soon as practicable after the appeal is intimated to the prosecutor.[2] A primary object of the section is to save expense and delay wherever the conviction is untenable or where some fatal flaw in the proceedings has been uncovered or when new facts undermining the conviction or disposal have come to the prosecutor's knowledge. It is not designed to enable the prosecutor simply and without independent check to reverse the sheriff or justice on a question of law; so, for example, when the prosecutor submitted at the end of the trial that the evidence was sufficient, and the judge agreed, and convicted, the question then arising, i e 'Was the judge *entitled* to convict?', was held to be a question of law to be answered by the appeal court, not by the prosecutor; cf *O'Brien v Adair*.[3] The procedure to be followed is very clearly set out in section 188(2)–(6). The minute must set forth the grounds on which the prosecutor is of opinion that the judgment of the inferior court cannot be maintained. The minute is signed by the prosecutor and written on the complaint or lodged with the clerk of court. The prosecutor must send a copy of the minute to the appellant or his solicitor and it is the duty of the clerk of court to ascertain as soon as possible from the appellant or his solicitor whether the appellant desires to be heard by the High Court before the appeal is disposed of. He notes on the record whether or not the appellant so desires and transmits the complaint and relative proceedings to the Clerk of Justiciary. He in turn lays those papers before a single judge of the High

Court in chambers. That judge hears parties if they desire to be heard. Then, whether or not he has heard parties, the single judge may set aside the conviction in whole or in part and award such expenses to the convicted person, both in the High Court and in the inferior court, as the judge may think fit.[4] Alternatively, he may refuse to set aside the conviction,[5] in which case the proceedings are returned to the clerk of the inferior court; the appellant is then entitled to proceed with his appeal in the same way as if it had been marked on the date when the complaint and proceedings were returned to the clerk of the inferior court.[6] The High Court would rarely insist upon a hearing if both the prosecutor and the convicted person were agreed that the conviction and/or sentence could not be sustained. It is accordingly important that the grounds upon which the prosecutor bases his opinion as to the unsoundness of the conviction/sentence should be clear and specific. If it is clear that the judgment in the inferior court is fatally flawed, the High Court is most unlikely to seek to enforce strictly the time limits in the section. Once the prosecutor sends the minute (under subsection (3)) the preparation of any draft stated case is delayed – effectively put on hold – until the High Court has taken its decision under section 188(4).

1   Criminal Procedure (Scotland) Act 1995, s 181(1).
2   *O'Brien v Adair* 1947 JC 180 at 181.
3   1947 JC 180.
4   CP(S)A 1995, s 188(4)(b).
5   *O'Brien v Adair* 1947 JC 180.
6   *O'Brien v Adair* 1947 JC 180 at 181, per LJ-G Cooper.

4.17   Crown appeal against unduly lenient or inappropriate sentence etc in solemn proceedings

Where a person has been convicted on indictment, the Criminal Procedure (Scotland) Act 1995, section 108, confers upon the Lord Advocate the right to appeal against any of the disposals specified in that section. In addition to his right to appeal on a point of law, section 108(2) enables the Lord Advocate to appeal on the ground that the sentence or other disposal was unduly lenient or on unduly lenient terms, or on the ground that the court's decision not to make a particular order or to remit to the Principal Reporter was inappropriate, or on the ground that a deferment of sentence was inappropriate or on unduly lenient conditions. These are not exactly the same tests and they may be applied differently by the High Court:[1]

'unduly lenient': The test that the disposal has been 'unduly lenient' is applied to the following disposals specified as discrete paragraphs in section 108:

(a)   a sentence passed on conviction;

(h)   an admonition;

(i)   an absolute discharge.

'inappropriate': The test that the decision was 'inappropriate' is applied to:

(b)   a decision under section 209(1)(b) not to make a supervised release order;

(c)   a decision under section 234A(2) not to make a non-harassment order;

(f)   a decision made under section 49(1) to remit to the Principal Reporter.

'unduly lenient or on unduly lenient terms': The test that the making of the order was 'unduly lenient or . . . on unduly lenient terms' is applied to:

(d)   a probation order;

(e)   a community service order.

'inappropriate or on unduly lenient conditions': The test of 'inappropriate or . . . on unduly lenient conditions' is applied to:

(f)   an order deferring sentence.

1   *HM Advocate v Lee* 1996 SCCR 205 (a deferment case).

4.18   The approach of the High Court to undue leniency appeals by the Crown

The Crown right of appeal has been used over 40 times since it was introduced by section 42 of the Prisoners and Criminal Proceedings (Scotland) Act 1993; the original provision has been much amended since then. About half of the Crown appeals have been successful. Several, whether successful or not, have resulted in criticism of the Crown's handling of the appeal.[1] The critical approach evident in some of the cases reflects the High Court's reluctance to interfere with the sentencing discretion of the judge of first instance[2] and perhaps a distaste for appeals taken against a background of media-generated or politically-inspired agitation. Leave to appeal is not required for a Crown appeal; and this means that the High Court 'is entitled to demand from the Lord Advocate and his advisers a high standard of care and accuracy from the outset in the handling of these appeals'.[3] The decision as to whether or not a disposal is in fact unduly lenient or inappropriate is for the High Court alone to make.[4] The quorum is three.[5] If the Lord Advocate appeals against a sentence or other disposal on the ground of undue leniency or inappropriateness, he must ensure that the basis for that challenge is properly laid in the trial court.[6] The High Court will have regard to its own past practice and to 'repeated warnings' which it has issued in the past as to the consequences for those committing particular types of crime.[7] For example, in a number of the cases referred to below, such as those involving dealing in Class A drugs, the High Court has made it plain that a custodial sentence is virtually inevitable. If a judge departs from such guidance the High Court may use an appeal by the Lord Advocate to reinforce the obligation not to depart from the publicised practice. The High Court may also give 'guidance' to sentencers generally or just to the particular judge whose sentence has been criticised[8]. The principal test applied by the High Court is that found in the opinion of the Lord Justice-General in *HM Advocate v Bell*:[9] 'The sentence must be seen to be *unduly* lenient. That means it must fall outside the range of sentences which the judge at first instance, applying his mind to all the relevant factors, could reasonably have considered appropriate.' In a case in which the High Court 'would have been inclined to select a substantially higher sentence' it was held that the sentencing judge was entitled to be lenient and the appeal was refused.[10] It has been said that it is implicit in the terms used in the statute that some degree of leniency may be appropriate in particular circumstances.[11] An important case in which the carefully reasoned approach of the sentencing judge was examined by the High Court with the utmost care, and found to be well justified, is *HM Advocate v Wheldon and Others*.[12] Another striking case is *HM Advocate v Jamieson*[13] in which the court decided that the sentence under appeal was unduly lenient, but nonetheless refused the appeal 'because the statute leaves a discretion in this court whether or not to interfere with the sentence imposed'. If the High Court decides that the sentence or disposal is to be quashed, the court will then approach the matter afresh and impose whatever sentence it considers just. Thus the High Court may take into account matters that were not before the court of first instance, such as the convicted person's current circumstances and any material changes since the sentence appealed against was passed.[14] If the High Court allows the Crown's appeal it will not necessarily impose a very much higher sentence than the one judged to be unduly lenient. In *HM Advocate v Wallace*[15] the court quashed a sentence of 30 months' imprisonment for wilful fire-raising by throwing a bottle filled with petrol into a house, with reckless disregard for the safety of the occupants, and replaced it with a sentence of four years. Even if the appeal on the ground of undue leniency is refused, the High Court may vary some aspect of the sentence, as in *HM Advocate v Duff*[6] in which the court refused the appeal against the sentences of imprisonment in respect of sexual offences but ordered a report from the local authority officer with a view to imposing a supervised release order.

1 *HM Advocate v Lee* 1996 SCCR 205; *HM Advocate v Bennett* 1996 SCCR 331; *HM Advocate v McKay* 1996 SCCR 410 – the Crown abandoned the appeal at the hearing.
2 *HM Advocate v May* 1995 SCCR 375; *HM Advocate v Heron* 1998 SCCR 449.
3 *HM Advocate v McKay* 1996 SCCR 410 at 417.
4 *HM Advocate v McPhee* 1994 SCCR 830; see also *H.M.Advocate v Davidson* 1999 SCCR 729.
5 Criminal Procedure (Scotland) Act 1995, s 103(2).
6 *HM Advocate v Bennett* 1996 SCCR 331; *HM Advocate v Donaldson* 1997 SCCR 738 at 742.
7 *HM Advocate v McPhee* 1994 SCCR 830.
8 *HM Advocate v Bell* 1995 SCCR 244.
9 At 250.
10 *H.M.Advocate v Gordon* 1996 SCCR 274. See also *HM Advocate v Campbell* 1997 SLT 354.
11 *HM Advocate v MacPherson* 1996 SCCR 802 at 807.
12 1998 SCCR 710, especially per the Lord Justice-General at 722.
13 1996 SCCR 836; see also *H.M.Advocate v Carnwall and Ors* 1999 SCCR 904.
14 *HM Advocate v Bell* 1995 SCCR 244 at 251.
15 1999 SCCR 309.
16 1999 SCCR 193.

4.19 Undue leniency appeals in summary proceedings

The provisions allowing a similar appeal by the prosecutor in summary cases are contained in the Criminal Procedure (Scotland) Act 1995, section 175(4). There is a time limit of four weeks for marking such an appeal and there is no provision for obtaining any extension.[1] The list of disposals that may be appealed on the ground of undue leniency and/or inappropriateness is the same as in solemn proceedings and the same grounds are applicable to each type of disposal.[2] The appeal is by note of appeal using Form 19.3-A. Section 175(4) provides that the appeal by the prosecutor may be made in any class of case specified by order made by the Secretary of State. The order that brought these provisions into force was the Prosecutors Right of Appeal in Summary Proceedings (Scotland) Order 1996, SI 1996/2548. The order specified '. . . any case in which, on or after 1 November 1996 – a sentence is passed, or (ii) a probation order,

community service order or order deferring sentence is made, or
(iii) the person is admonished or discharged absolutely' as the
class of case in which the prosecutor may appeal under section
175(4). A revised order is understood to be in course of preparation by the Scottish Ministers.

The principles and considerations that govern the approach of
the High Court in solemn proceedings apply also to appeals in
summary proceedings.

1   Criminal Procedure (Scotland) Act 1995, s 186(2)(b).
2   CP(S)A 1995, s 175(4A).

5. Human Rights, Devolution and Europe

5.01   The European Convention on Human Rights

The Convention for the Protection of Human Rights and Fundamental Freedoms (known as the European Convention on Human Rights, and here referred to as 'the Convention') was ratified by the United Kingdom government on 8 March 1951. Other member states of the Council of Europe followed, and the Convention came into force on 23 September 1953. It was not then incorporated into domestic law in the United Kingdom. Nor were the rights set forth in the Convention incorporated into our domestic law; they could not be relied upon directly as enforceable rights. In *Kaur v Lord Advocate*[1] Lord Ross held that the Convention was not part of the municipal law of Scotland and that a Scottish court was not entitled to have regard to it, whether as an aid to construction or otherwise. However, that strict view began to be modified under the influence of the somewhat different approach taken in England, notably by the House of Lords, and also by the fact that once individuals were given a right of individual petition to the European Court of Human Rights (ECt HR) – in 1966 – Scottish cases began to be decided by the ECt HR in Strasbourg and to have important consequences for Scottish criminal law and procedure.[2] Thus the importance and influence of the Convention were certainly already growing when, in 1998, the Parliament of the United Kingdom enacted the Scotland Act 1998 and the Human Rights Act 1998. Their effect has been to introduce Convention rights (as defined in the Human Rights Act 1998) into Scots law. The Convention is amended from time to time by Protocols. The date of entry into force of the latest version of the Convention, as amended by Protocol No 11, is 1 November 1998. The expression 'the Convention rights', as used in the Human Rights Act 1998, means:

'the rights and fundamental freedoms set out in—
(a) Articles 2 to 12 of the Convention ,
(b) Articles 1 to 3 of the First Protocol, and
(c) Articles 1 and 2 of the Sixth Protocol,
as read with Articles 16 to 18 of the Convention.'[3]

The whole subject is well introduced in *Human Rights Law and Practice* (Editors, Lord Lester of Herne Hill and David Pannick), published by Butterworths, 1999. There is a clear chapter by Lord Reed on the impact of the legislation on Scotland.

1   1980 SC 319.

2   Cf *Granger v United Kingdom* (1990) 12 EHRR 469; *Boner v United Kingdom* (1994) 18 EHRR 246; *Maxwell v United Kingdom* (1994) 19 EHRR 97.
3   Human Rights Act 1998, s 1. The rights are set out in full in Sch 1 to the Act.

5.02   Bringing the Convention into Scots law: the Scotland Act 1998

The domestication of these Convention rights, i e effectively giving them the force of law directly in Scotland, is achieved in two stages. The first was effected by the coming into force of the relevant provisions of the Scotland Act in May 1999; the second with the coming into force, in October 2000, of the Human Rights Act 1998. In relation to appeals in criminal cases, it is the effect of the Scotland Act 1998 upon the role and functions of the Lord Advocate that must be most particularly noticed here. For what is known as a 'devolution issue' in that Act may be raised in relation to the carrying out by the Lord Advocate of his functions, including the performance of his duties as public prosecutor. The Human Rights Act, however, also substantially impacts upon Scottish law, practice and institutions. In particular, section 6, which provides that any court is a 'public authority' for the purposes of the Act, makes it unlawful for a public authority to act in a way that is incompatible with a Convention right. The result is that the Convention rights become directly binding upon the Scottish courts, including the appeal court, and other public authorities. Furthermore, section 2 requires any court that is determining a question that has arisen in connection with a Convention right to take into account the case law of the European Court of Human Rights and certain opinions and decisions of Council of Europe institutions specified in that section.

5.03   The Scotland Act 1998 and the Lord Advocate

In terms of the Scotland Act 1998, section 44, the Lord Advocate became a member of the Scottish Executive. Section 57(2) provides:

'A member of the Scottish Executive has no power to make any subordinate legislation, or to do any other act, so far as the legislation or act is incompatible with any of the Convention rights or with Community law.'[1]

Section 126(1) provides that 'the Convention rights' has the same meaning as in the Human Rights Act 1998. Thus the Convention rights are not *all* the rights contained in the Convention itself but are the rights and fundamental freedoms set out in those parts of the Convention specified in the Human Rights Act 1998, section 1. The right themselves are set out in full in Schedule 1 to that Act, to which reference must be made for the necessary detail. They include the 'Right to a fair trial' (article 6).

1   s 57(3) provides that s 57(2) does not apply to acts of the Lord Advocate, as public prosecutor, which are carried out by him in terms of binding primary legislation, even if they are acts that may violate Convention rights.

5.04   Right to a fair trial: article 6

Article 6 of the Convention reads:

'Right to a fair trial
1. In the determination of his civil rights and obligations or of any criminal charge against him, everyone is entitled to a fair and public hearing within a reasonable time by an independent and impartial tribunal established by law. Judgment shall be pronounced publicly but the press and public may be excluded from all or part of the trial in the interest of morals, public order or national security in a democratic society, where the interests of juveniles or the protection of the private life of the parties so require, or to the extent strictly necessary in the opinion of the court in special circumstances where publicity would prejudice the interests of justice.
2. Everyone charged with a criminal offence shall be presumed innocent until proved guilty according to law.
3. Everyone charged with a criminal offence has the following minimum rights:
(a) to be informed promptly, in a language which he understands and in detail, of the nature and cause of the accusation against him;
(b) to have adequate time and facilities for the preparation of his defence;
(c) to defend himself in person or through legal assistance of his own choosing or, if he has not sufficient means to pay for legal assistance, to be given it free when the interests of justice so require;
(d) to examine or have examined witnesses against him and to obtain the attendance and examination of witnesses on his behalf under the same conditions as witnesses against him;
(e) to have the free assistance of an interpreter if he cannot understand or speak the language used in court.'

The rights contained within this article, as interpreted by the courts both in Strasbourg and in the United Kingdom, extend to the whole proceedings, including any appeal.[1] In implementing the rights in any particular case it may well be necessary to have regard to circumstances occurring outwith the proceedings themselves, if they might affect the fairness of the proceedings.

1   *Eckle v Federal Republic of Germany* (1982) 10 EHRR 1, paras 76-77;
Neumeister v Austria (1968) 1 EHRR 91 at para 19.

5.05   Devolution issues: what they are

A devolution issue is defined in the Scotland Act 1998, Schedule
6, Part I , paragraph 1.[1] The first two paragraphs read as follows:

'1. In this Schedule "devolution issue" means—
(a) a question whether an Act of the Scottish Parliament or any provision of an Act of the Scottish Parliament is within the legislative competence of the Parliament,
(b) a question whether any function (being a function which any person has purported, or is proposing, to exercise) is a function of the Scottish Ministers, the First Minister or the Lord Advocate,
(c) a question whether the purported or proposed exercise of a function by a member of the Scottish Executive is, or would be, within devolved competence,
(d) a question whether a purported or proposed exercise of a function by a member of the Scottish Executive is, or would be, incompatible with any of the Convention rights or with Community law,
(e) a question whether a failure to act by a member of the Scottish Executive is incompatible with any of the Convention rights or with Community law,
(f) any other question about whether a function is exercisable within devolved competence or in or as regards Scotland and any other question arising by virtue of this Act about reserved matters.
2. A devolution issue shall not be taken to arise in any proceedings merely because of any contention of a party to the proceedings which appears to the court or tribunal before which the proceedings take place to be frivolous or vexatious.'

Paragraph (a) relates to the legislative competence of the Scottish Parliament.

Paragraph (b) relates to the application of legislation allocating functions between Executive ministers, including the Lord Advocate.

Paragraph (c) relates to the powers of any member of the Scottish Executive: the issue is whether or not the law has given him the authority to exercise a particular function.

Paragraph (d) is really a special case of (c), because members of the Scottish Executive, including the Lord Advocate, have no legal authority – no *vires* – to exercise a function in a way incompatible with

Convention rights (i e European Convention on Human Rights) or with Community law (i e European Union law).

Paragraph (e) is really a special case of (d), because it makes it clear that a failure by a member of the Scottish Executive to act is to be treated as conduct incompatible with Convention rights or Community law if either of these sources of law obliges him to act.

Paragraph (f) is an all-inclusive category apparently designed to sweep up anything missed in the preceding paragraphs.

1   There are provisions in other statutes for other parts of the UK: cf the Northern Ireland Act 1998, Sch 10 and the Government of Wales Act 1998, Sch 8.

5.06   'Incompatible' acts of the Lord Advocate

As the Lord Advocate is a member of the Scottish Executive, he has no power to do any act so far as that act is incompatible with any of the Convention rights or with Community law.[1] The only exception is that noted earlier:[2] the Lord Advocate may do such an 'incompatible' act, whether in prosecuting an offence or in his capacity as head of the systems of criminal prosecution and investigation of deaths in Scotland, if, but only if, having regard to primary legislation (of the UK Parliament) he could not have acted differently, or (in the case of an alleged omission) was not able to act in the way that it is suggested he should have acted.

1   Scotland Act 1998, s 57(2).
2   See n 4 above.

5.07   Who may raise a devolution issue?

The Scotland Act 1998, Schedule 6, paragraph 4(3) [*Institution of Proceedings*] provides: 'This paragraph is without prejudice to any power to institute or defend proceedings exercisable apart from this paragraph by any person.' 'Person' obviously includes the accused. However, persons other than the accused may be involved in criminal proceedings and may be able to found upon a devolution issue. In *Kelly v Vannet*,[1] for example, the accused's solicitor brought a bill of suspension to challenge the grant by a sheriff of a warrant sought by the Crown to precognosce him (the solicitor) on oath. Such an issue might now be presented as a devolution issue.

1   1999 SCCR 169.

5.08   Devolution issues: challenging incompatible acts

The principal result of these provisions for present purposes is that if, in the course of criminal proceedings prosecuted by or on behalf of the Lord Advocate, an accused alleges that the prosecutor has acted or is about to act[1] in breach of any restriction placed upon the Lord Advocate by the Scotland Act 1998, section 57(2), the person so alleging may be able to challenge the Lord Advocate's act or omission, by bringing it before the court as a devolution issue . The Lord Advocate has issued an instruction that the Crown is not to present any argument to the effect that, when acting under summary procedure, a procurator fiscal does not act as his representative[2]. The effect is that a person can seek to raise a devolution issue in respect of any allegedly incompatible act (or omission) by a procurator fiscal or by Crown counsel. A person who wishes to raise a devolution issue may do so by using the procedures provided for in the new Chapter 40 of the Act of Adjournal (Criminal Procedure Rules) 1996, SI 1996/513. It is not the intention of the authors to deal in this text with the law in relation to raising a devolution issue at first instance. However, a good illustrative example of how the procedure was used in proceedings on indictment is to be found in *Little v HM Advocate*.[3]

1   *Paton v Ritchie* 2000 SCCR 151.
2   *Brown v Stott* 2000 SLT 379.
3   1999 SCCR 625.

5.09   Devolution issues: the impact

In *HM Advocate v Montgomery and Coulter*, the Lord Justice-General said: 'it would be wrong ... to see the rights under the European Convention as somehow forming a wholly separate stream in our law; in truth they soak through and permeate the areas of our law in which they apply.' There is an ever-growing number of cases in which devolution issues have been raised and have reached the appeal court: they tend to be dealt with, at least at the first stage, very quickly. The reported cases include the following examples:

McNab v H.M. Advocate[1] (admissibility of evidence)

H.M. Advocate v Dickson[2] (challenge to the *vires* of the Act of Adjournal (Devolution Issue Rules) 1999 SI 1999/1346)
Gayne v Vannet[3] (whether fixed fees system in legal aid amounted to oppression by militating against fairness of proceedings)
McLean v H.M. Advocate[4] (delay, and specification of charge: article 6)
H.M. Advocate v Danskin[5] (whether publishing report of earlier proceeding prejudiced right to fair trial)
McFadyen v Gatley[6] (expenses in extradition proceedings, articles 6 and 7)
Paton v Ritchie[7] (if police interview in absence of solicitor violates article 6)
McKenna v H.M. Advocate[8] admissibility of hearsay of deceased person)
Brown v Stott above (Crown relying on self-incriminating statement obtained under compulsory powers in road traffic legislation)
Starrs v Ruxton[9] (prosecuting before temporary sheriff)
Hoekstra & Ors v H.M. Advocate[10] (disqualifying a bench of the appeal court on basis of perceivable lack of impartiality on part of one of its members).
HM Advocate v Fraser[11] (prejudicial pre-trial publicity)
HM Advocate v Nulty[12] (hearsay evidence of a mentally ill person)
Cumnock (Scotland) Ltd v HM Advocate[13] (delay in a case of scientific complexity)

1 1999 SLT 99.
2 1999 SCCR 859; 2000 JC 93.
3 2000 SCCR 5.
4 2000 SCCR 112.
5 2000 SCCR 101.
6 2000 SCCR 123.
7 2000 SCCR 151.
8 2000 SCCR 159.
9 2000 SLT 42.
10 2000 SCCR 367.
11 2000 SCCR 412
12 2000 SCCR 431
13 2000 SCCR 453

5.10 The Devolution Issue Rules

These are contained in Chapter 40 of the Act of Adjournal (Criminal Procedure Rules) 1996, SI 1996/513, as amended. This new chapter was added by the Act of Adjournal (Devolution Issue Rules) 1999, SI 1999/1346 ('the Devolution Issue Rules') which came into force on 6 May 1999. They regulate the procedure that has to be followed where a devolution issue arises in any proceedings. They include important definitions. They also provide for such matters as giving intimation to others specified in the rules of the intention to raise a devolution issue, the prescribed forms to be used, the timetables to be observed and the methods to be used by others seeking to enter the proceedings. They also deal with references to the High Court and to the Judicial Committee of the Privy Council, interim regulation of matters relating to the proceedings and all consequential matters. There are some differences in detail between the steps to be taken in proceedings on indictment,[1] summary proceedings[2] and other criminal proceedings[3] (the latter to include appeals to the High Court).

The practitioner must consult the Devolution Issue Rules themselves in order to be sure that the steps to be taken at first instance are taken correctly and on time. As this book is concerned with criminal appeals, first instance procedure is not dealt with here unless it is necessary to explain some aspect of appeal procedure. It has also to be borne in mind that the Devolution Issue Rules are liable to be changed in the light of experience, because this is a rapidly expanding field of criminal procedure and practice, and new aspects of the operation of the law arise frequently.

Solemn proceedings

In *HM Advocate v Montgomery and Coulter*[4] the court discussed the interrelation of devolution issue procedure and preliminary diet procedure. The Lord Justice-General observed that a challenge to a provision in an Act of the Scottish Parliament on the ground that it is incompatible with any of the Convention rights might take the form of a plea to the competency or relevancy of the indictment, and it would therefore come within the scope of the Criminal Procedure (Scotland) Act 1995, section 72(1)(a)(i), while also being regulated by Chapter 40 of the Act of Adjournal (Criminal Procedure Rules) 1996, SI 1996/513. He stated that 'when a devolution issue is involved, however, the procedures in Sections 72 to 75 and 79 (Preliminary Pleas) must be melded, so far as possible, with those in Chapter 40 of the Act of Adjournal'. In that case, although the procedure followed at first instance was flawed, the High Court treated the Crown appeal as if taken under section 74(1) of the 1995 Act. It was also observed by the Lord Justice-General that Chapter 40 of the Criminal Procedure Rules 1996 contained no specific provisions for a hearing on a devolution issue minute. He added:

'The inference is that devolution issues are to be considered under existing procedures' and

'While the authority now given to Convention rights in our law means that, when considering what constitutes a fair trial, the court must take account of Convention law and jurisprudence, the issue will still fall to be dealt with under our existing procedures Cf. *McLeod v HM Advocate (No 2)*[5] 1998 JC 67, at p. 77 D-E per the Lord Justice-General. In other words, even when relying on an alleged breach of Article 6 on the part of the Crown, an accused person may still seek to focus the issue by means of a plea of oppression.'

These observations apply to appeals against decisions at first instance on devolution issues. It follows that after the indictment has been served, but before the trial, it would be appropriate to proceed by way of preliminary diet procedure under sections 72 ff. If the matter does not fall within those listed in section 72(1)(a)–(c) it might fall under section 72(1)(d), provided that the party raising the devolution issue correctly judges that it is a matter that could be resolved with advantage before the trial. However, one of the possible problems with 'melding' the preliminary diet procedure and the devolution issue procedure is that the periods within which notice should be given are not always the same. The period specified in paragraph 40.2 of the Criminal Procedure Rules is 'not later than 7 days after the date of service of the indictment'. In respect of preliminary diets the period is 'the appropriate period' which varies according to the character of the matter to be raised.[6] Rule 40.5(1) provides that no party to criminal proceedings shall raise a devolution issue in those proceedings except in accordance with the preceding rules 'unless the court, on cause shown, otherwise determines'.[7]

Additionally, when a party to proceedings on indictment proposes to raise a devolution issue he has to give notice not only to the court and to the other parties (as in preliminary diet procedure) but also to 'the relevant authority'[8] which, in criminal cases, means the Advocate General for Scotland. The Advocate General may enter the proceedings by taking the steps specified in Rule 40.2(3). Rule 40.2 is 'without prejudice to any right of or requirement upon a party to the proceedings to raise any matter or objection or to make any submission or application under section 72 [of the 1995 Act]'.[9]

Even if the matter cannot be raised under the preliminary diet procedure, it may be possible to raise it as a ground of appeal after the verdict in the ordinary way. Rule 40.4 applies to 'criminal proceedings which are not proceedings on indictment or summary proceedings'. If a devolution issue is raised during the course of the trial, Rule 40.7(3) applies. It reads: 'Where the court determines that a devolution issue may be raised during a trial, the court shall not refer the devolution issue to the High Court but shall determine the issue itself.' So there is no appeal at that stage, unless possibly by bill of advocation, although proceeding by bill of advocation during trial is rarely competent. The words 'Where the court determines that a devolution issue may be raised during a trial' appear to refer back to the right of the court to rule that the contention of the party that there is a devolution issue is 'frivolous or vexatious'[10] and that accordingly no devolution issue is raised. They may also refer to the right of the court on cause shown to allow certain matters to be raised even although the prescribed time for raising the point may have passed.[11]

Summary proceedings
Devolution issues may give rise to objections to competency or relevancy. The Criminal Procedure (Scotland) Act 1995, section 144(4) provides that any objection to the competency or relevancy of a summary complaint or the proceedings thereon, or any denial that the accused is the person charged by the police with the offence, shall be stated before the accused pleads to the charge. Subsection (5) provides that no such plea can be advanced at any later stage except with leave of the court on cause shown. Section 145 enables the court to adjourn the case; this allows the matter to be properly debated later. Section 174 provides that, with leave of the court, and in accordance with such procedure as may be prescribed by Act of Adjournal, a party may appeal to the High Court against a decision of the court of first instance relating to an objection or denial of the kind mentioned in section 144(4). It follows, given the approach of the court in *HM Advocate v Montgomery and Coulter*,[12] that a devolution issue may be raised under section 144 and appealed to the High Court, with leave, under section 174. Although that is so, the time prescribed for raising an issue under the two forms of procedure are not the same. However, as the Lord Justice-General pointed out in the somewhat special circumstances of that case, but under reference to the broadly similar provisions in section 73(1) of the 1995 Act, 'there will probably be few cases in which a presiding judge will think it right to grant leave at this stage since such an appeal will be liable to lead to additional delays'. The general guidance that can properly be taken from that observation is that the possibility of additional delay is a factor to be taken into account by a court when deciding whether or not to grant leave.

As section 174 itself re-affirms, there may be a right of appeal in the ordinary way, under section 175(1); and section 191 preserves the right to appeal by bill of suspension, after conviction. It may be possible to raise a devolution issue by bill of advocation,[13] but the right to proceed by bill of advocation is very limited.[14] This is discussed further in Chapter 3 above.

1 Acts of Adjournal (Criminal Procedure Rules) 1996, SI 1996/513, Rule 40.2.
2 Criminal Procedure Rules, Rule 40.3.
3 Criminal Procedure Rules, Rule 40.4.
4 1999 SCCR 959.
5 1998 SCCR 77 at 96.
6 Criminal Procedure (Scotland) Act 1995, s 72(1) and (2).
7 For an example, see *HM Advocate v Nulty* 2000 SCCR 431.
8 Criminal Procedure Rules, Rule 40.2(1).
9 Criminal Procedure Rules, Rule 40.2(5).
10 Scotland Act 1998, Sch 6, para 2.
11 Criminal Procedure (Scotland) Act 1995, s 79(1) and Rule 40.5(1).
12 1999 SCCR 959.
13 See *McLeay v Hingston* 1994 SCCR 116.
14 See *Khalid v HM Advocate 1994* SCCR 47, and Sheriff Gordon's note thereon at 50.

5.11   Making a reference to the High Court

There is a third possibility, provided for by rule 40.7 of the Criminal Procedure Rules. That rule takes account of the fact that the Scotland Act 1998, Schedule 6, paragraph 9 allows a court, other than any court consisting of two or more judges of the High Court of Justiciary, to refer any devolution issue which arises in criminal proceedings before it to the High Court of Justiciary.[1] Although this provision does not allow an appeal, as such, it enables the court of first instance to have the devolution issue resolved by the High Court during the first instance proceedings, but not during the trial itself.[2] If the court does make a reference to the High Court under Rule 49.7. it must pronounce an order giving directions to the parties about the manner and time in which the reference is to be drafted. It must also give its reasons for making the reference and cause those reasons to be entered in the record or minutes of proceedings, as the case may be, and continue the proceedings from time to time as may be necessary for the purposes of the reference.[3] The reference has to be adjusted as appropriate at the sight of the court. That means that the parties draft it but the court must approve the draft to ensure that the issue is properly defined. After approval, the reference has to be transmitted by the clerk of the court of first instance to the Clerk of Justiciary with a certified copy of the record or minutes of proceedings, as the case may be, together, where applicable, with a certified copy of the relevant indictment or complaint.

1 See also Sch 10, para 27 and Sch 8, para 17.
2 See above, r 40.7(3) Act of Adjournal (Criminal Procedure Rules) 1996, SI 1996/513.
3 Criminal Procedure Rules, rule 40.7(1).

5.12 Raising a new devolution issue on appeal

A devolution issue is able to be raised in the form of a ground of appeal or in a statement of matters which the appellant desires to bring under review by way of a stated case appeal. If the devolution issue is not sought to be raised until after leave to appeal has been granted in respect of grounds specified in the letter formally intimating the grant of leave, the appellant will need to seek leave of the High Court as permitted by the Criminal Procedure (Scotland) Act 1995, section 107(8) for solemn appeals or 180(8) or section 187(7) for summary appeals. If leave is to be sought under these sections the timetables contained in the same sections must be observed.

5.13 Right of appeal for Advocate General

By a new provision[1] inserted into the Criminal Procedure (Scotland) Act 1995 by the Scotland Act 1998, Schedule 8, paragraph 32 the Advocate General for Scotland may refer to the High Court for its opinion any devolution issue which has arisen in criminal proceedings to which the Advocate General was a party in pursuance of paragraph 6 of Schedule 6 to the 1998 Act. The right to a reference arises if in those proceedings a person has been acquitted or convicted of a charge, whether on indictment or in summary proceedings.

1 s 288A.

5.14 Reference to the Judicial Committee of the Privy Council

There are provisions in the Rules, Rule 40.9. to cover the situation that arises when a court consisting of two or more judges of the High Court of Justiciary decides to refer a devolution issue to the Judicial Committee of the Privy Council, under the Scotland Act 1998, Schedule 6, paragraph 11:[1] or where a court is required by a relevant authority to refer a devolution issue to the Judicial Committee. Rule 40.9 should be referred to for its terms, which explain in a straightforward way what the referring court is to do and how the Judicial Committee (Devolution Issue) Rules 1999, SI 1999/665 ('the Judicial Committee Rules') apply. It will be observed that a reference to the Judicial Committee must include such matters as may be required by the Judicial Committee Rules, Rule 2.9. The first sub-paragraph of that rule specifies all the details that have to go into the reference. It must be referred to for its precise terms by those who are drafting a reference, so that it may be done accurately. It provides:

'2.9—(1) The reference shall set out the following—
(a) the question referred;
(b) the addresses of the parties;
(c) the name and address of the person who applied for or required the reference to be made;
(d) a concise statement of the background to the matter including—
  (i) the facts of the case, including any relevant findings of fact by the referring court or lower courts ; and
  (ii) the main issues in the case and the contentions of the parties with regard to them;
(a) the relevant law, including the relevant provisions of the Scotland Act 1998;
(b) the reasons why an answer to the question is considered necessary for the purpose of disposing of the proceedings.'

The second sub-paragraph requires that there shall be annexed to the reference all judgments already given in the proceedings, including copies of any interlocutors and any notes attached to such interlocutors. Rule 2.10 of the Judicial Committee (Devolution Issue) Rules 1999 provides that any party to the proceedings in the court making the reference who intends to participate in the proceedings in the Judicial Committee must, within 14 days of the service upon him of the copy reference, enter appearance and give notice to the other parties that he has done so. Any Law Officer who is not already a party to the proceedings may intervene;[2] but in criminal proceedings under the Criminal Procedure (Scotland) Act 1995 the Crown is always a party.

---

1 Or Sch 10, para 29 or Sch 8, para 19.
2 Judicial Committee (Devolution Issue) Rules 1999, SI 1999/665, r 2.11.

5.15 Appeals to the Judicial Committee of the Privy Council

If the High Court determines the devolution issue, the decision may be appealed, with leave of the High Court, to the Judicial

Committee of the Privy Council. The Scotland Act 1998, Schedule 6, paragraph 13 provides inter alia:

'An appeal against a determination of a devolution issue by – (a) a court of two or more judges of the High Court of Justiciary (whether in the ordinary course of proceedings or on a reference under paragraph 9) . . . shall lie to the Judicial Committee, but only with leave of the court concerned or, failing such leave, with special leave of the Judicial Committee.'

The procedure is governed by the Judicial Committee (Devolution Issue) Rules 1999, Rule 2.12.[1] If leave to appeal to the Privy Council has been obtained from the court that has determined the issue, the appellant has to lodge a petition of appeal within six weeks of the date on which leave to appeal was granted. If leave to appeal has not been granted by the court that has determined the issue, the person who desires to appeal must obtain special leave to appeal from the Judicial Committee and thereafter lodge a petition of appeal within 14 days of the grant of special leave. Special leave to appeal is governed by Chapter V of the Judicial Committee Rules. Chapter V is very detailed indeed and must be consulted for its exact terms. It includes provisions regarding time limits (petition to be lodged within 28 days of judgment appealed against), the form of the petition, service, the number of copies required, entering appearance, lodging additional papers, written submissions and oral hearings (if referred by the Board for oral hearing, lodging petitions out of time) and various incidental matters. Reference should also be made to the Scotland Act 1998 (Consequential Modifications) Order 1999 SI 1042 and the comment thereon by Sir Gerald Gordon in the Note appended to the report of *Hoekstra v H.M. Advocate* in 2000 SCCR at 383.

1 Contained in the schedule to the Judicial Committee, Rules.

5.16 Procedure following disposal of reference, or appeal, by Judicial Committee

Under the Act of Adjournal (Criminal Procedure Rules) 1996, SI 1996/513, Rule 40.10, once the Judicial Committee has determined a devolution issue, the determination is intimated to the clerk of the court that made the reference. The determination is laid before the court. The court then gives directions for further procedure and intimates those directions to the parties. In the case of an appeal, once the Judicial Committee has made its judgment, the High Court, on the application of any party to the proceedings, fixes a diet for dealing with the consequences.[1]

1 Act of Adjournal (Criminal Procedure Rules) 1996, Rule 40.11.

5.17 The Human Rights Act 1998

This Act is likely to be of increasing importance in the development of the criminal law in the United Kingdom. That is because the Act requires United Kingdom courts and tribunals to take account of judgments, decisions, declarations and advisory opinions of the ECt HR (referred to as the 'jurisprudence' of the Court), and of certain opinions of the Commission and certain decisions of the Committee of Ministers.[1] Appropriate rules of court may be made governing the manner in which such material is to be placed before the Scottish courts. Hitherto the courts have found no difficulty in relying upon the reports contained in the unofficial European Human Rights Reports (EHRR). These reports are not, however, exhaustive; some cases may not be reported in them. Furthermore, the courts frequently consider cases from other jurisdictions concerning similar human rights issues. In *Brown v Stott*[2] the opinions refer to reports of cases from Canada, South Africa and the United States of America, amongst others. The Human Rights Act 1998 requires that all legislation be read and given effect to in a way that is compatible with the Convention rights.

1 Human Rights Act 1998, s 2.
2 2000 SLT 379.

5.18 Incompatible acts by public authorities (section 6)

Of even greater importance is the fact that section 6 of the Human Rights Act 1998 makes it unlawful for any public authority to act in a way that is incompatible with a Convention right (unless required to do so by primary legislation). A court is a public authority (as are tribunals and certain persons whose functions are or include functions of a public nature). Section 7 contains provisions relating to the bringing of proceedings against a public authority in respect of an alleged contravention of a relevant Convention right. Section 7 enables a person who claims that a public authority has acted (or proposes to act) in a way that is made unlawful by section 6(1) to 'bring proceedings against the authority under the Act in the appropriate court or tribunal'. That right is, however, heavily qualified, in respect of a court, by section 9, which provides that section 7 proceedings in respect of a judicial act[1] may be brought only by exercising a right of appeal, or by judicial review or in such other forum as may be prescribed by rules.[2] This means that the rights themselves can be claimed in court proceedings. Section 9 also enables a person to 'rely on the Convention right or rights concerned in any legal proceedings'. A person may proceed against a public authority only if he is, or would be, a 'victim'[3] of the unlawful act. The term 'legal proceedings' includes an appeal against the decision of a court or tribunal. Section 8 specifies the judicial remedies that are available. Where the act to be challenged under section 7 is a judicial act (as defined in section 9(5) to mean 'a judicial act of a court, including an act done on the instruction, or on behalf, of a judge') then proceedings may be brought only '(a) by exercising a right of appeal; (b) on an application(in Scotland a petition) for judicial review; or (c) in such other forum as may be prescribed by rules.'[4]

1   Defined in Human Rights Act 1998, s 9(5).
2   Defined in HRA 1998, s 7(9).
3   Within the meaning of art 34 of the Convention.
4   All such rules are now published on the internet: http://www.scotcourts.gov.uk (Scottish Court Service website) and http://www.hmso.gov.uk/stat.htm (Stationery Office website).

REFERENCES TO COURT OF JUSTICE OF THE EUROPEAN COMMUNITIES

5.19   The nature of a reference

A 'reference' to the Court of Justice of the European Communities ('the European Court') (not to be confused with the European Court of Human Rights), by means of which a 'preliminary ruling' is sought on a 'question' (as defined in the next paragraph), is not in the strict sense an appeal from a decision of the court which makes the reference. However, despite the possible ambiguity in the term 'preliminary ruling', the judgment of the European Court finally determines the issues raised by the reference; and the Scottish court which has made the reference is obliged to accept the ruling made by the European Court and apply it to the case in respect of which the ruling was made. Such a reference is therefore treated in this book alongside ordinary appeal procedure.

5.20   The European Community and the European Court

What is now called the European Union consists of three Communities. The first to come into existence was the European Coal and Steel Community (ECSC) created by the Treaty of Paris, which came into force in 1952. The two others, the European Economic Community (EEC) and the European Atomic Energy Community (Euratom), were created by the Treaties of Rome, the EEC Treaty and the Euratom Treaty respectively, which took effect in 1958. In 1967 the three Communities were merged and, after signing the Treaty of Accession in 1972, the United Kingdom became a member of each of the three merged Communities. The Court of Justice of the European Community (referred to as 'the European Court') is common to all three Communities. The language used in article 31 of the ECSC Treaty to describe the role of the European Court is slightly different from that used in the EEC and Euratom Treaties in articles 164 and 136 respectively; but the effect is the same: the European Court has the responsibility of ensuring that, in the interpretation and application of all the treaties and of any rules made for their implementation, 'the law' is observed. The jurisdiction of the court in relation to the giving of preliminary rulings is conferred by separate articles in each of the three Treaties. The one most commonly invoked is article 177 of the EEC Treaty. Detailed consideration of these matters is beyond the scope of this book.[1] All that need be observed for present purposes is that a 'question' which may arise for reference to the European Court is defined in the Act of Adjournal (Criminal Procedure Rules) 1996 SI 1996, 513, Rule 31.1 to mean 'a question or issue under Article 177 of the EEC Treaty, Article 150 of the Euratom Treaty or Article 41 of the ECSC Treaty'.

There are also many other important treaty documents, for example the Single European Act [1986], the Treaty of European Union ('the Maastricht Treaty') [1992] and the Treaty of Amsterdam [1998]. As the treaty texts are able to be altered it will be necessary to consult the current text of the relevant treaty if a question is thought to be likely to arise. However, the procedure for referring a 'question' from a Scottish court remains unaltered by recent treaty developments.

---

1   A simple introduction to the European legal order and the institutions will be found in Lord Mackenzie Stuart's 1977 Hamlyn Lectures, *The European Communities and the Rule of Law*. A fuller, up-to-date explanation may be found in PSRF Mathijsen's *A Guide to European Union Law* (7th edn 1999).

5.21 European questions

The rules governing the reference to the European Court of questions arising in solemn and in summary cases are contained in Chapter 31 of the Act of Adjournal (Criminal Procedure Rules) 1996, SI 1996, 513. This chapter of the Rules is written with commendable clarity and should be easy to follow. It should be consulted directly by practitioners who are thinking of raising a European Union 'question' in criminal proceedings, as these Rules are likely to be altered in the light of experience, especially now that a 'question' within the meaning of this chapter might also be a devolution issue within the meaning of Chapter 40 of the same Rules. In brief, the current procedure prescribed by Chapter 31 where a European 'question' is to be raised is as follows.

Solemn procedure

(1) Notice of intention to raise the question has to be given to the court before which the trial is to take place, and also to the other 'parties' (including co-accused), not later than 14 days after service of the indictment.

(2) The notice has to be recorded on the record copy of the indictment or in the record of proceedings, as the case may be, and the court, in chambers, must reserve consideration of the question to the trial diet.

(3) The court may order that witnesses and jurors are not to be cited to attend at the trial diet.

(4) At the trial diet, the court, after hearing parties, may determine the question or may decide that a preliminary ruling should be sought.

(5) If the court determines the question without making a reference, the accused are then called upon to plead to the indictment (if it is otherwise appropriate for them to do so). The court is empowered to prorogate the time for lodging any special defence and to continue the diet to a specified time and place. If witnesses and jurors have not been cited to attend the trial diet, the court must continue the diet and order the citation of witnesses and jurors to attend the continued diet. No period during which the diet is so continued is to be longer than 21 days, but that period can be lengthened by the court, on special cause shown, on the application of the prosecutor or the defence. The time of any period granted must be taken into account for the purposes of determining whether any time limit has expired.[1]

Summary procedure

In summary proceedings at first instance the notice of intention to raise a 'question' has to be given before the accused is called upon to plead to the complaint. A record of the notice has to be entered in the minute of proceedings and the accused is not called upon to plead. The court may hear parties on the 'question' forthwith or may adjourn the case to a specified date for a hearing. After the hearing, whenever it is heard, the court may either determine the 'question' or decide that a 'preliminary ruling' should be sought. If the court determines the 'question' (by deciding the point at issue) the accused is then called upon to plead to the complaint, where appropriate, i e if there is still a complaint to plead to.

1   Act of Adjournal (Criminal Procedure Rules) 1996, SI 1996/513, Rule 31.2.

5.22   Preliminary ruling

As Professor Mathjisen points out in *A Guide to European Union Law*, at p 140: 'the responsibility for applying Community Law rests, in the first place, with the national judge'. Reference to the European Court ensures uniformity in the interpretation and application of the law. If the question arises, whether in solemn or in summary proceedings, in a court from which there is a right of appeal, that court may determine the issue, subject to appeal, or may make a reference. Where, however, the question arises in a court from which there is no right of appeal, that court must make a reference – subject, however, to exception in cases where the answer is clear and beyond reasonable doubt, as discussed below. If such a court makes an order making a reference, any party to the proceedings who is aggrieved by the order may appeal against the order to the High Court sitting as a court of appeal. The appeal to the High Court must be taken within 14 days after the date of the order.[1]

1   SI 1996/513, Rule 31.7.

5.23   Deciding if reference to be made

The court of first instance, after hearing parties, may determine the question or may decide that a preliminary ruling – from the European Court – should be sought. This provision echoes the Treaty provisions which empower the court to refer 'if it considers that a decision on the question is necessary to enable it to give judgment'.

DECIDING IF REFERENCE TO BE MADE **5.23**

In an English case in the House of Lords[1] Lord Diplock, with whom all the other judges agreed, stated that:

'in a criminal trial on indictment it can seldom be a proper exercise of the presiding judge's discretion to seek a preliminary ruling before the facts of the alleged offence have been ascertained, with the result that the proceedings will be held up for nine months or more. . . It is generally better . . . that the question be decided by [the presiding judge] in the first instance and reviewed thereafter if necessary throughout the hierarchy of the national courts.'

Clearly, the considerations that lay behind that statement are also material in Scotland; but there are in Scotland other relevant considerations. The Scottish courts are in certain respects more accustomed to deciding questions of law in advance of the determination of the facts: this circumstance is reflected in the existence of the preliminary and first diet procedure contained in the Criminal Procedure (Scotland) Act 1995, sections 71–74 and 144. An accused is entitled under these provisions to raise a matter relating to the competency or relevancy of the indictment or complaint and to obtain a diet to determine the matter. Most questions (as defined in the Act of Adjournal (Criminal Procedure Rules) 1996, SI 1996/513, Rule 31.1(1)) would relate to competency or relevancy. Accordingly, as Rules 31.2(4) and 31.3(4) provide, the accused, or the Crown, is entitled to obtain either a decision on any question raised or a reference for a preliminary ruling by the European Court. The judge's options are to make a reference or to decide the 'question'. Whatever he may do, he cannot postpone a decision on any question of relevancy or competency raised at a preliminary diet until after 'the facts of the alleged offence have been ascertained' (as favoured by Lord Diplock); there is no proof before answer on indictment. If he grants leave to appeal under section 74 or section 174(1) then the case goes to the High Court on appeal and the High Court 'shall proceed to make a reference' if the (European) question is still raised on appeal and has to be decided. Despite this wording and the corresponding requirements of the treaties, it is not necessary for the High Court, despite there being no appeal from its decisions (unless a devolution issue is raised), to make a reference if the answer to the 'question' is 'so obvious as to leave no scope for reasonable doubt'. This is how the matter was stated by the Lord Justice-General in *Jardine v Crowe*,[2] following *Orru v HM Advocate*[3] and *Westwater v Thomson*.[4] Even without leave to appeal, the Crown may appeal to the High Court by bill of advocation; and, if it does so, there must be a reference of any European question which has to be decided in the appeal – unless, again, the answer is so obvious as to render a reference unnecessary. In *Wither v Cowie; Wither v Wood,*[5] a summary case, the court appeared to suggest that it would have been better for the sheriff to deal with the matter and hear the evidence before deciding if a preliminary ruling should be sought. That would appear to be the course least likely to lead to long delay; a proof before answer would make sense in this context.

1   *R v Henn* [1981] AC 850.
2   1999 SCCR 52.
3   1998 SCCR 59, a case on indictment appealed after conviction.
4   1992 SCCR 624.
5   1990 SCCR 741.

5.24 Form of reference

If the court decides that a preliminary ruling should be sought, the duties of the court, regardless of whether it is a summary or a solemn court, are those set out in the Act of Adjournal (Criminal Procedure Rules) 1996, SI 1996/513, Rule 31.5, to which reference should be made. The court must give reasons for its decision to make a reference and cause those reasons to be recorded in the record or minute of proceedings. The court must also continue the proceedings from time to time as may be necessary for the purposes of the reference. The reference has to be drafted as in Form 31.5 and the court also gives directions as to the drafting and adjustment of the case for reference. The court approves the reference after adjustment and transmits it to the Registrar of the European Court, when the period for appeal allowed by Rule 31.7 has expired.[1]

1   Act of Adjournal (Criminal Procedure Rules) 1996, SI 1996/513, Rule 31.5.

5.25 Appeal against reference order

If a party does not want there to be a reference he can appeal against the making of the order. This appeal procedure is regulated by the Act of Adjournal (Criminal Procedure Rules) 1996, SI 1996/513, Rule 31.7. Where an order making a reference is made, 'any party to the proceedings who is aggrieved by the order' may appeal against the order within 14 days after its date. The right to appeal against the making of an order for a reference is not available against a decision of the High Court sitting as a court of appeal or exercising the *nobile officium* The words 'any party to the proceedings' are broad enough to include a co-accused who has raised no European question but who objects to the reference, possibly because he is anxious to avoid the inevitable delay in proceeding to trial. Although the appeal against the making of the order must be taken within 14 days, it is clear from *HM Advocate v Wood; HM Advocate v Cowie*[1] that the High Court may in the exercise of the *nobile officium* relieve a party from the consequences of an excusable failure to comply with the statutory timetable. The appeal against the order making the reference is made by lodging with the clerk of court that made the order a note of appeal in the form of Form 31.7 of the Criminal Procedure Rules. In that form the appellant must set forth details of the order appealed against and also the grounds for appeal. The form must be signed by the appellant or his solicitor and a copy of the note of appeal must be served by the appellant on each other party to the proceedings. The clerk of court records the lodging of the note and transmits it to the Clerk of Justiciary with the record or minute of proceedings and a copy of the relevant indictment or complaint.

1   1990 SCCR 195. But see *Connolly, Petitioner* 1997 SCCR 205.

5.26   Disposing of the appeal

The Act of Adjournal (Criminal Procedure Rules) 1996, SI 1996/513, Rule 31.7(5) empowers the High Court to sustain or dismiss the appeal, and in either case remit the proceedings to the court of first instance with instructions to proceed as accords. That was the order made by the High Court in *Jardine v Crowe*,[1] where the case reached the High Court by way of note of appeal against a decision on competency after the sheriff decided not to make a reference; the suggestion that a reference was necessary was renewed in the grounds of appeal and rejected.

1   1999 SCCR 52.

5.27   Appeal against a refusal to refer

There is no provision in the rules contained in the Act of Adjournal (Criminal Procedure Rules) 1996, SI 1996/513 Chapter 31 governing an appeal against a refusal by the trial court to seek a preliminary ruling. If the judge in the court of first instance does not decide to make a reference then he must decide

161

the question himself. In that event, the decision he makes may be appealable at that stage, if necessary with leave, under the ordinary procedures, or after the verdict in the court of first instance. *Jardine v Crowe*[1] is an example of an appeal against a decision on competency that depended upon determining a European question. *Orru v HM Advocate*[2] is an example of an appeal after conviction raising a European question.

1   1999 SCCR 52.
2   1998 SCCR 59.

5.28   Preliminary ruling – final procedure

When a preliminary ruling has been given by the European Court on a question referred to it and the ruling has been received by the clerk of the referring court, the clerk lays it before the referring court, which then gives directions as to further procedure. The directions have to be intimated by the clerk, with a copy of the ruling, to each of the parties to the proceedings. These directions will almost invariably be that the case will be put out for (further) hearing.

If the European Court's ruling exhausts the only live questions remaining in the case the court, after hearing parties, will simply apply the ruling and decide the case in accordance with it. If the ruling is not exhaustive of the issues the court will, after hearing parties, apply the ruling and decide the case in accordance with it and with the findings in fact and the relevant domestic law. Any statement of the relevant law contained in a preliminary ruling is in effect treated as if it were a matter of fact.

5.29   European 'questions' and 'devolution issues' in the same case.

It has been noted elsewhere[1] that, in terms of section 57 of the Scotland Act 1998, the Lord Advocate, as a member of the Scottish Executive, has no power to do any act so far as that act is incompatible with Community law.[2] Section 126(9) of the same Act details what is referred to as Community law in that Act. Schedule 6 to that Act provides that 'devolution issue' means inter alia:

'(d) a question whether a purported or proposed exercise of a function by a member of the Scottish Executive is incompatible with . . . Community law ; (e) a question whether a failure to act by a member of the Scottish Executive is incompatible with . . . Community law'.

It is clear that in criminal proceedings a matter of the applicability of Community law may arise, and may fall to be treated both as a 'devolution issue' and as a 'question' in terms of Rule 31.1(1) of Chapter 31 of the Act of Adjournal (Criminal Procedure Rules) 1996, SI 1996/513. If that happens and a party to the proceedings seeks to raise the matter in both senses it will be necessary to comply with the requirements of both sets of rules, namely those in Chapter 40 and those in Chapter 31. They are different but not incompatible. The time limits are not the same and the requirement for notice and intimation may differ. It is therefore essential for the practitioner to ensure that he complies with both sets of rules in such a case, as well as any procedural requirements imposed by the ordinary provisions applicable to preliminary diets or to diets for disposing of preliminary pleas in summary cases if these procedures are applicable.

1   para. 5.06.
2   NB the exception in Scotland Act 1998, s 57(3).

6. Powers of the court

FUNDAMENTAL NULLITY

SCOTTISH CRIMINAL CASES REVIEW COMMISSION

SOLEMN

6.01 Disposal of appeal against decision at a first diet or a preliminary diet

This matter is dealt with at 2.09 above. In brief, in disposing of an appeal under the Criminal Procedure (Scotland) Act 1995, section 74(1), the High Court may affirm the decision appealed against or may remit the case to the court of first instance with such directions in the matter as the High Court thinks fit. If the court of first instance has dismissed the indictment or any part of it, the High Court has power to reverse that decision and to direct the court below to fix a trial diet. The High Court may also on cause shown extend the period mentioned in section 65(1), namely the 12 months commencing with the accused's first appearance on petition.

6.02 Powers incidental to a full appeal hearing

The Criminal Procedure (Scotland) Act 1995, section 104, which is without prejudice to any existing power of the High Court, enables the court to employ various methods for the purpose of enabling it properly to determine an appeal under section 106(1), (any appeal against conviction or sentence or both) or section 108 (Lord Advocate's right of appeal against disposal). The court may order the production of any document or other thing connected with the proceedings.[1] This provision would, for example, allow the appeal court to order the production of an article that should have been produced at the trial but was not[2] because it had been temporarily mislaid; if it later appears to be of materiality the court may order its production. The court may hear any evidence relevant to any alleged miscarriage of justice or order such evidence to be heard by a judge of the High Court or by such other person as it may appoint for that purpose.[3] The appeal court may take account of any circumstances relevant to the case which were not before the trial judge.[4] The effect of these provisions became clear in *Carrington v H.M. Advocate*[5] in which the section's predecessor – section 252 of the Criminal Procedure (Scotland) Act 1975 – was considered. That was a case in which the appellant appealed against his conviction, although he had been convicted following his own 'guilty' plea. The court decided to consider new evidence which, the appellant submitted, would show that he was suffering from total alienation of reason at the time of the offence. In *Rubin v HM Advocate*[6] Lord Justice-General Emslie expressed the opinion obiter that the power now contained in section 104(1)(c) was designed for use only in appeals against sentence. Lord Cameron was not, without fuller argument and consideration, prepared so to restrict its application. *Carrington* decided that the section (now 104(1)(b)) was in such unqualified terms that the court would be entitled to hear the evidence tendered. Accordingly the powers are available in all appeals and are provided in addition to the power to hear fresh evidence under section 106(3). These provisions could cover, for example, those cases in which material is put before the appeal court either by the Crown or by the appellant, but which is not put forward as evidence at the trial. In *McDonald v HM Advocate*[7] the court, though without reference to any statutory power under section 252(c) of the 1975 Act, took account of circumstances highly relevant to the case which were not before the trial judge or the jury, principally the fact that during the course of the trial, but during an adjournment and therefore outwith the presence of the judge and jury, one of the witnesses (McLeod) who had not yet concluded his evidence, was charged with perjury. The Crown continued to present the witness to the trial court as worthy of credit and to assert to the jury that statements which the witness had made were true, although in the perjury charge the same statements were averred to be false. The appeal court's knowledge of these circumstances came not from the evidence or from the presenting of additional evidence but to some extent from assertions and explanations by Crown counsel. In *McColl v HM Advocate*[8] the appeal court took account of representations as to matters of fact, made to the appeal court by counsel for the appellant, as to what had happened between the clerk of court and the jury in the course of the jury's deliberations and also of statements by the clerk of court and the trial judge on the same events. On that basis the appeal court concluded that there had been a miscarriage of justice in that part of the trial had taken place outwith the presence of the accused, contrary to section 145(1).[9] In *McCadden v HM Advocate*[10] the court, again without specific reference to paragraph (c), took account of precognitions from persons bearing upon a juror's alleged prejudicial statements about an appellant during the trial; the appellant's motion (which was refused) was to order an inquiry into the matter by a suitable person in terms of paragraph (d). It may well be, however, that the High Court does not need the statutory authority that paragraph (c) of section 104 confers, as the High Court's 'existing power' is extremely wide and constantly finds new expression. The power to remit to any fit person to inquire and report in regard to any matter or circumstance affecting the appeal is contained in paragraph (d) of section 104. The competency of such a proceeding was affirmed in *McCadden*.[11] In a summary case, *Bradford v McLeod*,[12] the appeal court remitted to the sheriff principal to inquire and report in relation to the conduct of the sheriff who, it was said, had on a social occasion made remarks about miners in a context which disqualified him from sitting as the trial judge in relation to certain charges brought against miners shortly thereafter. The report was fully taken into account by the appeal court. In *Crossan v HM Advocate*[13] the appellant had been charged with murder. In the course of the trial, his counsel, acting on oral instructions, tendered a plea of guilty to murder. The trial judge convicted him in terms of the power conferred by section 137A(2) of the 1975 Act – now section 95(2) of the 1995 Act. The case was then by agreement adjourned until the next morning. When the case called then, the appellant sought to withdraw his plea of guilty. The trial judge held that this could not competently be done. Both then and at the appeal hearing it was clear that there was a serious dispute as to the circumstances in which the plea had been instructed and tendered. The court decided to remit to a High Court judge to enquire into that dispute and report under paragraph (d) of the section, and held further that the circumstances revealed by the report could be taken account of by the appeal court under paragraph (c). The evidence had to be heard in public as in an ordinary criminal trial.[14]

Finally, the court may appoint a person with expert knowledge to act as assessor to the High Court in any case where it appears to the court that such expert knowledge is required for the proper determination of the case. In *Carraher v HM Advocate*[15] Lord Justice-General Cooper said that this power (then contained in section 6 of the Criminal Appeal (Scotland) Act 1926) had never been exercised and was one that should be used with the greatest reserve. That remains the position. If additional expert evidence is needed the court can obtain it, as in *Duff v HM Advocate*,[16] where the court did not explain the source of its power to call upon the psychiatrists who had submitted written reports to the trial court to give oral evidence to the appeal court, which was considering an appeal against sentence only. That case was concerned with medico-legal questions as to diminished responsibility, and risk.

1 Criminal Procedure (Scotland) Act 1995, s 104.
2 As in *MacNeil v HM Advocate* 1986 SCCR 288.
3 CP(S)A 1995, s 104(b).
4 CP(S)A 1995, s 104(c).
5 1994 SCCR 567.

6 1984 SCCR 96.
7 1986 SCCR 376 at 380.
8 1987 SCCR 153.
9 1989 SCCR 229.
10 See also *Cunningham v HM Advocate* 1984 SCCR 40.
11 1985 SCCR 282.
12 1985 SCCR 282 at 289.
13 1985 SCCR 379.
14 1996 SCCR 279.
15 CP(S)A 1995, s 104(2) and (3).
16 1946 JC 108.
17 1983 SCCR 461.

6.03   Other routine incidental powers

The High Court sitting as a court of appeal makes such orders or gives such directions as are reasonably incidental to and necessary for determining any appeal. It may decide to remit to the judge in the inferior court for clarification of some matter that has not been adequately dealt with in any report or case that he may have prepared. If the court decides to allow additional or amended grounds of appeal it may remit to the inferior court for an additional report. It may allow the Crown to amend the indictment in an appeal being heard by the court if that is appropriate. It may order a transcript of any part of the proceedings[1] including proceedings at a preliminary diet. The statutory power to require the judge who presided at the trial to produce his trial notes[2] was repealed by the Criminal Justice (Scotland) Act 1995. The court can adjourn an appeal to await the result of other proceedings, as happened in *Mitchell v HM Advocate.*[3] In that case the appellant lodged as additional evidence[4] an affidavit of another man, Chapman, to the effect that it was he (Chapman), not the appellant (Mitchell) who had carried out the crime of which Mitchell had been convicted. When the Crown informed the court that Chapman was to be tried on a charge of attempting to pervert the course of justice by swearing a false affidavit (the one being relied upon by Mitchell), the appeal court postponed any further hearing of the appeal until after the trial.[5] The court may, as an exceptional indulgence, permit part of an appeal to be presented by counsel and part by the appellant himself.[6] When the appeal court continues or adjourns a case for what is likely to be a long period it may grant bail.[7] The court can also call for reports, such as social inquiry reports, community service reports or medical or psychiatric reports. Where the court below has failed in its statutory duty to obtain some such report the appeal court can quash the sentence, call for the necessary report and, at a later date, decide what sentence to impose in the light of the report. The court may extend time limits or excuse non-compliance with them and with most rules of practice for the time being in force: section 129. The exception relates to rules under section 60 (Appeals against hospital orders).[8] It has no power to award expenses (in solemn appeals).[9] The appeal court now issues written opinions.[10] No conviction, sentence, judgment, order of court or other proceeding is to be quashed for want of form.[11]

1 Provided that one exists: see *Carroll v HM Advocate* 1999 SCCR 617.
2 Criminal Procedure (Scotland) Act 1975, s 237.
3 1989 SCCR 502.
4 In terms of the Criminal Procedure (Scotland) 1975, s 228(2).
5 See 1989 SCCR 502 at 510 A–E.
6 *Montgomery v HM Advocate* 1987 SCCR 264.
7 Criminal Procedure (Scotland) Act 1995, s 112(1); even if the conviction was for murder, as in *Campbell (T) v HM Advocate* 1998 SCCR 214.
8 CP(S)A 1995, ss 103(5) and 129.
9 CP(S)A 1995, s 128.
10 CP(S)A 1995, s 118(9).
11 CP(S)A 1995, s 118(8)(a) (solemn), s 192(3)(a) (summary).

6.04 Frivolous appeals

The provision formerly contained in the Criminal Procedure (Scotland) Act 1975, section 256, allowing the High Court to dismiss summarily an appeal against conviction if the appeal was judged to be frivolous or vexatious, was removed by the Criminal Justice (Scotland) Act 1995, it having become unnecessary in the light of the requirement to obtain leave to appeal.

6.05 Disposal of appeal against conviction

The leading section regulating the powers of the High Court in disposing of an appeal against conviction in solemn proceedings is the Criminal Procedure (Scotland) Act 1995, section 118. Subsection (1) of this section empowers the High Court to dispose of the appeal by:
(a) affirming the verdict of the trial court, or
(b) setting aside the verdict of the trial court and either quashing the conviction or substituting therefor an amended verdict of guilty; or
(c) setting aside the verdict of the trial court and quashing the conviction and granting authority to bring a new prosecution in accordance with section 119.
The wording of paragraph (c) was altered in the 1995 Act, even although it was a consolidation measure, in order to make it

clearer that, whether or not the court decided to grant authority to bring a new prosecution, the conviction had to be quashed. The full background is discussed in *Campbell (T) v HM Advocate.*[1] An amended verdict of guilty substituted under subsection (1)(b) must be one that could have been returned on the indictment before the trial court. If the court sets aside a verdict but the appellant still stands convicted – whether because the court has substituted an amended verdict of guilty, or because he remains convicted on other charges on the same indictment and in respect of which the verdict was not set aside (or for both these reasons) – the court may pass another, but not more severe, sentence. The court has 'an entirely free hand' to reduce or effectively to re-impose the original sentence(s), though it may not increase any sentence or substitute a more severe disposal when exercising the relevant power under section 118(3).[2]

Appellant insane
If, in relation to any appeal,[3] it appears to the High Court that the appellant committed the act(s) charged against him but was insane when he did so, the court is obliged to act in accordance with the Criminal Procedure (Scotland) Act 1995, section 118(5). It must, therefore, (a) set aside the verdict of the trial court and substitute therefor a verdict of acquittal on the ground of insanity,[4] and (b) quash any sentence imposed on the appellant (or disposal or order made) as respects the indictment and make an order of the kind mentioned in section 57(2): the provisions of subsections (3) and (4) of section 57 apply to such an order. Section 118(5)(b)(ii), however, permits the court to make no order after setting aside the verdict and substituting a verdict of acquittal on the ground of insanity.

1   See 1998 SCCR 214, per Lord McCluskey at 257 ff.
2   *Caringi v HM Advocate* 1989 SCCR 223.
3   ie against conviction, sentence or both.
4   Cf Criminal Procedure (Scotland) Act 1995, s 54.

6.06   Setting aside the verdict

If the High Court sets aside the verdict it may simply quash the conviction. If the convictions on all charges are set aside, and no amended verdict of guilty is substituted therefor, all the sentences must be quashed. If the appellant was convicted on several charges and is successful in his appeal against some of the convictions, but not others, the court is entitled to reconsider and may alter the sentences imposed in respect of the convictions which still remain standing.[1] Such sentence or sentences can therefore be reconsidered whether the trial court imposed separate sentences for each charge in respect of which the appellant was found guilty, or imposed one cumulo sentence or some mixture of separate and cumulo sentences. When dealing with an appeal against conviction alone,[2] the court has no power to increase the sentences imposed in the trial court. The court may quash a conviction and substitute therefor an amended verdict of guilty, provided that the amended verdict is one which the trial court jury could have returned on the indictment before them. The appeal court may, for example, substitute a verdict of culpable homicide for one of murder, or of reset for one of theft or of a statutory offence for a common law crime, if that could have been done on the trial indictment, as in *McKenzie v HM Advocate*.[3] In *Salmond v HM Advocate*[4] the court substituted a verdict of 'guilty of assault under extreme provocation' for a verdict held to be incompetent, i e 'guilty (of attempted murder) by reason of reckless indifference with extreme provocation'; the sentence was then reduced from five years' imprisonment to three years': for other examples, see the Criminal Procedure (Scotland) Act 1995, Schedule 3, paragraphs 7 ff. As the amended verdict must be one that could competently have been returned on the indictment before the trial court, it follows that if, after a partly successful appeal, the appellant stands convicted of some of the charges of which he was convicted in the trial court, and is newly convicted by the appeal court of amended offences in relation to other charges of which he was convicted in the trial court, (but in respect of which he has been acquitted on appeal), the appeal court will then have a free hand – subject to section 118(3) – to reconsider all questions of sentence in relation to the actual convictions which are recorded against the appellant at the conclusion of the appeal. Thus the only formal limitation upon its power is the statutory requirement not to impose a more severe sentence than those quashed.[5] The appeal court is not bound by the trial judge's view. The High Court may impose a probation order or a community service order; the appellant then remains subject to the jurisdiction of the High Court and if he transgresses the conditions can be brought back before that court to be dealt with. The court may issue a warrant for the arrest of a person who it decides should appear before it again, or issue a citation to such a person to appear. The appeal court can also defer sentence and it sometimes does. There is no appeal against any sentence imposed by the appeal court: section 124(2).[6] A technical error by the court can be remedied.[7]

1   *Caringi v HM Advocate* 1989 SCCR 223 at 225B, per Lord Justice-Clerk Ross, delivering the opinion of the court.
2   But contrast Criminal Procedure (Scotland) Act 1995, s 118(4), appeals against sentence etc.
3   1959 JC 32.
4   1991 SCCR 43.
5   CP(5)A 1995, s 118(3).
6   Cf *Perrie, Petitioner* 1991 SCCR 475; but see *Express Newspapers plc, Petitioners,* 1999 SCCR 262 and 6.13 below.
7   See *Perrie, Petitioner* 1991 SCCR 475 at 481A, and the case of *James McLellan* there referred to; *Heywood, Petitioner* 1998 SCCR 335.

6.07   Authority for new prosecution

If the High Court, in disposing of an appeal against conviction, sets aside a verdict of a trial court, it may grant authority to bring a new prosecution in accordance with the Criminal Procedure (Scotland) Act 1995, section 119.[1] Exactly similar provisions confer the same power on the High Court in relation to appeals in summary proceedings.[2] In either case (solemn or summary), if authority is granted, the accused may be prosecuted in respect of the same or any similar offence arising out of the same facts which gave rise to the conviction which the court has set aside. In a new prosecution (whether solemn or summary) the accused cannot be charged with an offence more serious than that of which he was convicted in the earlier proceedings.[3] This amendment, made by section 46 of the Criminal Justice (Scotland) Act 1995, effectively overruled *HM Advocate v Boyle*.[4] If the successful appellant is later convicted in the new proceedings which have taken place under such authority, no sentence may be passed on conviction unless it could have been passed on conviction under the earlier proceedings. If new prosecution proceedings are to be brought they must be commenced within two months of the date on which authority to bring the new prosecution was granted.[5] However, a new prosecution may be brought under section 119 notwithstanding that any *other* time limit for the commencement of proceedings has elapsed.[6] If the two months prescribed by section 119(5) pass and no new prosecution has been brought, the order setting aside the verdict has the effect, for all purposes, of an acquittal.[7] The new proceedings are deemed to be commenced on the date on which a warrant to apprehend or cite the accused is granted, provided such warrant is executed without unreasonable delay; in any other case the proceedings are deemed to be commenced on the date on which the warrant is executed. There is no power to extend the two-month limit. The subject of 'unreasonable delay' in the execution of warrants is much litigated, but it lies outwith the scope of this book.[8]

1 Criminal Procedure (Scotland) Act 1995, s 118(1)(c).
2 CP(S)A 1995, ss 183(1)(d), 185 and 191(3) and (4) – appeal by suspension or advocation.
3 CP(S)A 1995, s 119(2).
4 1992 SCCR 939.
5 CP(S)A 1995, s 119(5).
6 CP(S)A 1995, s 119(4).
7 CP(S)A 1995, ss 119(9) and 185(9).
8 Cf *Renton and Brown* paragraph 9.48 and Stoddart *Criminal Warrants* (2nd edn, 1999) para 2.15.

6.08 New prosecutions: the practice

The first case in which the High Court granted authority to bring a new prosecution was *Mackenzie v HM Advocate*.[1] The trial judge had misdirected the jury (in a case of alleged murder by stabbing) by erroneously withdrawing the defence of accident. Lord Justice-Clerk Wheatley observed that the new statutory provisions left the matter of granting authority for a new prosecution to the discretion of the court without specifying any grounds on which that course was warranted.

'Each case will require to be dealt with on its own facts. Where it is not suggested that there was not sufficient evidence to warrant the conviction, or any fault on the part of the Crown, and the one thing which has led to the setting aside of the verdict is a material misdirection in law by the trial judge, that is something which, in the interests of justice and the public interest, must be seriously taken into account when deciding whether to grant authority to bring a new prosecution instead of simply quashing the conviction.'[2]

Mackenzie had originally been charged with murder; the Crown brought a new prosecution charging him with culpable homicide, which charge was found not proven.[3] In *King v HM Advocate*,[4] where the one successful ground was a material misdirection for which the trial judge alone was responsible, authority was granted for a new prosecution: one was successfully taken. In *Cunningham v HM Advocate*[5] the trial judge erred in giving instructions to the jury outwith the presence of the accused, in contravention of section 145 of the Criminal Procedure (Scotland) Act 1975. A new prosecution was authorised because the error was purely that of the judge and was 'procedural in character'.[6] The new prosecution resulted in a verdict of not proven (some five months after the appeal). In *McGhee v HM Advocate*[7] the trial judge's error consisted of making improper comments on the appellant's answers at judicial examination; but, as there was adequate evidence, authority was granted; the new prosecution resulted in a conviction. The fault that warranted the setting aside of the verdict of *Slater v HM Advocate*[8] was purely procedural: the jury, under direction, returned an ambiguous verdict to an ambiguous partial plea of guilty. The Crown successfully moved the appeal court to grant authority under section 254(1)(c) of the 1975 Act, now section 118(1) of the Criminal Procedure (Scotland) Act 1995. In *Sinclair v HM Advocate*,[9] essentially a misdirection case, the court granted authority to the Lord Advocate to bring a new prosecution despite a 'suggestion' of fault on the part of the Crown, any such fault being described as 'not of great significance'. In the event, no new prosecution was taken.[10] Absence of any fault on the part of the Crown is a factor in favour of granting authority to bring a new prosecution.[11] Contributory fault on the part of the Crown is not decisive against granting authority: the court's view of the public interest is more important: *Miller v Lees*[12] and *McNicol v HM Advocate*[13]. If the setting aside by the appeal court is based on what is truly a technical error (but a vital one), as in *McGowan v Ritchie*,[14] the court is more likely to grant authority.

1 1982 SCCR 499.
2 1982 SCCR 499 at 505–506.
3 See Sheriff Gordon's editorial note at 1982 SCCR 508.
4 1985 SCCR 322.
5 1984 SCCR 40.
6 1984 SCCR 40 at 57, per Lord Hunter.
7 1991 SCCR 510.
8 1987 SCCR 745.
9 1990 SCCR 412.
10 1990 SCCR 412: editor's note at 416.
11 *McDade v HM Advocate* 1994 SCCR 627.
12 1991 SCCR 799 at 803.
13 1993 SCCR 242 at 250.
14 1997 SCCR 322.

6.09 New prosecutions: refusal of authority

There are no cases in which the court has authorised a new prosecution after upholding an appeal on the ground that the evidence adduced at the trial was insufficient in law to warrant conviction. In *Hogg v H.M. Advocate*[1] where that situation arose, the Crown conceded the point: the logic of it is that, because the evidence was insufficient to convict, the appellant should have been acquitted at the first trial. To allow a new prosecution in any such case would be to allow the Crown two bites at the cherry. A similar situation arose in *McGeary v HM Advocate*;[2] the trial jury had deleted all the specification in the libel but nonetheless convicted the appellant. That was properly a verdict of acquittal in respect of the facts libelled and it would be inconsistent with such a verdict to allow a new prosecution.[3] In *Kerr v HM Advocate*[4] the jury in the original trial had voted, seven for guilty, and four each for not proven and not guilty; that was properly seen as a verdict of acquittal and authority for a new prosecution was refused. Authority was refused in a summary case, *Kelly v Docherty*:[5] that was a case in which the sheriff was held not to have taken the correct and necessary steps to satisfy himself as to the capacity of a child witness, aged seven, to distinguish between telling lies and telling the truth. Although this was a technical judicial error (especially in a summary case), authority for a new prosecution was refused, having regard to the young age of the child – who was an essential corroborating witness – the lapse of time which might affect his evidence and the possibility of distress to the child if he were to be required to give evidence again. It thus appears that if the admissible evidence has been ruled to be insufficient or if the evidence is likely to have degraded because of the passage of time and the age of important witnesses or other reasons (e g death or disappearance since trial of vital witnesses) or if the error that resulted in the quashing of the conviction is a material one for which the Crown must bear the responsibility, then the court will be slow to allow a fresh prosecution. However, the mere passage of time, though an important consideration, is not necessarily decisive[6] In *Cameron v HM Advocate*[7] the appellant had faced two trials, and had had a long period on remand; nearly three years had elapsed since the events giving rise to the prosecution. Authority was refused in *Jones v HM Advocate*[8] in which the appellants, after their conviction but before their convictions were set aside on appeal, gave evidence at the trial of *socii*; it was held that the setting aside of the convictions operated retroactively and that they were therefore immune from prosecution having given evidence as witnesses adduced by the Crown. No doubt the point could have been taken as a plea in bar of trial if the court had granted authority and the Crown had raised a fresh indictment.

It is possible to think of other factors that would militate against granting authority for a new prosecution, such as wide adverse publicity for the appellant after the conviction, or the character of the evidence, e g identification depending on momentary glimpse by a stranger, or the fact that the appellant had substantially served the sentence imposed or was terminally ill; but as more cases are decided further relevant criteria will emerge and be more clearly defined. The existence of this relatively new power has probably had an important bearing upon the appeal court's exercise of its jurisdiction to allow an appeal on the ground of 'alleged miscarriage of justice'.[9]

1   1998 SCCR 8.
2   1991 SCCR 203.
3   The trial judge should have invited the jury to reconsider their verdict.
4   1992 SCCR 281.
5   1991 SCCR 312.
6   Cf *McGroarty v H.M. Advocate* 1991 SCCR 708 (2½ years from event to appeal); *Brims v MacDonald* 1993 SCCR 1061; *McPhelim v H.M. Advocate* 1996 SCCR 647.
7   1999 SCCR 11.
8   1991 SCCR 290.
9   See chapter 7.

6.10   Disposal of appeal against sentence

The powers of the High Court in relation to disposal of an appeal against sentence[1] are available to the court both when disposing of an appeal against sentence alone and also when disposing of an appeal against both conviction and sentence. The same powers are available in a case in which the appellant, having brought an appeal against both conviction and sentence, abandons the appeal in so far as it is against conviction but proceeds with it against sentence alone, under section 116(2). If, however, an appellant appeals against both conviction and sentence but, before the hearing, abandons the appeal against sentence and proceeds with his appeal against conviction alone, the appeal court, though it may substitute a different sentence for the one imposed in the trial court, cannot impose a more severe sentence. The Court has power to defer sentence and, additionally, to call for reports to be made available to the Court at the next diet; the membership (ie the composition) of the Bench at the next diet need not be the same as it was at the diet when sentence was deferred. Appeals against sentence alone are usually dealt with by a bench of two judges: section 103(2).

1   Criminal Procedure (Scotland) Act 1995, s 118. The term 'sentence' is used here to include all disposals mentioned in s 106(1).

6.11   Power to increase sentence

Accordingly, in disposing of any appeal in which the appellant has put sentence in issue and has not timeously abandoned his appeal against sentence, the High Court has power, in terms of the

Criminal Procedure (Scotland) Act 1995, section 118(4)(b), not only to affirm the sentence but also 'if the court thinks that having regard to all the circumstances, including any evidence such as is mentioned in section 106(3) of this Act, a different sentence should have been passed' to quash the sentence and pass another sentence 'whether *more* or less severe' in its place.[1] The court may choose to defer sentence and to call for reports available to the court at the next diet; the membership of the court at the second diet need not be the same as at the diet when sentence was deferred. The power to increase a sentence is used when the court, after the appeal hearing has started, concludes that the sentence appealed against is inadequate. Examples of the exercise of the power to increase a sentence appealed against include *O'Neil v HM Advocate*[2] where a party appellant argued that a two-year sentence (then the sheriff court maximum) imposed in the sheriff court, for masked armed robbery, was excessive: the High Court described that sentence as 'grossly inadequate' and increased it to five years.[3] *Connolly v HM Advocate*,[3] though partly overruled in effect by section 254 of the Criminal Procedure (Scotland) 1975 Act (now section 118 of the 1995 Act), is still authority for the rule that the High Court can impose a sentence greater than any sentence that could competently have been imposed by the sheriff, if the sheriff could have remitted for sentence. In *Grant v HM Advocate*[4] two appellants (represented by counsel and agents) submitted that their consecutive sentences of three years' imprisonment in respect of (1) a counterfeiting charge and (2) a Firearms Act charge were excessive. A vain attempt was made to abandon one of the appeals during the course of the hearing; but the appeal court refused to allow it to be abandoned. The sentences were described as 'inadequate' and the court increased each sentence from three years' to five years' imprisonment, the sentences to run consecutively. In *Walker v HM Advocate*[5] a woman appealed against two sentences, each of one year's imprisonment, for possession of drugs contrary to sections 5(2) and 5(3) of the Misuse of Drugs Act 1971; the trial judge had ordered that the two sentences should run consecutively. The appeal was persisted in despite the trial judge's statement in his report that 'it would be easier to criticise my sentences as too light rather than excessive'. The appeal court considered both sentences to be inadequate and doubled each to two years, but ordered the two sentences to run *concurrently*: what was lost on the swings was gained on the roundabout. The appeal court may choose to make even a modest increase in a sentence: in *Donnelly v HM Advocate*[6] a 16-year-old first offender who appealed against a sentence of 18 months' detention for possessing a CS gas grenade at a football match had his sentence increased to two years. In *Reid v Normand*[7] a concurrent sentence imposed in respect of a bail charge was altered to run consecutively. In *Stephen v H.M. Advocate,*[8] a drugs case, concurrent sentences of 12 months' imprisonment were appealed as excessive: the court increased them to two years' imprisonment, also to run concurrently. There appears to have been a decline in the number of occasions on which the power to increase a sentence has been exercised, possibly because the requirement to obtain leave to appeal has reduced the number of worthless appeals against sentence. The fact that the Lord Advocate can appeal against a sentence as unduly lenient also has a bearing on this. The power of the High Court to pass any sentence under Part VIII of the 1995 Act can be exercised in relation to an appellant even if he is absent.[9]

1   Criminal Procedure (Scotland) Act 1995, s 118(4)(b).
2   1976 SLT (Notes) 7.
3   1954 JC 90.
4   1985 SCCR 431.
5   1987 SCCR 379.
6   1988 SCCR 386.
7   1994 SCCR 475.
8   1993 SCCR 660.
9   CP(S)A 1995, ss 120(2), 192.

6.12   Time spent pending appeal

Where, under the Criminal Procedure (Scotland) Act 1995, section 112, an appellant has been admitted to bail pending determination of his appeal or any relevant appeal by the Lord Advocate under section 108 or 108A, the period beginning with the date of his admission to bail and ending on the date of his re-admission to prison in consequence of the determination or abandonment of the appeal is not to be reckoned as part of any term of imprisonment under his sentence, in so far as he was not in custody during that period.[1] If, however, the appellant was in custody for any part of the time pending the determination of his appeal, whether because he was not admitted to bail or because his bail was recalled and he was, in consequence of that recall, returned to custody, the time actually spent in custody is reckoned as part of any term of imprisonment under his sentence, although the High Court may give a direction to the contrary.[2] The power of the High Court to give a direction that any time spent in custody pending appeal is *not* to be reckoned as part of the sentence of imprisonment is rarely used, but is available and was used in respect of an appeal considered to be frivolous: in *Scott (J N) v HM Advocate*,[3] this was the test applied in relation to the exercise of a similar power in section 9(4) of the Criminal Appeal (Scotland) Act 1926. As leave to appeal is now necessary, it seems highly unlikely that an appeal deemed arguable by the sifting judges would be treated as frivolous in character.

1   Criminal Procedure (Scotland) Act 1995, s 125(1).
2   CP(S)A 1995, s 125(2).
3   1946 JC 68.

6.13   Finality of proceedings

Subject to the provisions of the Criminal Procedure (Scotland) Act 1995, Part XA (Scottish Criminal Cases Review Commission), section 124(2) provides that 'every interlocutor and sentence pronounced by the High Court under this Part [solemn procedure] of this Act shall be final and conclusive and not subject to review by any court whatsoever and it shall be incompetent to stay or suspend any execution or diligence issuing from the High Court under this Part of this Act'. It is, however, clear that the High Court in the exercise of its *nobile officium* can, in very special circumstances, alter or correct an order pronounced by the court in exercise of its appellate jurisdiction. It can correct a clear error, as in *James McLellan, Petitioner*, referred to in *Perrie, Petitioner*.[1] It can correct an error resulting from the High Court's having done something that it was not authorised by Parliament to do: *Allan, Petitioner*,[2] where the court had imposed a sentence in respect of a conviction that had not been brought before the court in the appeal proceedings. It has a power to correct entries in various records: see section 299(4). In *Express Newspapers plc, Petitioners*[3] the court pointed out that section 124(2) applied in solemn proceedings only, and therefore did not apply to an interlocutor or sentence pronounced in proceedings by way of petition and complaint for contempt of court but also reaffirmed that the *nobile officium* can be used to remedy defects in the proceedings of the High Court itself. In *Hoekstra & Others v H.M. Advocate* a court consisting of three judges set aside an interlocutor pronounced in appeal proceedings some weeks earlier, on 28 January, by an appeal court, (also consisting of three judges) on the ground that as one of the judges in the court that pronounced that interlocutor 'was not objectively impartial and ought therefore to have excused himself, we must set aside the purported interlocutor of

28 January on the basis that it was pronounced by a court which was not properly constituted by three impartial judges'. No reference was made to the *nobile officium* or to section 124(2). In *Express Newspapers plc* the opinion of the court stated that it was for the court to determine what was the appropriate quorum for the hearing of classes of business.

1   1991 SCCR 475 at 481. But see *Heywood, Petitioner,* 1998 SCCR 335.
2   1993 SCCR 686.
3   1999 SCCR 262.

SUMMARY

6.14   Disposal of pre-trial appeals

Appeals may be taken pre-trial in certain circumstances: see 3.01 ff above. Certain objections if not taken timeously cannot be competently taken on appeal.[1] The High Court may affirm the decision of the court of first instance or may remit the case to it with such directions as the High Court thinks fit:[2] see 3.04 above.

1   Criminal Procedure (Scotland) Act 1995, s 192(3).
2   CP(S)A 1995, s 174(4).

6.15   Powers incidental to an appeal hearing

The Criminal Procedure (Scotland) Act 1995, section 182(5), which is without prejudice to any existing power of the High Court, empowers the court to employ various methods for the purpose of enabling it to determine properly an appeal by way of stated case. The powers which are contained in paragraphs (a), (b), (c), (d) and (e) of section 182(5) are identical to those conferred upon the court in solemn proceedings by section 104. Those powers are discussed at 6.02 above. Both the 'existing powers' and these statutory powers are available to the High Court in dealing with summary appeals by bill of suspension or by advocation as well as with stated cases.[1] Additionally, the High Court may, in hearing a stated case, '(f) take account of any matter proposed in any adjustment rejected by the trial judge and of the reasons for such rejection' and 'take account of any evidence contained in a note of evidence such as is mentioned in section 179(7) of the Act'.[2] The appeal court can also remit the stated case back to the inferior court to be amended and returned. It should also be noted that the High Court may at the hearing of an appeal take into account an allegation relating to an alleged mis-carriage of justice which has been made by the appellant in his application for a stated case or in any duly made amendment or addition to that application, even although the inferior court itself was unable to take the allegation into account in preparing the stated case.[3] There may be circumstances relevant to an alleged miscarriage of justice of which the trial judge knows nothing and upon which he is therefore unable to comment, as in *McDonald v HM Advocate.*[4] See also *Crossan v H.M. Advocate.*[5]

1   Criminal Procedure (Scotland) Act 1995, s 191(3).
2   See CP(S)A 1995, s 179(7)(a) and (b): see also 6.16 below.
3   CP(S)A 1995, s 182(2).
4   1987 SCCR 153; cf 159 (ground 5).
5   1996 SCCR 279.

6.16   Stated case: special powers

In terms of paragraphs (f) and (g) of the Criminal Procedure (Scotland) Act 1995, section 182(5), the High Court has certain powers exercisable in hearing a stated case which are related to the modern statutory provisions for the proposing of adjustments and the treatment of rejected adjustments:[1] see 3.30 above. The appeal court can take account of any matter proposed in any adjustment rejected by the trial judge and of the reasons for such rejection. It can also take account of any evidence contained in a note of evidence appended to the case by the trial judge, in terms of section 179(7). The cases referred to at 3.30 above illustrate how the High Court exercises these powers.

1   Criminal Procedure (Scotland) Act 1995, s 179.

6.17   Disposal of appeals against conviction by stated case

The principal statutory provisions regulating the powers of the High Court in disposing of an appeal by way of stated case (unless the High Court considers that the appellant was insane at the material time)[1] are those contained in the Criminal Procedure (Scotland) Act 1995, section 183 (all of the relevant powers are available in relation to bills of suspension and advocation).[2] The appeal court may remit the cause to the inferior court with their opinion and any direction thereon.[3] In *Aitchison v Rizza,*[4] where the sheriff declined to admit evidence tendered by the Crown, the High Court upheld the Crown's appeal and remitted to the sheriff to proceed as accords, making it plain to him that that meant he had to hear the evidence he had previously refused to hear. Thus where, for example, the sheriff upon a mistaken view of the law of corroboration has acquitted, the court may answer the appropriate questions and remit the case to the sheriff with a direction to convict, as in *Tudhope v Smellie*[5] or in *McLeod v Mason*.[6] If the inferior court improperly sustains an accused's submission of no case to answer, the court will deliver an opinion on the points at issue and remit the case to the sheriff to proceed as accords with the trial, as in *Galt v Goodsir*.[7] The appeal court may affirm the verdict of the inferior court.[8] Although it is not necessary in terms of the statute for the court to deliver an opinion in this or various other types of disposal, it has become the practice for the appeal court to deliver an opinion setting out its reasoning in almost all appeals which are finally disposed of at a hearing. Paragraph (c) of section 183(1)) empowers the court to set aside the verdict of the inferior court and either quash the conviction or substitute for that conviction an amended verdict of guilty, provided that such amended guilty verdict could have been returned on the same complaint in the inferior court: these powers are conferred in the same terms as the powers exercisable in solemn appeals: reference should therefore be made to 6.05 and 6.06 above. Similarly, the powers of the High Court in relation to dealing with sentences when any verdict of the inferior court is set aside or amended, contained in section 183(4), are in the same terms as those exercisable in solemn appeals.[9] The discussion at 6.06 above applies to those powers; see also Schedule 3 to the 1995 Act, which relates both to indictments and to complaints.

1   See 6.25 below.
2   Criminal Procedure (Scotland) Act 1995, s 191(3).
3   CP(S)A 1995, s 183(1)(a).
4   1985 SCCR 297.
5   (1977) SCCR Supp 186.
6   1981 SCCR 75.
7   1981 SCCR 225.
8   CP(S)A 1995, s183(1)(b).
9   See 6.10 and 6.11 above.

6.18   Authority to bring new prosecution

If the High Court, in disposing of an appeal by stated case, or an appeal by bill of suspension or by bill of advocation,[1] sets aside the verdict of the inferior court, it may grant authority to bring a new prosecution in accordance with the Criminal Procedure

(Scotland) Act 1995, section 185. The relevant provisions governing the powers of the court in this regard are effectively in the same terms as those applicable to solemn appeals. Reference should therefore be made to 6.07 to 6.09 above.

1 Criminal Procedure (Scotland) Act 1995, ss 183(1)(d) and 191(3).

6.19 Appeal against acquittal

The provisions governing the powers of the High Court when an appeal against acquittal is sustained are specified in the Criminal Procedure (Scotland) Act 1995, section 183(6)–(10). Where an appeal against acquittal is sustained, the High Court may convict and sentence the respondent (the accused in the complaint). If the High Court itself proceeds to sentence it cannot impose a sentence on the respondent beyond the maximum which could have been passed by the inferior court from which the prosecutor has successfully appealed.[1] Alternatively, the High Court may remit the case to the inferior court with instructions to convict and sentence the respondent. In that event, the respondent must attend any diet fixed by the inferior court for that purpose (convicting and sentencing). The third option is to remit the case to the inferior court along with the opinion of the High Court: this would be the appropriate course to follow when further evidence (for example, evidence wrongfully excluded at the trial) might be placed before the inferior court, or when the case cannot be decided without some step or decision which only that court can make.

1 Criminal Procedure (Scotland) Act 1995, s 183(7).

6.20 Disposal of appeal against sentence

Whether the appeal against sentence is taken as an appeal against sentence alone or is combined with an appeal against conviction the disposal of the appeal against sentence is regulated by the Criminal Procedure (Scotland) Act 1995, section 189.[1] In a summary appeal the appeal court cannot increase the sentence beyond the maximum sentence that could have been passed in the inferior court.[2] In other respects the considerations discussed in relation to the similarly worded statutory provisions governing solemn appeals apply also to summary appeals against sentence: see 6.10 and 6.11 above.

1 By virtue of s 183(3) and (5).
2 Criminal Procedure (Scotland) Act 1995, s 189(2).

6.21 Disposal of bills

If the appeal has come before the High Court by way of bill of suspension the court has the incidental powers already noted at 6.15 above. Under the Criminal Procedure (Scotland) Act 1995, section 191(3) the High Court has power to set aside the verdict of the inferior court and grant authority for a new prosecution, as in an appeal by stated case: see 6.17 above. In setting aside a verdict the High Court may quash any sentence and proceed as in a stated case hearing: cf 6.06 above. The court has power to pass the bill and to suspend any sentence, order, judgment or proceeding to which it relates and to order repayment of any fine, penalty or expenses paid in terms of the findings and orders of the inferior court. The court may suspend the proceedings in part and sustain them in part or amend or alter or vary them, provided the good and the bad portions are distinctly separable.[1] If the court refuses the bill, it may re-commit the appellant to prison if that is appropriate. The court has powers to remit the case to the inferior court with specific instructions as to how to proceed or with instructions to proceed 'as accords'. In that event the High Court will usually make it clear in an accompanying opinion just what that entails. The court may alter the conviction and/or sentence and also remit to the inferior court with instructions. The foregoing powers are available to the court not only in bills of suspension but also in bills of advocation. Such a bill may be passed in whole or in part and the subject matter of the inferior court's decision may be dealt with by the High Court; the case may be remitted to the inferior court with instructions as to how to proceed in relation to that subject matter.

1 *Moncrieff* chapter III, section II, p 178.

6.22 Expenses

The High Court has power in an appeal arising out of summary proceedings, whether by stated case or by bill, to award such expenses both in the High Court and in the inferior court as it may think fit.[1] The power is discretionary and the conduct of the parties to the appeal is relevant. Expenses usually follow success and are almost always modified by the High Court in proceedings for review: cf *Gallacher, Petitioner*.[2] The same practice of modification obtains when the parties before the High Court are private parties. The sum to which any expenses are modified tends to be one of several standard sums which occasionally increase over time, but there is no mechanism for regular updating. Currently (since October 1993) the sums awarded in stated cases (not legally aided) are usually modified as follows, in accordance with guidance prepared by the Clerk of Justiciary:

STATED CASES:

A. a wholly successful appellant (accused) who has printed the stated case: £280;

B. a wholly successful respondent (accused) who has not printed: £140;

C. a wholly unsuccessful appellant (accused) who has printed: Crown's expenses modified to, say, £70;

D. a wholly unsuccessful respondent (accused) who has not printed: Crown's expenses modified to, say, £140;

E. a partly successful appellant (accused) who has printed: £140;

F. a partly successful respondent (accused) who has not printed: no expenses due or by either party.

An accused who successfully appeals against sentence alone can expect an award modified to £105. An appellant may get an award of expenses if the prosecution consents to set aside the conviction: see 4.15–4.16 above. The restriction formerly imposed by statute[3] has been removed.[4] Awards in bills of suspension or advocation tend to follow the same guidelines although the sum awarded may be less because the printing costs tend to be less. In legally aided cases no expenses are granted irrespective of the result. Accounts may be remitted in exceptional circumstances to the Auditor of the Court of Session for taxation.

1 Criminal Procedure (Scotland) Act 1995, s 183(9).
2 1990 SCCR 492 at 496, per Lord Justice-General Hope.
3 *Hamilton v Friel* 1992 SCCR 67, 1992 SLT 819.
4 CP(S)A 1995, s 188(4)(a)(i).

6.23 Warrants or sentence orders

Where, following an appeal, the appellant remains liable to imprisonment or detention under the sentence of the inferior court, or is so liable under a sentence passed in the appeal proceedings, the High Court has power, where at the time of disposal of the appeal the appellant was at liberty on bail, to grant warrant to apprehend and imprison (or detain) the appellant for a term. The term of imprisonment or detention, which is to run from the date of his apprehension under the warrant, cannot be longer than that part of the term or terms of imprisonment (or detention) specified in the sentence brought under review which remained unexpired at the date of liberation. The Crown will formally move the court to grant any necessary warrant. If at the time of disposal the appellant was in custody serving one or more terms of imprisonment in detention imposed in relation to a conviction subsequent to the conviction appealed against, the High Court has power to exercise the like powers in regard to him as may be exercised, in relation to an appeal abandoned, under the Criminal Procedure (Scotland) Act, section 177(6) by a court of summary jurisdiction: see 3.32 above and *Proudfoot v Wither*.[1] If disqualification for driving has been suspended pending the outcome of an appeal and at the hearing the appeal court refuses to suspend the disqualification or imposes a sentence of disqualification, the Crown moves the court to recall the interim suspension, and the unexpired portion of the disqualification starts to run from the date of the hearing. If the appeal court quashes an order for disqualification but exercises some other penalty power it may need to consider if an order should be made in respect of penalty points. If the appeal court interferes with a sentence involving disqualification or endorsation or recalls an interim suspension of disqualification, the High Court will direct the clerk of the sentencing court to intimate the result of the appeal to the police and driving licence authorities.

1   1990 SCCR 96.

6.24   Limitations upon the powers of the court

The High Court cannot quash proceedings in an inferior court on certain grounds unless the point has been raised timeously in the inferior court. This matter is discussed at 3.48 above. An incidental limitation upon the power of the court came to light in *Farmer v Guild*[1] where it was observed that neither the inferior court exercising powers of interim regulation nor the appeal court had any power to suspend a community service order. However, the Criminal Procedure (Scotland) Act 1995, section 193A[2] now provides that where a convicted person, or the prosecutor, appeals to the High Court under section 175, the court may, on the application of the appellant, direct that the whole or any remaining part of a relevant sentence shall be suspended until the appeal, if it is proceeded with, is determined: for this purpose

' "relevant sentence" means any one or more of the following:
   (a) a probation order;

(b) a supervised attendance order made under section 236(6) of this Act;

(c) a community service order;

(d) a restriction of liberty order.'

The procedure for applying for suspension is governed by the Act of Adjournal (Criminal Procedure Rules) 1996, Rule 19.10A. The application must be made with the application for a stated case or the note of appeal as the case may be and the court has to grant or refuse it within seven days.

If the court has exercised this power to suspend, the convicted person, unless excused, has to appear personally in court on any day fixed for the hearing of his appeal.[3] If he fails to do so, the court's powers are set out in section 193A(3): if the convicted person has brought the appeal the court may decline to consider it in his absence and dismiss it summarily. Whoever has taken the appeal the court has power to consider and determine it or to make such other order as it thinks fit.

1   1991 SCCR 174.
2   Added by the Crime and Punishment (Scotland) Act 1997.
3   s 193A (2).

6.25   Appellant insane: disposal of appeal

The governing statutory provisions, in the Criminal Procedure (Scotland) Act 1995, section 190, relate to any appeal by a convicted person in respect of whom it appears to the High Court that the appellant committed the act charged against him but that he was insane when he did so. They are in virtually the same terms[1] and have the same effects as the powers available to the court in appeals for solemn proceedings;[2] see 6.05 above.

1   Except for the provision in the Criminal Procedure (Scotland) Act 1995, s 57(3) about a person charged with murder.
2   CP(S)A 1995, ss 118(5) and (6).

THE *NOBILE OFFICIUM*

6.26   Petitions to *nobile officium*

The High Court of Justiciary has an inherent and necessary jurisdiction to take effective action to vindicate the authority of the court and to preserve the due and impartial administration of justice.[1] It is an exclusive power enabling the High Court (quorum of three), but no other court, to provide a remedy for all extraordinary or unforeseen occurrences in the course of criminal business before any criminal court.[2] It may be exercised to provide a remedy to a person adversely affected by criminal proceedings, eg as a witness or a potential witness.[3] It is an extraordinary power which is exercised inter alia to fill gaps in the criminal procedural law. It does not allow the High Court to review the exercise by a Secretary of State (or the Scottish Ministers) of a statutory power in relation to the release of prisoners, as this is a matter for the Court of Session.[4] It may be invoked by the Crown, by an accused or convicted person, by witnesses or persons cited as witnesses, by solicitors involved in proceedings and by others, e g persons who are the owners of goods forfeited from the possession of an offender.[5] The older history of this power and some modern examples of its exercise are discussed in an article by CN Stoddart in 1974 SLT (News) 27.[6] A short, authoritative and much-quoted passage on the scope and purpose of this exceptional jurisdiction is contained in the opinion of the court delivered by Lord Justice-General Emslie in *Anderson v HM Advocate*,[7] which is a leading authority. The *nobile officium* jurisdiction is also discussed in the opinion of the court in *Macpherson, Petitioners*.[8]

1   *Cordiner, Petitioner* 1973 JC 16 at 18.
2   Alison, ii, 13, p 23.
3   *Gerrard, Petitioner* 1984 SCCR 1.
4   *Newland and Maguire, Petitioners* 1994 SCCR 254.
5   *Lloyds and Scottish Finance Ltd v HM Advocate* 1974 JC 24.
6   Cf also Alison, ii, 13, pp 23(5).
7   1974 SLT 239.
8   1989 SCCR 518. See also *Renton and Brown* Chapter 34.

6.27   Illustrative cases

There have been many cases in which the power has been invoked by a petitioner, not always successfully. Many reported cases arise out of summary proceedings but there are many examples of petitions to the *nobile officium* arising out of solemn proceedings: see, for example, *Wylie v HM Advocate*[1] and *Evans, Petitioner*.[2] In *Evans* the petitioner was one of several accused on trial on indictment in the High Court in Aberdeen. On the second day of his trial he tendered certain pleas of guilty through his counsel. The Crown accepted these pleas and the jury returned guilty verdicts, as directed by the trial judge.[3] On the following day the accused sought leave of the trial judge to withdraw some of his pleas of guilty on the ground that they had been tendered under a substantial error and misconception. That motion was refused on the next morning (Thursday 1 November 1990) on the ground that it was not competent for the trial judge to annul the jury's verdict after it had been recorded; the accused then intimated his intention to petition the *nobile officium*. The trial was then adjourned until the Monday following. The petition was heard on Friday 2 November 1990 in the High Court sitting in Edinburgh. The prayer of the petition was:

'MAY IT THEREFORE PLEASE YOUR LORDSHIPS to appoint this petition to be intimated to Her Majesty's Advocate and to be intimated on the Walls in common form and thereafter to appoint a diet to allow said plea of guilty *quoad* charge (4) to be withdrawn and *quoad ultra* to do further or otherwise in the premises as your Lordships shall seem proper.'[4]

The court refused the prayer because it considered (1) that there existed another remedy, namely an appeal under section 228(1) of the Criminal Procedure (Scotland) Act 1975, to correct any miscarriage of justice, such an appeal being competent even after a plea of guilty;[5] and (2) that to exercise the *nobile officium* in the circumstances of this case would be to override an express provision of the statute and to act in conflict with the statutory intention express or implied. *Evans* illustrates the flexibility of the courts and of the procedure when an extraordinary situation develops and also the speed with which, when necessary, procedural emergencies can be addressed and resolved. It also illustrates that the *nobile officium* will be exercised only when no other remedy exists. In *Black, Petitioner*[6] the court said: It is clear . . . that the court will only exercise the *nobile officium* when the circumstances are extraordinary or unforeseen, and where no other remedy or procedure is provided by law.' Such a situation arose in *Hughes, Petitioner*[7] where the trial judge deserted a diet of trial *pro loco et tempore* after it came to his notice that one juror had spoken to her fellow jurors in a way that could have been prejudicial to one of the accused; the trial judge concluded that he could not solve the problem by discharging all the jurors and empaneling a fresh jury under the provisions of section 129. The accused presented a petition to the *nobile officium* and the High Court recalled the desertion *pro loco et tempore*, directed the trial judge to excuse the 15 empanelled jurors and ordered the trial to proceed with a new jury. This was another case in which the High Court moved with exceptional speed to deal with an emergency situation. The court will not exercise its *nobile officium* to entertain arguments that might have formed good grounds of appeal where it is plain that the statute applicable to the situation deliberately excluded any right of appeal.[8] In *Draper, Petitioner*[9] it was held to be competent to invoke the *nobile officium* to challenge (i e effectively appeal against) a judge's recommendation of a minimum sentence on a murder charge, there having been no statutory right of appeal against such a recommendation at the time when the judge made it. The challenge was successful.

1   1966 SLT 149.
2   1991 SCCR 160.
3   This procedure has now been changed: cf the Criminal Proceedure (Scotland) Act 1995, s 95(2).
4   Cf 1991 SCCR 160 at 161.
5   *Boyle v HM Advocate* 1976 JC 32; cf also *MacGregor v MacNeill* 1975 JC 57; and *Pirie v McNaughton* 1991 SCCR 483.
6   1991 SCCR 1.
7   1989 SCCR 490.
8   *City of Edinburgh District Council, Petitioners* 1990 SCCR 511.
9   1996 SCCR 324.

6.28   *Nobile officium* not exercised where other remedy available

An unusual case in which the court declined to exercise the power because another remedy existed arose in *Clayton, Petitioner*.[1] The petitioner had been sentenced in November 1988 in the High Court to six years' detention and, a week later, by a sheriff to four months' detention, consecutive to the former sentence. The petitioner mistakenly believed that the two sentences would be aggregated for the purpose of allowing his early release on licence under section 25(1) of the Prisons (Scotland) Act 1989. When he discovered, late in 1990, that the effect of the consecutive sentence imposed by the sheriff would be to prevent his release while his six-year sentence was being served, he petitioned the *nobile officium*, asking the court to quash the sentence of four months' detention, on the basis that it was too late to appeal against that sentence as exercised in the circumstances. The court held that his remedy was to apply under the Criminal Procedure (Scotland) Act 1975, sections 453B(6) and 444 for a further period of time to lodge an appeal; the petition to the *nobile officium* was therefore dismissed as incompetent. He later obtained leave to appeal late and his appeal was allowed to the extent of ordering the four-months sentence to run from the date of its being imposed.[2]

If, however, a petition to the *nobile officium* falls to be dismissed because the petitioner had a statutory right to seek review by a different procedure but neglected to use it, the court, to avoid further expense and to afford the petitioner a remedy to which he appears to be entitled, may treat the petition as if it were an application of the appropriate kind made in the appropriate way: *Gilchrist, Petitioner.*[3] In that case, in which the court considered that the petitioner could have used his statutory right under section 299 of the 1975 Act to have his bail conditions reviewed, the Crown consented to the petition being treated as if it were a bail appeal but it is not clear that the Crown's consent is essential. If, however, there were good grounds for the withholding of consent by the Crown, the court would be unlikely to treat an incompetent petition to the *nobile officium* as if it were a different form of application.

In *Boyle, Petitioner*[4] the court did not exercise the *nobile officium* as the issue raised was identified as one of competency, and therefore an issue for the appeal court to decide. However, as the matter raised by the petition was whether or not the appeal court had, in earlier proceedings, acted in excess of its statutory powers, the petition to the *nobile officium* was a competent petition. In *McGregor, Petitioner*[5] it was held that a supervised attendance order was not a sentence passed on conviction and could not be appealed. However, as it appeared to the court that the proceedings had resulted in an injustice and oppression it was held appropriate to give a remedy by using the *nobile officium*. In *Windsor, Petitioner*[6] it was held that the emergence of new evidence after the appeal had been concluded was not an unforeseen or extraordinary circumstance warranting the use of the *nobile officium* as the legislation then in force permitted a person to found on new evidence and that the Secretary of State could refer the case to the court.

1   1991 SCCR 261.
2   Editor's Note, *Clayton, Petitioner* 1991 SCCR 261 at 265.
3   1991 SCCR 699.
4   1992 SCCR 949.
5   1999 SCCR 225.
6   1994 SCCR 59.

6.29   Where remedy excluded by statute

The court will not exercise the *nobile officium* to do that which is clearly prohibited by statute. Accordingly the High Court refused a petition to the *nobile officium* in a case in which the effect of entertaining the petition would have been to bring under review a decision of the High Court itself, sitting as an appeal court, contrary to the Criminal Procedure (Scotland) Act 1995, sections 262 and 281, which provide that 'Interlocutors' (meaning any judgment or order pronounced by the court) are final and conclusive and not subject to review by any court whatsoever.[1] The circumstances were highly unusual in that the ruling which the petitioner sought to challenge was a ruling by an appeal court of three judges holding as incompetent and inadmissible evidence which the petitioner, as an appellant against conviction, was seeking to adduce before that appeal court. The evidence was being tendered to the court following an earlier decision of that court[2] to hear additional evidence relevant to an alleged miscarriage of justice, the character of that proposed evidence having been fully disclosed by the lodging of affidavits. However, despite the terms of sections 262 and 281, the court altered a previous order of the appeal court in *James McLellan, Petitioner*.[3] There the appeal court quashed an earlier decision of the appeal court which was based on an error which the court had made; this was done by an exercise of the *nobile officium*. It was not opposed by the Crown. The court obviously has power to put right its own typographical or similar errors if it is necessary to do so to remedy an injustice. Very wide powers to excuse compliance with rules, statutory or otherwise, governing appeal procedure are contained in section 277; this section should be consulted before an appellant thinks of petitioning the *nobile officium*. A petition to the *nobile officium* was dismissed as incompetent when it appeared that the petitioner was inviting the court to have the merits of his conviction reviewed, having already proceeded by way of stated case and lost.[4]

1   *Perrie, Petitioner* 1991 SCCR 475; but see *Hoekstra v HM Advocate* (No 2) 2000 SCCR 367.
2   See *Perrie v HM Advocate* 1991 SCCR 255 at 256.
3   Unreported, but mentioned in *Perrie, Petitioner* 1991 SCCR 475 at 481.
4   *Anderson v HM Advocate* 1974 SLT 239.

6.30   Failure to comply with timetable

The court refused to exercise the *nobile officium* to allow an appeal by stated case against conviction to proceed after the appeal had been deemed to have been abandoned because the principal copy of the stated case was not lodged timeously, owing to the negligence of the solicitors acting for the appellant.[1] The current position in such cases is discussed in *Berry, Petitioner*[2] and in the Editor's note to the report of that case. The remedy provided by statute is contained in section 181(1)–(3) of the Criminal Procedure (Scotland) Act 1995 which gives the court power to direct that further time be allowed to an applicant for a stated case who has failed to intimate his adjustments (or that he has none to propose) within the period allowed by section 179(1) or has failed to cause the stated case to be lodged within the one week prescribed by section 179(a). The power must be exercised with regard to the same considerations (of avoiding injustice or oppression) as in the exercise of the *nobile officium*.[3] As Sheriff Gordon implies it is not easy to envisage a continuing role for the *nobile officium* in such cases. A similar comment can be made about solemn cases, given the terms of section 129.

1   *Brown, Petitioner* (1974) SCCR Supp 71.
2   1985 SCCR 106.
3   1985 SCCR 106 at 112 per Lord Emslie.

6.31   Excusing procedural lapse

Generally, the High Court is reluctant to exercise the *nobile officium* to put an appeal process back on the rails if the appeal has been dismissed owing to a failure by the appellant's solicitor to take a mandatory step in the process.[1] In *Fenton, Petitioner*[2] the court declined to grant the prayer of a petition to the *nobile officium* (inviting the court to admit the petitioner to bail) in a case in which the petitioner who was appealing against sentence had omitted to lodge his appeal against the sheriff's refusal of bail within the time prescribed by what is now the Criminal Procedure (Scotland) Act 1995, section 177(2). It was said that the court would not exercise its power under the *nobile officium* simply because an accused or his legal advisers had been 'mindless of a statutory timetable'. If the failure to comply with the mandatory timetable is not mindless, but is explicable and explained the court may, however, exercise the *nobile officium* effectively to allow the time limit to be extended if it is considered to be in the interest of justice to do so.[3] But the circumstances must always be such that something extraordinary or unforeseen has occurred and that the court can properly hold that it is necessary for the proper administration of justice that the *nobile officium* be exercised. So the court refused to exercise it where, an appeal having been dismissed for want of insistence because the appellant did not appear and was not represented when his case was called before the appeal court, he later sought to have the appeal reinstated, explaining that his failure to attend court resulted from his having gone to live at an address different from that of his domicile of citation. A change of address without having the domicile of citation changed provided no basis for an excuse in the circumstances condescended on: *Manson, Petitioner.*[4] Section 117, which inter alia prescribes a 24-hour time limit for proceeding by note of appeal in relation to bail, contains no dispensing power such as is found in section 181; accordingly it might be competent to petition for the exercise of the *nobile officium* in a case where the failure to adhere to that statutory time limit was excusable and not to entertain the late appeal would result in oppression or injustice. Thus, for example, if because of some emergency such as a riot or a fire, all prisoners were locked in their cells during the 24-hour period, an appellant who as a result could not have his note of appeal processed timeously would be able to petition for the exercise of the *nobile officium.* Where an appellant abandoned his appeal on the basis of what was later shown to be incomplete and inaccurate legal advice, and the appeal was deemed to be dismissed, the appellant succeeded in invoking the *nobile officium* to have the appeal reinstated.[5]

1   *McLeod, Petitioner* (1975) SCCR Supp 93.
2   1981 SCCR 288.
3   *HM Advocate v Wood*; *HM Advocate v Cowie* 1990 SCCR 195.
4   Printed as a note at 1991 SCCR 472.
5   *McIntosh, Petitioner* 1995 SCCR 327.

6.32   *Nobile officium* reviews in respect of legal aid applications

In a number of cases, decisions in relation to legal aid applications have been considered by the courts. The varied fates of these applications well illustrate certain of the criteria governing the exercise of this exceptional jurisdiction. In *Rae, Petitioner*[1] the petitioner, a solicitor, invited the court to exercise its *nobile officium* by reviewing the refusal of the trial judge, at a High cCourt trial, to grant to the petitioner a certificate under paragraph 13(2) of the (now repealed) Act of Adjournal (Criminal Legal Aid Fees) 1964, SI 1964/1410, as amended, which allowed additional remuneration in certain circumstances. The court had previously held in *Heslin, Petitioner*[2] that the court would not, in the exercise of its *nobile officium,* entertain an application seeking review of the refusal by a trial judge to grant a paragraph 13(2) certificate, because the Act of Adjournal had not intended that the exercise by a trial judge of his discretion on this matter should be reviewed on appeal. But in *Rae* the court concluded that the trial judge had not exercised his discretion at all and therefore remitted the application with a direction to the trial judge to dispose of the application upon its merits. In *Harper, Petitioner*[3] the court refused to exercise the *nobile officium* in a paragraph 13(2) case in which the sheriff declined to consider a paragraph 13(2) application on its merits because, in the circumstances disclosed to the sheriff, he decided that paragraph 13(2) did not apply. The court agreed with that decision and rejected a submission that there was a *lacuna* or *casus omissus* in the failure of paragraph 13(2) to provide for the making of an application in the circumstances which had arisen. In *McLachlan, Petitioner*[4] a stipendiary magistrate had refused legal aid. Although the appeal court considered that the decision was plainly wrong, it refused to intervene in the exercise of the *nobile officium* because it felt obliged to hold that the stipendiary magistrate had in fact exercised his discretion; so the petition had to be dismissed as incompetent. A person's entitlement to legal aid cannot be terminated by any court unless he has been heard on the matter, and if legal aid is withdrawn by the court without hearing him he can petition the *nobile officium*.[5]

1   1981 SCCR 356.
2   1973 SLT (Notes) 56 (followed in *Mullane, Petitioner* 1990 SCCR 25).
3   1981 SCCR 363.
4   1987 SCCR 195.
5   *Lamont, Petitioner* 1995 SLT 566.

6.33   Additional inquiry

If on the first hearing of a petition to the *nobile officium* the court considers that it needs additional information in response to averments in the petition or statements made at the bar, the court may continue the case for answers, for some form of investigation or inquiry or for a report from the court in which the proceedings giving rise to the petition took place.[1]

1   *Lau, Petitioner* 1986 SCCR 140.

6.34   Crown applications to *nobile officium*

The Lord Advocate may petition the High Court to exercise the *nobile officium*.[1] *Keegan* was a bail case in which the sheriff did not exercise any judgment in relation to a bail application because he believed, wrongly, that the application for bail had not been disposed of within 24 hours, as required by what is now section 23(7) of the Criminal Procedure (Scotland) Act 1995, and therefore liberated the applicant forthwith. In *MacDougall, Petitioner*[2] the procurator fiscal successfully applied by petition to the *nobile officium* when the sheriff refused the Crown's application to state a case against a decision to uphold a submission of no case to answer;[3] the High Court directed the sheriff to state a case within three weeks, as craved in the petition.

1   *HM Advocate v Keegan* 1981 SLT (Notes) 35; *HM Advocate v Wood; HM Advocate v Cowie* 1990 SCCR 195.
2   1986 SCCR 128.
3   See now the Criminal Procedure (Scotland) Act 1995, s 160.

FUNDAMENTAL NULLITY

6.35   Fundamental nullity

In the course of criminal proceedings some of the errors which are perpetrated are of such a character that everything that follows the error is irredeemably flawed. Such errors give rise to fundamental nullity, sometimes described as fundamental irregularity or illegality. For example, if a person is charged with committing a statutory offence on a date before the relevant statutory provision has come into force or after it has been repealed, the charge is fundamentally null and all subsequent proceedings following upon it are fundamentally flawed. So, even if an accused pleads guilty to such a charge, or to a charge which does not disclose a known crime or offence, the conviction and sentence following the plea cannot stand. In *Aitkenhead v Cuthbert*[1] the accused pled guilty and appealed to the High Court against sentence only. In the course of the hearing, however, the appellants argued that the complaint was incompetent because it charged an offence which did not exist.[2] The High Court agreed and, despite recognising that the defect could easily have been remedied had the objection been taken before conviction, concluded that it could not properly allow the accused to stand convicted of a non-existent offence. The conviction was quashed. Similarly, if the court which convicted an accused had no jurisdiction to do so, whether the want or defect of jurisdiction was geographical or flowed from the court's lack of statutory power to deal with the crime or offence charged[3] the conviction is fatally flawed. Even in an otherwise straightforward case which starts and proceeds at first in a regular way, some vital procedural step may be missed or some positive procedural blunder perpetrated, with the result that all that follows it is vitiated. Thus, for example, failure to serve an indictment upon an accused was fatal to all the proceedings which purportedly followed against him upon that indictment;[4] though failure to serve a complaint did not result in a fundamental nullity in *Scott v Annan*.[5] The error will usually be made by the prosecutor; but it may be made by the court. Thus, for example, because all criminal diets are peremptory and all cases which are called have to be adjourned by the court to a specified time and place, if a case is called but not adjourned to a fixed diet then, in the absence of any saving statutory provision, the instance dies at midnight of the day on which the case has been called; any proceedings following thereon are fatally flawed and fundamentally inept or illegal.[6] See also *Hull v HM Advocate*[7] where, in solemn proceedings, the court failed to deal at all with the case at a peremptory diet; that was a fundamental nullity which rendered all subsequent proceedings *funditus* null and void. *Heywood v Stewart*[8] is a striking case of fundamental irregularity. In that case the accused pled guilty, the Crown accepted the plea and the court adjourned the case for three weeks for preparation of a social inquiry report; but the court failed to minute the adjournment of the diet. Even although both the accused's agent and the Crown were prepared to overlook the absence of the minute, the sheriff held that the failure to sign a minute adjourning the diet was a fundamental defect which was incapable of being cured. The High Court, after discussing the relevant authorities, agreed. There are, of course, many errors that may be perpetrated in the bringing or handling of a case which are capable of being remedied by amendment,[9] or by correcting the official record under section 299 of the Criminal Procedure (Scotland) Act 1995; there are other procedural errors or omissions which are not challengeable after a certain stage in the proceedings has been passed.

Thus, for example, a defect in the name or designation of an accused person may sometimes be cured by amendment if the court in the exercise of its discretion decides to allow amendment of the complaint or indictment.[10] If a remediable defect is not in fact remedied before conviction the conviction may (or may not) be treated as *funditus* null and void. There is statutory provision[11] cutting off the right to object (except by leave) after a specified preliminary stage in the proceedings. The question of what is or is not a fundamental nullity can be a difficult one. This is well illustrated by *HM Advocate v McDonald*[12] where the accused were indicted for trial on 18 June 1984 without having been given the minimum statutory induciae of 29 'clear days' between the service of the indictment and the trial diet, as required by the Criminal Procedure (Scotland) Act 1975, section 75 (now

6.35 *FUNDAMENTAL NULLITY*

Criminal Procedure (Scotland) Act 1995, section 66(6)(b)). When the trial diet was called, each of the accused took objection to the competency of the proceedings as being fundamentally flawed by the failure to give the requisite induciae. The trial judge, and two consulted judges, concluded that the events which had happened disclosed a fundamental nullity, and that the trial could not proceed even although the accused could point to no prejudice. An appeal court of five judges took the opposite view, holding that no fundamental irregularity was disclosed but a mere defect in citation which, not having been objected to at a preliminary diet, could not be raised later without leave. See also *Rendle v Muir*[13] where nice distinctions were drawn between fundamental nullity and mere irrelevancy. Similar difficulties of analysis and classification have emerged in other cases concerned with procedure. Contrast *Beattie v McKinnon*[14] with *Scott v Annan*;[15] cf the editorial discussion of the two cases in 1981 SCCR at page 176. Nice distinctions between procedural blunders which are fatal and others which are not also emerge in the discussion in *Heywood v Stewart* above of *Pettigrew v Ingram*.[16] In *Robertson v H.M. Advocate*[17] the judges disagreed as to whether a statutory provision which the prosecutor had not complied with was mandatory or merely directory: only if it fell to read as mandatory would failure to comply with it inevitably result in a fatal incompetency. The cases also illustrate that, in giving effect to a plea of fundamental nullity, the High Court is not applying the miscarriage of justice test.[18]

1 1962 JC 12.
2 Illegal fishing for salmon on a Sunday by persons acting together.
3 *Gallaghan v HM Advocate* 1937 JC 27.
4 *Hester v MacDonald* 1961 SC 370.
5 1981 SCCR 172.
6 *Lafferty v Jessop* 1989 SCCR 451.
7 1945 JC 83.
8 1992 SCCR 42.
9 Cf Criminal Procedure (Scotland) Act 1995, ss 96 and 159.
10 Cf *Hoyers (UK) Ltd v PF Lanark* 1991 SCCR 919. See also the article by Gerald H Gordon 'Fundamental nullity and the power of amendment' 1974 SLT (News) 154.
11 CP(S)A 1995, ss 72(1), 79 and 144(4), (5).
12 1984 SCCR 229.
13 1952 JC 115.
14 1977 JC 64.
15 1981 SCCR 172.
16 1982 SCCR 259.
17 1995 SCCR 152
18 See 7.01–7.05 below.

200

6.36   Raising fundamental nullity on appeal

It is not within the scope of this book to examine all the defects that may in certain circumstances be regarded by the court as giving rise to a fundamental irregularity or to attempt to produce a rationale for distinguishing between borderline cases. Cases illustrating such distinctions are referred to in *Renton and Brown* at paragraphs 20–21 and 20–22. It is, however, important to note that any error that is truly characterised as a fundamental nullity can be raised on appeal and dealt with by the High Court even although the matter has not been raised or even foreshadowed in the grounds of appeal, in the questions in the stated case or in the averments or the pleas in the bill of suspension or of advocation.[1] The High Court will itself raise any issue of fundamental irregularity that is discovered, whether by itself, as in *Hull v HM Advocate*,[2] or by a reporting judge, or by the sifting judges. The court has an inherent power to consider such a matter[3] even if review is expressly excluded or is permitted only by means of a prescribed procedure which the appellant has not invoked. It is obvious, however, as some of the preceding cases illustrate, that, although the court will always take note of a true fundamental nullity, it can be difficult to predict whether or not any particular irregularity will be treated as fundamental – unless there is a clear precedent for so treating it. Thus any point of relevancy or competency or any irregularity should be raised and made the subject of objection or submission as early as the procedure allows.

1   *Christie v Barclay* 1974 JC 68; *Robertson v Aitchison* 1981 SCCR 149.
2   1945 JC 83.
3   *O'Malley v Strathern* 1920 JC 74.

SCOTTISH CRIMINAL CASES REVIEW COMMISSION

6.37   Membership, powers and criteria

Until Part XA was inserted into the Criminal Procedure (Scotland) Act 1995 by the Crime and Punishment (Scotland) Act 1997,[1] the statutory position was that 'The Secretary of State, on the consideration of any conviction of a person or the sentence ... passed on a person who has been convicted, [may], if he thinks fit, at any time and whether or not an appeal against such conviction or sentence has previously been heard and determined by the High Court, refer the whole case to the High Court'. The case had then to be heard and determined, subject to any directions the High Court might make, as if it were an appeal under Part VIII of the 1995 Act.[2] Section 124 was radically altered by the 1997 Act. The effect of the 1997 amendments has been:

(1)   to preserve the prerogative of mercy, under section 124(1);

(2)   to provide that the finality of interlocutors and sentences pronounced by the High Court is not to prevent the High Court from dealing with a case referred to it under Part XA;

(3)   to create a commission, the Scottish Criminal Cases Review Commission, to take over the Secretary of State's functions in relation to sending cases to the High Court where there is sufficient reason to believe that a miscarriage of justice may have occurred and that it is in the interests of justice that a reference should be made.[3]

Like so much else in relation to the reform of appeal procedure in the 1997 Act, the amendments effected by that Act in this regard largely derive from a recommendation made by the Sutherland Committee.[4] The recommendation was 'to remove the Secretary of State from the process altogether and to establish a new body, completely independent of the Executive, with powers to consider alleged miscarriage of justice cases and to refer deserving cases to the Appeal Court for determination'. This, as the Committee noted, was the model recommended by the Royal Commission on Criminal Justice and legislated for in the Criminal Appeal Act 1995. Under the previous system there was no provision for summary cases to be referred to the High Court by the Secretary of State. As the Committee noted,[5] a miscarriage of justice in such cases might be reviewed either by way of a bill of suspension or an application by minute by the Crown to set aside a conviction under the Criminal Procedure (Scotland) Act 1975, section 453(1)(b).[6] The Royal Prerogative of Mercy was available in such cases also. The Committee recommended that the remit of the new body should be restricted initially to solemn cases but that the legislation should provide for the remit to be extended by order to particular categories of summary case, or summary cases as a whole. When the government introduced the Crime and Punishment (Scotland) Bill it contained no provision for the setting up of such a Commission, the government having decided against implementing that recommendation. However, at the last moment, and under pressure from the House of Lords the government introduced amendments to create what is now Part XA of the 1995 Act. The legislation, though based upon the corresponding English legislation, was hastily drafted and was not discussed at all in either House of Parliament. Section 194B subsection (1), as now amended, reads:

'(1) The Commission on the consideration of any conviction of a person or of the sentence (other than sentence of death) passed on a person who has been convicted on indictment or complaint may, if they think fit, at any time, and whether or not an appeal against such conviction or sentence has previously been heard and determined by the High Court, refer the whole case to the High Court and the case shall be heard and determined, subject to any directions the High Court may make, as if it were an appeal under Part VIII or, as the case may be, Part X of this Act.' [emphasis added].

The Commission, consisting of seven members, came into operation on 1 April 1999. Its remit was in fact extended to summary cases as well as to solemn cases. The basis of the reference to the High Court by the Commission includes the availability of new evidence. The legislation has not yet been critically examined in the High Court. The first case to be referred to the High Court related to a conviction obtained in the High Court in Dundee in May 1948. The convicted person[7] had been sentenced to seven years in prison and his appeal against conviction rejected.

The power of referral arises in relation to conviction, sentence or both. The Commission may refer a case even where an appeal has not previously been heard, although in practice the Commission would expect special reasons to be advanced for considering such an application. Such special reasons might include evidence that the applicant was prevented from appealing by serious threats made against him or his family, or where only the special powers of investigation which the Commission has under statute can uncover the fresh evidence needed to support the application. The Commission may exercise its power whether or not the person convicted/sentenced has petitioned for the exercise of the prerogative of mercy.[8] The Commission may also refer where a person charged with the commission of an offence has been found to be insane, where a court has found that an accused person who is insane has committed the act or omission as charged, and even where the person convicted is deceased.[9]

'The grounds upon which the Commission may refer a case to the High Court are that they believe—
(a) that a miscarriage of justice may have occurred; and
(b) that it is in the interests of justice that a reference should be made.'[10]

The Commission may refer a case to the appeal court even where no application for a reference has been made.[11] Section

194E extends the Commission's remit to summary cases and the necessary order, with effect from 1 April 1999, came into force on that date.[12] The order amended section 194B by inserting the words 'or complaint' after the word 'indictment' in the original enactment.

The Commission may take any steps it considers appropriate for the exercise of its functions and may in particular itself undertake inquiries and obtain statements, opinions or reports, or request the Lord Advocate or any other person to undertake such inquiries or obtain such statements, opinions or reports.[13] Thus the Commission can request the assistance of the Crown Office, and thus obtain the assistance of the police, in the investigation of applications. Obviously, however, the principal source of information is likely, in most cases, to be the convicted person; his lawyers can greatly assist the thorough and prompt investigation by the Commission of their cases if they submit as much appropriate material as is available. The Commission has power to apply to the sheriff under section 194H to have a person cited to appear before the sheriff for precognition on oath by a member of the Commission or a person appointed by it to act in that regard.[14] The Commission also has power, under section 194I, to obtain documents. The provisions in Part XA contain much more detail about the powers of investigation and in relation to possible offences in that connection, these provisions in the statute, which may be amended by statutory instrument in certain respects, should be consulted directly if necessary. It should, however, be noted that under section 194I the Commission's power to obtain documents or other material can be exercised both in relation to persons and in relation to public bodies. A 'public body' is defined as meaning:

'(a) any police force;
(b) any Government department, local authority or other body constituted for the purposes of the public service, local Government or the administration of justice; or
(c) any other body whose members are appointed by Her Majesty, any Minister or any Government department or whose revenues consist wholly or mainly of money provided by Parliament.'[15]

The same subsection defines both 'Minister' and 'police force'.

When the matter comes before the court, it is treated as an ordinary appeal. The court itself has the power to allow fresh grounds of appeal to be presented and existing grounds to be amended.[16] There is no reason to suppose that the approach of the court will be any different under the new provisions from the approach that was developed over the years in relation references by the Secretary of State. The history of such references is detailed in chapter 5 of the Sutherland Committee Report where it narrates that 14 individuals had their cases referred back to the Appeal Court since 1928, when the arrangements for the involvement of the Secretary of State were first introduced. Six convictions were quashed. The number of referrals increased latterly and the Committee expected that there would be more referrals as a result of the setting up of the Commission. The previous history of the Secretary of State's reference is discussed at paragraph 5.25 of the first edition of this book. The prerogative function has been devolved to the Scottish Ministers.[17]

The Commission supplies forms for any person who seeks to invite the Commission to have a conviction or sentence reviewed. The application form, and assistance in dealing with what is required, can be obtained from:

Scottish Criminal Cases Review Commission
Portland House
17 Renfield Street
Glasgow
G2 5AH.

The other details are:
Telephone: 0141-270 7030
Fax: 0141-270 7040
e-mail   info@sccrc.co.uk

The Commission has published its priority criteria in the following terms:

'The Scottish Criminal Cases Review Commission

Commission's Priority Criteria

The criteria applied by the Commission in prioritising cases are as follows:
A   Cases where the applicant is in custody will be prioritised over cases where the applicant is at liberty
B   Cases will be prioritised where the applicant is suffering from a life threatening illness
C   Age will only be used as a basis for prioritising where the applicant is very young and vulnerable
D   Cases will be prioritised where a key witness is likely to become unavailable or where evidence is likely to deteriorate
E   In exceptional circumstances priority may be given to a case because of its impact upon public confidence in the criminal justice system
F   Sometimes prioritisation may be justified for operational reasons (e.g. in related cases, where on applicant is in custody and the other is now at liberty)

G Seriousness of offence may also be a basis for prioritisation (as a rough rule of thumb, an offence for which 5 years' imprisonment or more was awarded is treated as being a serious offence).

NOTE If two or more cases are accorded the same priority status on the basis of the foregoing criteria (e.g. if there are several applicants in custody and none of the other priority criteria applies to any of them) the cases will be dealt with in order of receipt of the applications by the Commission.

1 With practical effect from 1 April 1999.
2 See Criminal Procedure (Scotland) Act 1995, s 124, before amendment in 1997.
3 CP(S)A 1995, s 194C, as amended.
4 Report, para 5.50.
5 Report, para 5.22.
6 Now CP(S)A 1995, s 188.
7 George Fraser.
8 CP(S)A 1995, s 194B(2).
9 CP(S)A 1995, s 194B(4).
10 CP(S)A 1995, s 194C.
11 CP(S)A 1995, s 194D.
12 The Scottish Criminal Cases Review Commission (Application to Summary Proceedings) Order 1999 SI 1999/1181.
13 CP(S)A 1995, s 194F.
14 CP(S)A 1995, s 194H.
15 CP(S)A 1995, s 194I(4).
16 See *Kilpatrick and McEwan* v. *H.M. Advocate* 1 November 1991; *Beattie* v *HM Advocate* 1995 SCCR 93.
17 Scotland Act 1998, s 53, Sch 5, para 2(1)(a).

7. Miscarriage of justice and grounds of appeal

MISCARRIAGE OF JUSTICE

PARTICULAR GROUNDS OF APPEAL

MISCARRIAGE OF JUSTICE

7.01   The new law (post-1997)

In the first edition of this book (stating the law as at 1 May 1992) there was a discussion of the development of the law which was introduced in 1980[1] and altered the grounds of appeal. Since 1992 there have been significant developments in case law, although some of the concepts, terms, principles and tests in use before and after 1980 have survived and form part of the law at the present time. More importantly, very far-reaching changes have been made by the Crime and Punishment (Scotland) Act 1997, which followed the publication (in June 1996) of the Report by the Committee on Criminal Appeals and Miscarriages of Justice, the chairman of which was Professor Sir Stuart Sutherland and whose members included the then Lord Justice-Clerk (Lord Ross) and Sheriff (now Sir Gerald) Gordon. Its terms of reference were:

'To examine the current criteria for consideration of appeals by the Appeal Court in Scotland; to consider possible changes to the statutory criteria contained in sections 228 and 442 of the Criminal Procedure (Scotland) Act 1975; and to make recommendations, having regard to the interests of justice, including the need for fairness to the appellant and to the principle of finality in criminal proceedings.

To examine the current procedures under section 263 of the Criminal Procedure (Scotland) Act 1975 for referral of cases to the Appeal Court by the Secretary of State; to consider options for change to the procedures for considering alleged miscarriages of justice in Scotland; and to make recommendations on whether and what changes may be required to those procedures, having regard to the efficient use of resources throughout the criminal justice system'.

The parliamentary history of the enactment of what are now the main statutory provisions is discussed in *Campbell (T) v HM Advocate*.[2] In the light of the readiness of the courts to look at the parliamentary record of legislation, following *Pepper v Hart*,[3] it may prove helpful, if questions of interpretation arise, to look at that parliamentary history; but it is not proposed here to add to the discussion of it in *Campbell*. The report of the Sutherland Committee is itself a valuable guide for the understanding of the new provisions.

1   Criminal Justice (Scotland) Act 1980, s 33 and Sch 2.
2   1998 SCCR 214, in the opinion of Lord McCluskey.
3   [1993] AC 593.

7.02   The current grounds of appeal

Solemn proceedings
The right of appeal (with leave) was contained in the Criminal Procedure (Scotland) Act 1995, section 106(1) until amendment in 1997. The grounds of appeal *before* the 1997 amendments were then stated in subsection (3) in the following terms:

'By an appeal under subsection (1) above a person may bring under review of the High Court any alleged miscarriage of justice in the proceedings in which he was convicted, including any alleged miscarriage of justice on the basis of the existence and significance of additional evidence which was not heard at the trial and which was not available and could not reasonably have been made available at the trial.'

This wording dates back to 1980. This short subsection was replaced by the more detailed provisions in section 17 of the Crime and Punishment (Scotland) Act 1997, which inserted the new provisions into section 106 of the 1995 Act. These new provisions, which were largely based on recommendations in Chapter 2 of the Sutherland Committee Report, were in the terms following:

'**106(3)** By an appeal under subsection (1) above a person may bring under review of the High Court any alleged miscarriage of justice, which may include such a miscarriage based on—
   (a) subject to subsections (3A) to (3D) below, the existence and significance of evidence which was not heard at the original proceedings; and
   (b) the jury's having returned a verdict which no reasonable jury, properly directed, could have returned.
(3A) Evidence such as is mentioned in subsection (3)(a) above may found an appeal only where there is a reasonable explanation of why it was not so heard.
(3B) Where the explanation referred to in subsection (3A) above or, as the case may be, (3C) below is that the evidence was not admissible at the time of the original proceedings, but is admissible at the time of the appeal, the court may admit that evidence if it appears to the court that it would be in the interests of justice to do so.
(3C) Without prejudice to subsection (3A) above, where evidence such as is mentioned in paragraph (a) of subsection (3) above is evidence—
   (a) which is
      (i) from a person; or
      (ii) of a statement (within the meaning of section 259(1) of this Act) by a person,
   who gave evidence at the original proceedings; and

(b) which is different from, or additional to, the evidence so given, it may not found an appeal unless there is a reasonable explanation as to why the evidence now sought to be adduced was not given by that person at those proceedings, which explanation is itself supported by independent evidence.

(3D) For the purposes of subsection (3C) above, 'independent evidence' means evidence which—

(a) was not heard at the original proceedings;

(b) is from a source independent of the person referred to in subsection (3C) above; and

(c) is accepted by the court as being credible and reliable.'

Summary proceedings

The grounds of appeal in cases appealed from summary proceedings are supposed to be the same [see the Sutherland Report, paragraphs 2.80 and 2.81]. They are the same, except that the provisions applicable to appeals in summary proceedings contained a drafting error pointed out in *Ward v Crowe*;[1] the error was removed in 1998.[2] The provisions relating to appeals in summary proceedings are now contained in the Criminal Procedure (Scotland) Act 1995, section 175, as amended. As they are in identical terms to those in section 106 (although the numbering of the subsections is different) it is unnecessary to deal separately with them.

1   1999 SCCR 219 at 222.
2   Crime and Disorder Act 1998, Sch 8, para 123.

7.03   Comparing the old and the new statutory provisions

1.   The basic ground for reviewing a conviction remains the same: 'a person may bring under review of the High Court any alleged miscarriage of justice' (see the opinion of the Lord Justice-Clerk in *Campbell (T) v HM Advocate*.[1] The concept of 'miscarriage of justice' is discussed at 7.09 ff below.

2.   The words 'in the proceedings in which he was convicted' have been deleted, as recommended in paragraph 2.30 of the Sutherland Committee Report. The Lord Justice-Clerk commented upon this alteration in *Campbell* at page 239.

3.   In the amended sections of the 1975 Act (sections 228 and 442) as worded in and after 1980, the only instance given of a specified ground was expressed in the words:

'including any alleged miscarriage of justice on the basis of the existence and significance of additional evidence which was not heard at the trial and which was not available and could not reasonably have been made available at the trial.'

The Criminal Procedure (Scotland) Act 1995, section 106 as now in force, following the 1997 amendment, gives two instances or examples of miscarriage, by referring to:

'any alleged miscarriage of justice, which may include such a miscarriage based on—
(a) subject to subsections (3A) to (3D) below, the existence and significance of evidence which was not heard at the original proceedings; and
(b) the jury's having returned a verdict which no reasonable jury, properly directed, could have returned.'

4.   One effect of the new subsections (3A) to (3D) is to remove the requirement that the evidence 'not heard' has to be 'additional evidence'; and also to remove the requirement that the evidence not heard has to be evidence that was 'not available and could not reasonably have been made available at the trial'.

5.   The removed requirements were replaced by more specific and detailed requirements, which in effect impose new conditions which have to be complied with before the court can assess the allegation of miscarriage of justice on the basis of 'the evidence not heard' (commonly referred to – as in the Sutherland Report – as 'fresh evidence'). The new conditions vary according to the nature and source of the fresh evidence.

6.   The conditions are:
(i) the evidence was 'not heard at the original proceedings';[2]
(ii) there is a reasonable explanation of why it was not heard at the original proceedings.[3]

7.   If the explanation advanced as a reasonable explanation of why the evidence was not heard at the original proceedings is that it was not admissible according to the rules of evidence or procedure prevailing at the time of the trial, but that the rules have changed so that the evidence would be admissible in a trial held at the date of the appeal, then 'the court may admit the evidence if it appears to the court that it would be in the interests of justice to do so'.[4]

8.   There is provision for the special circumstance in which the evidence that was not heard at the original proceedings, but

which it is now sought to present as fresh evidence, is evidence derived from a person who gave evidence at the original proceedings. Whether the fresh evidence tendered is to be in the form of evidence to be given by the person himself from the witness box or is to be in the form of a statement of that person admissible by reason of section 259(1) of the 1995 Act[5] there has to be a reasonable explanation as to why the evidence now sought to be adduced was not given by that person at those proceedings, which explanation is itself supported by independent evidence.[6]

9. 'independent evidence' is defined as evidence

    'which—
    (a) was not heard at the original proceedings;
    (b) is from a source independent of the person referred to in subsection (3C) above; and
    (c) is accepted by the court as being credible and reliable'.

1 1998 SCCR 214 at 239 *Kidd v HM Advocate* 2000 SCCR 513 at 528.
2 Criminal Procedure (Scotland) Act 1995, 106(3)(a).
3 CP(S)A 1955, s 106(3A).
4 CP(S)A 1955, s 106(3B).
5 For example, because he is dead, unfit to give evidence or cannot be brought to court: CP(S)A 1995, 259(2).
6 CP(S)A 1995, 106(3C).

7.04 The pre-1997 law: gone but not forgotten

'Additional evidence'
The requirement that the fresh evidence be 'additional' has now gone. This change in the law (coupled with the new subsection (3C)) means that cases such as *Mitchell v HM Advocate*,[1] *Jones v HM Advocate*,[2] *Maitland v HM Advocate*[3] and *Brodie v HM Advocate*[4] – in which the court held that evidence of a person who had already given evidence as a witness in the original trial, and now wished to change that evidence, could not be regarded as evidence that was 'additional' (for it was merely 'different') – are no longer of importance in that respect. This change in wording also disposes of the unsatisfactory decision in *McCormack v HM Advocate*[5] in which the accused was charged with and convicted of strangling his wife. At the trial he gave evidence of a struggle followed by memory loss; the next thing he claimed to remember was seeing his wife strangled on the floor. He accepted that he must have strangled her. The fresh evidence tendered at the appeal, to support a reduction of the murder conviction to a lesser

charge by reason of provocation, was that he had now recovered his memory and now remembered that he had been provoked by his wife asserting that he was not the father of her child. The court held that such evidence would not be additional; it would merely be different. The court did not seem to entertain the possibility that it might be both different and additional. A person who says on one occasion 'I do not remember'; and, on a second occasion, says 'I now remember' is no doubt saying something 'different'. If he then proceeds to say what it is that he now remembers, although he could not remember it before, it is difficult to see why the newly remembered matter should not have been regarded as 'additional'. The thinking of the court in these cases was influenced by the considerations present in *Temple v HM Advocate*.[6] The current position (post-1997) is that any evidence 'not heard at the original proceedings' is *potentially* admissible as fresh evidence.

'Not available and could not reasonably have been made available at the trial'
With these words now removed, less weight attaches to the actual decisions in a number of cases in which these words were interpreted and applied. However, cases decided under the old provisions still have some relevance. The earlier decisions are discussed in the first edition. The word 'reasonably' finds an echo in the uses of the expression 'reasonable explanation' in subsections (3A) and (3C)(b). It is noteworthy that the words 'the existence and significance of evidence . . . not heard' are repeated in subsection (3)(b) of the amended section 106. The concepts of 'reasonableness' and 'significance' are analysed in the reasoning and decisions in a number of cases; they may shed some light on how the court will apply the reasonableness test derived from the new provisions. Thus in *MacKenzie v HM Advocate*[7] the Lord Justice-General said that 'evidence which an accused is unable to give at his trial but is able to give later . . . may be regarded as evidence which was not available to him and which could not reasonably have been made available by him at the trial'; but that an accused who chose, through fear of the consequences, not to give evidence at the trial could not later claim that the evidence that he chose not to give was 'not reasonably available' at the trial. The reasoning was that it was 'his choice not his inability to give it' that resulted in the evidence not being given at the trial.[8] This reasoning would be likely to support the view that an explanation on similar lines would not count as a reasonable explanation. In *Carr v Lees*,[9] in the absence of any explanation in the affidavits as to why the fresh

evidence to be given by a new witness (a friend of the accused) had not been discovered before the trial, it could not be said that the evidence was not reasonably available. Again, the reasoning in this case may shed useful light on the concept of reasonable explanation.[10]

1 1989 SCCR 502.
2 1989 SCCR 726.
3 1992 SCCR 759.
4 1993 SCCR 371.
5 1993 SCCR 581.
6 1971 JC 1.
7 1995 SCCR 141 at 151.
8 Contrast with the case of *McCormack v HM Advocate* 1993 SCCR 581.
9 1993 SCCR 316.
10 See also *Cameron v HM Advocate* 1994 SCCR 502.

7.05   Inadmissibility at the original trial: the rule in *Conway v HM Advocate*[1]

In this case it was held that before the court could be satisfied that there had been a miscarriage of justice on the ground of fresh evidence the evidence had to be evidence that would have been relevant and admissible at the original trial. This rule is swept aside by the Criminal Procedure (Scotland) Act 1995, section 106(3B) which provides that evidence not admissible at the trial which has become admissible by the date of the appeal may be admitted 'if it appears to the court that it would be in the interests of justice to do so'. There is no further statutory provision to guide or restrict the court in its assessment of the interests of justice in any particular case.

1   1996 SCCR 569.

7.06   Fresh evidence: the requirements (post-1997)

1. *Miscarriage of justice*
The basic requirement is to satisfy the High Court that there has been a miscarriage of justice. This is dealt with at 7.09 below.

2. *Evidence 'not heard'*
Clearly, the words 'evidence which was not heard' are not meant to be construed literally as referring to evidence received through the ears. Evidence may be adduced in various ways, for example,

through showing television images from an unmanned, automatic closed circuit television system, or by displaying photographs, or plans, or diagrams, or by being the subject of agreement under the Criminal Procedure (Scotland) Act 1995, section 256, or as being deemed to be proved as 'uncontroversial evidence' under section 258, or by letter of request procedure under section 272, or even by a witness silently displaying his scars to the court. Accordingly, what the words 'not heard' convey is that the evidence was not presented to, and admitted by, the court in the original proceedings.

3. *'The existence and significance of evidence . . . not heard'.*
The court has to be satisfied that what is said to be fresh evidence exists as evidence capable of being adduced in court. That requirement imposes upon the appellant and his advisers a preliminary obligation to present the material in a suitable form. Sworn affidavits may be required.[1] However, the court has often looked at precognitions,[2] experts' reports, letters and other material said by the appellant to show, or tend to show, the existence of evidence which has not been heard.[3] In *Ward v Crowe*[4] what was submitted to be fresh evidence was tendered in the form of a copy of an initial writ in which certain averments of fact had been made on behalf of the pursuer by his solicitor. That pursuer had given important evidence at the appellant's trial and it was submitted on behalf of the appellant that the averments constituted fresh evidence of the pursuer/witness. No affidavit was produced from that person. The court held that averments in an initial writ did not constitute 'evidence' for the purposes of the section.

There are many cases in which the court has had regard to the possible 'significance' of fresh evidence without hearing it. In some cases the court has found it possible, simply upon the basis of the affidavits, precognitions, reports or other material presented, to conclude that the fresh evidence could not be significant even if it met all the other conditions imposed by section 106. In other cases it has been thought appropriate to postpone any determination of the significance of the material until it has been properly presented as evidence to the court.[5] In some instances, of course, the possible significance becomes a vital ingredient of the final judgment as to whether or not there has been a miscarriage of justice.[6] In *Baikie v HM Advocate*[7] the appellant had been convicted of and sentenced for attempted murder in 1996. He was later transferred from prison to the State Hospital at Carstairs. In 1998 he lodged a note of appeal against sentence on the basis that new medical reports now revealed that, although it had not been realised at the time of the offence or at the date of the trial, he was suffering from schizophrenia at the time of the offence. The court continued the appeal to allow the Crown to have the appellant medically examined. When the Crown obtained a report confirming that the appellant's behaviour in relation to the offence was likely to have been secondary to his mental illness, the court held that had the sentencing court known at the time of sentencing what had subsequently become known, it would probably have received, and given effect to, a recommendation for a hospital order. On that basis the appeal court quashed the sentence and replaced it with a hospital order under sections 58 and 59 of the 1995 Act, restricting discharge.

In *Hynes v HM Advocate*,[8] discussing the former test of reasonable availability at the trial, the court said:

'there is no rule of practice which requires that a final decision on the question of availability must be taken before the court hears the alleged additional evidence. There may be cases where this issue can be decided against the appellant at the first stage by looking simply at the affidavits or statements of the proposed witnesses. It may be clear from what has been produced in support of the appeal that the statutory tests cannot be satisfied, in which case there would be no point in hearing the evidence and the appeal can be disposed of by being refused at that stage. There may, however, be other cases where this issue cannot be resolved one way or another without hearing the evidence and it will always be open to the court, where it decides to hear the evidence, to review the whole matter once the evidence has been led from the reposed witnesses. The question whether the statutory tests are satisfied must be determined at that stage in the light of what the witnesses have said in the witness box. It is their evidence, not what they said in their statements to the solicitor, which must be examined at that stage. As the present case demonstrates, it is not unknown for a witness to give evidence that contradicts what he said in his statement to the solicitor. He may depart entirely from what he said in that statement or provide further details which alter the whole effect of it. It would be pointless for the court to hear his evidence if it had to proceed instead on the affidavits and reach a decision which was contrary to the evidence.'

These observations are apt also in relation to the test of significance. In relation to other such issues the court has also employed the two-stage approach[9] allowing crucial decisions to be postponed until the fresh evidence had been heard and properly assessed.

4. *Reasonable explanation*

Subsection (3A) makes it an essential condition for the taking into account of fresh evidence that there is a reasonable explanation of why it was not heard at the trial. The use of this expression in the subsection was first fully discussed in *Campbell (T) v HM Advocate*.[10] At page 240 of that report the Lord Justice-Clerk referred to the recommendations of the Sutherland Committee and noted the recommendation 'that there should be a reasonable explanation for the failure to adduce the evidence and we would not wish to try to circumscribe what might be a reasonable explanation in any particular circumstances. We believe that is a matter for the Court to decide'. The Lord Justice-Clerk also quoted the words of Lord Justice-Clerk Thompson in *Gallagher v HM Advocate*,[11] referring to 'the dominating consideration that we may order new evidence if we think it necessary or expedient in the interests of justice'. Against that background the Lord Justice-Clerk concluded that, in determining whether or not the terms of subsection (3A) have been satisfied, 'the court should have regard to the interests of justice according to the circumstances of the particular case'. It is clear that it is for the appellant to show that the test has been satisfied, but it is equally clear that the appellant does not have to establish that the explanation is the truth. It has to be shown to be 'genuine' or it is not regarded as an explanation at all. It must be sufficient to account for the fact that the evidence was not heard. A deliberate tactical decision not to lead certain evidence would be most unlikely to provide a basis for a reasonable explanation within the meaning of subsection (3A). The underlying intention of the new legislation is that the court should take a broad and flexible approach in taking account of the circumstances of the particular case.[12] The court has to be satisfied that there is a reasonable explanation before it attempts to assess the significance of the evidence. The full details of the reasoning of the judges in *Campbell (T) v HM Advocate* are to be found in the report referred to at pages 240 ff (LJ-C), pages 261 ff (Lord McCluskey) and pages 270 ff (Lord Sutherland). These tests, which are not, and cannot be, very precise, have been applied in a number of cases since *Campbell (T) v HM Advocate*. These may be referred to in order to see how the test came to be applied in very different circumstances. In *Hall v HM Advocate*[13] the test was applied in an old (1988) case referred to the High Court by the Secretary of State. The same test was considered a second time after the evidence had been heard.[14] The Lord Justice-Clerk then said:

'The terms of subsection (3A) suggest that the matter should be looked at from the point of view of those who represented the appellant at the time of the trial, which includes, of course, the period in which the defence was being prepared. Thus, if it is shown that, despite reasonable steps having been taken to investigate the case, it did not appear that a person would provide information which would be of assistance, whether by way of challenging the Crown case or advancing the case for the defence, there could be a reasonable explanation of why he was not adduced at the trial to give the evidence which he is now asked to give. It follows that, in a case where the requirements of subsection (3A) have to be satisfied, it is important that the appellant should be able to point to information as to what was known to those who represented the appellant at that time and what steps they took to investigate the defence'.

The same approach is taken in *Barr v HM Advocate*.[15] In *Mills v HM Advocate*[16] the court had to consider whether or not the fact that the fresh evidence was to come from a person who had been a co-accused at the original trial of itself amounted to 'a reasonable explanation' within the meaning of subsection (3A). Although the authority of the decision is weakened by the fact that it proceeded upon a concession made by the Crown, the court was careful to point out that there existed an alternative way of proceeding in circumstances where it became evident before the trial that the co-accused's evidence might be essential for one of the other accused. The Lord Justice-General added:

'One might therefore have expected that the appellant would have moved the court to separate the trials of Reilly (the co-accused) and the appellant, so that Reilly, . . . could have been called to give evidence.'

In that case also the court reiterated the view that a tactical decision not to adduce evidence would render it extremely difficult to establish a reasonable explanation. It is thus clear that if an accused considers that the evidence of his co-accused is necessary for the proper presentation of his case, the most careful consideration should be given to making a motion before trial for separation of trials. If the motion is made but is refused then it would be difficult to resist the conclusion that there was a reasonable explanation for not adducing the co-accused's evidence at the trial.

It is considered unnecessary to discuss here every reported case in which the 'reasonable explanation' requirement imposed by subsection (3A) has been applied. The circumstances always vary. The requirement has always to be met and satisfied. Accordingly the full presentation of the explanation of why the evidence was not heard at the original proceedings forms an essential part of the application for leave to appeal and of the presentation of the appeal itself.

1 As in *Maitland v HM Advocate* 1992 SCCR 759, *Carrington v HM Advocate* 1994 SCCR 567, *MacKenzie v HM Advocate* 1995 SCCR 141 and *Karling v HM Advocate* 1999 SCCR 359.
2 Taken by a suitably qualified person: *Allison v HM Advocate* 1985 SCCR 408; see also *Reid v HM Advocate* 1994 SCCR 755.
3 *Salusbury-Hughes v HM Advocate* 1983 SCCR 461.
4 1999 SCCR 219.
5 As in *Karling v HM Advocate* 1999 SCCR 359.
6 As in *Marshall v Smith* 1983 SCCR 156.
7 2000 SCCR 119.
8 1994 SCCR 602 at 607.
9 *Mitchell (S.P.) v HM Advocate* 1996 SCCR 477 at 481.
10 1998 SCCR 214.
11 1951 JC 38 at 45.
12 *Barr v HM Advocate* 1999 SCCR 13.
13 1998 SCCR 525.
14 See *Hall v HM Advocate (No 2)* 1999 SCCR 130.
15 1999 SCCR 13.
16 1999 SCCR 202.

7.07 Change of evidence by a witness

The Sutherland Committee[1] considered an amendment of the law to alter the rule applied in *Mitchell v HM Advocate*[2] and *Brodie v HM Advocate*.[3] That rule prevented the court from hearing, as fresh evidence, sworn testimony from a witness who was by the date of the appeal prepared to say that the evidence he gave at the trial was wrong. The Committee argued:[5]

'It cannot be right that a person should be excluded from bringing before the Court truthful evidence which might exculpate him or at least throw a reasonable doubt on his conviction. Nevertheless there must be a real risk of abuse if changes of evidence were allowed to be heard, without any additional supporting evidence.'

The recommendation[5] was in the following terms:

'We *recommend* that an appeal based on fresh evidence in the form of a change of witness testimony should be possible. To avoid the very obvious pitfalls of opening the door to this kind of appeal, we further *recommend* that the reasons given for the change of testimony should be supported by some additional credible and reliable evidence. If the change of testimony is so supported, it should be considered. If it is not so supported, it should not be considered. *This supporting evidence need not necessarily be new* [emphasis added]. Evidence led at the trial might, in certain circumstances, take on a quite different significance when viewed in the context of a change of evidence by a witness. This is a matter which we are content for the Court to develop. All other tests relating to fresh evidence appeals discussed in the previous section would, of course, still require to be applied by the Court.'

In *Campbell (T) v HM Advocate*,[6] the Lord Justice-Clerk said:[7] 'The provisions of subsections (3C) and (3D) broadly reflect the recommendations of the Sutherland Committee. However they are in certain respects more stringent.' That is clearly correct; but, in one very important respect, the new statutory provisions are less stringent and wider than what was recommended by the Sutherland Committee. From the whole discussion of the matter in the Sutherland Committee Report it is clear that what was being contemplated by the Committee was that a witness who gave evidence at the original proceedings might *change* his evidence *thereafter*. Thus the discussion in paragraph 2.54 – which has a sidenote, 'Change of evidence by a witness' - looks at 'the current position' by reference to the opinion of the Lord Justice-General (Emslie) in *Mitchell v HM Advocate*[8] where his Lordship said, 'Putting the matter shortly, we shall say that the Court will never entertain an appeal upon the proposition that a witness who has given evidence at a trial merely wishes to change his story'. The recommendation in paragraph 2.58 is specifically related to 'a change of witness testimony'. Subsection (3C), however, requires that the fresh evidence (i e not heard at the original proceedings) should – in this special case – have the following features:

(a) it must be
    '(i) from a person; or
    (ii) of a statement (within the meaning of section 259(1) of this Act)
        by a person, who gave evidence at the original proceedings; and
(b) which is different from, or additional to the evidence so given . . .'

An examination of subsection (3C) and section 259 shows that the fresh evidence, the evidence not heard at the original proceedings, may come in the form of a statement from a person who is, by the date of the appeal, dead, unfit, untraceable etc, as provided for in section 259(2). There is no provision that the fresh evidence has to be evidence that somehow came into existence *after* the person gave evidence as a witness at the original proceedings. It is at least conceivable that a person would give evidence as a witness at the original proceedings, being evidence which pointed to the guilt of the accused; but that thereafter he might die and only then might it emerge that *before* or during the trial at which he gave his incriminating evidence he had made a statement admissible under section 259 which was exculpatory of the accused or at least wholly contradictory of the witness's incriminating evidence.[9] That would be evidence which was 'not heard at the original proceedings' but it could hardly be described as a 'change' of evidence by a witness after he gave his evidence at the original proceedings. To this extent at least the provision in subsection (3C) opens the door significantly wider than was proposed by the Sutherland Committee. The importance of the reference to section 259(1) is discussed in *Campbell (T) v HM Advocate*,[10] although at that point the discussion relates to the interpretation of the words 'a reasonable explanation' in subsection (3C). Accordingly it is clear that the section permits the court to consider as fresh evidence, evidence which differs from or is additional to evidence given by a witness at the trial even if the new material submitted as fresh evidence existed prior to the giving of evidence by that witness at the original proceedings. A reasonable explanation is, of course, required by subsection (3A). This requirement is discussed in at 7.04 and 7.06 above.

The concept of 'a reasonable explanation' in subsection (3C)
It is now important to consider the requirement of this subsection that the evidence coming from a person who gave evidence at the original proceedings 'may not found an appeal unless there is a reasonable explanation as to why the evidence now sought to be adduced was not given by that person at those proceedings'. This gave rise to some disagreement amongst the judges in *Campbell (T) v HM Advocate*. Subsection (3C), in laying down the conditions that have to be satisfied before the court will have regard to fresh evidence from a person who gave evidence at the original proceedings, begins with the words 'Without prejudice to subsection (3A) above'. As subsection (3A) imposes a condition – 'only where there is a reasonable explanation' – and subsection (3C) itself also imposes a condition – 'unless there is a reasonable explanation' – an issue that arises is whether two reasonable explanations are needed, or only one. Is the repetition significant or not? Do the two reasonable explanations have to come from different sources? This curious issue was much debated in *Campbell (T) v HM Advocate*. The judges agreed that the words 'a reasonable explanation' must have the same meaning in subsections (3A) and (3C). They disagreed about the significance of the opening phrase in subsection (3C). Lord Sutherland considered that the requirement for a reasonable explanation appearing in subsection (3C) added something distinctive to the requirement

in (3A). The distinction, it was said, lay in the source of the explanation. Lord Sutherland concluded, in relation to a subsection (3C) reasonable explanation, 'In my view there is *only one person* who can give that explanation, namely the witness who wishes to alter or add to his evidence' [emphasis added]. Lord McCluskey[11] disagreed, referring particularly to subsection (3C)(a)(ii), which allows 'fresh' evidence from beyond the grave[12] from a person who was dead before the appeal was taken. The Lord Justice Clerk did not find it necessary to resolve this issue. It is suggested that subsection (3C), which was added hastily at the last moment in the parliamentary proceedings, is not at all well drafted and that undue significance should not be attached to the opening phrase of that subsection. The issue as to who has to provide the reasonable explanation required by subsection (3C) remains unresolved. A decision on that point was reserved in *Hall v HM Advocate*.[13] That case, however, sheds useful light on the application of the adjective 'reasonable' and the need for an appellant to specify clearly what the proffered explanation is.[14]

'Independent evidence' needed to support a (3C) 'reasonable explanation'
The subsection (3C) reasonable explanation has to be 'supported by independent evidence'. Subsection (3D) provides that what is meant by 'independent evidence' is evidence which:

'(a) was not heard at the original proceedings;
(b) is from a source independent of the person referred to in subsection (3C) . . . ; and
(c) is accepted by the court as being credible and reliable.'

It is clear from the opinions in *Campbell (T) v HM Advocate*[15] that the subsection (3C) explanation needs to be corroborated by evidence which was not heard at the trial and is *accepted* by the court as being both credible and reliable. The Lord Justice-Clerk, in that case,[16] pointed out that the provision in subsection (3D)(a) was in addition to what the Sutherland Committee had recommended. In short, therefore, the corroboration of the reasonable explanation must itself be fresh, i e unheard, evidence. The parliamentary proceedings indicate that the government, in inserting subsection (3D), was deliberately not implementing the suggestion in the Sutherland Committee[17] that 'Evidence led at the trial might, in certain circumstances, take on a quite different significance when viewed in the context of a change of evidence by a witness.' The reference in subsection (3D)(b) to 'a source independent of the person referred to in subsection (3C)' expresses clearly the need for true corroboration. The words 'credible and reliable' in subsection (3D)(c) are directed not at the significance of the evidence; the 'significance' test is imposed by subsection 3(a). Accordingly, if the other conditions imposed elsewhere in the section are met, or at least if the court has not yet decided that any other essential condition has not been met, it will usually be necessary, for the purposes of subsection (3B), for the court to hear the evidence which is said to be 'independent'. However, the term used in the subsection is 'accepted by the court'; and it may well be that the court could accept evidence as being credible and reliable without necessarily hearing it. The matter might be conceded by the Crown and that concession might be acceptable by the court. The evidence in question may come from an unimpeachable and unimpeached source and thus may be regarded by the court as able to be accepted as being credible and reliable. If necessary, however, it will hear the evidence before making a judgment as to credibility and reliability. The whole court may choose to hear the evidence or may order the evidence to be heard by a judge of the High Court (or other such person as it may appoint for the purpose), in terms of section 104(1)(b). That power was invoked in the case of *Mellors v HM Advocate*,[18] a case under subsection (3A). Although the cases decided so far under the newly worded subsections contain no clear guidance on how the court may approach the matter dealt with in subsection (3D)(c), the words used there, 'credible and reliable', are obviously to be used in their ordinary sense. They were so used, but not in this exact context, in *Hall v HM Advocate (No 2)*.[19]

1 Report; paras 2.54–2.58.
2 1989 SCCR 502.
3 1993 SCCR 371.
4 para 2.57.
5 para 2.58.
6 1998 SCCR 214.
7 1998 SCCR 214 at 246.
8 1989 SCCR 502.
9 As happened in *McLay v HM Advocate* 2000 SCCR 579.
10 1998 SCCR 214 at 263–264, in the opinion of Lord McCluskey.
11 At 264.
12 See the discussion in the preceding paragraph, suggesting that the 'fresh', i e unheard, evidence might have come into existence before the trial but remained undiscoverable by the accused.
13 1998 SCCR 525 at 538.
14 See p 538.
15 1998 SCCR 214.
16 At 246.
17 para 2.58.
18 1999 SCCR 869.
19 1999 SCCR 130.

7.08   Significance of evidence not heard: miscarriage of justice

The potential significance of the fresh evidence will have to be considered at the first stage when the court is invited to allow the fresh evidence to be heard.[1] If it could not be significant, even if true, the court will not hear it. If, however, the evidence is in fact heard by or otherwise presented to the court, it becomes necessary again to consider its significance to determine whether or not there has been a miscarriage of justice.

1   See 7.06 above.

7.09   Miscarriage of justice and discretion of High Court

The Sutherland Committee recommended (paragraph 2.29) retention of the one general ground of appeal, 'that a miscarriage of justice has occurred'. The Crime and Punishment (Scotland) Act 1997 proceeded upon an acceptance of this recommendation. Thus the pre-1997 cases about the concept of miscarriage of justice remain of importance.

The effect to be given to the pre-1997 provisions was the subject of the opinion of the Lord Justice-Clerk (Wheatley) in *McCuaig v HM Advocate*,[1] an opinion with which the other judges agreed. In that case there was undeniably a breach of the Criminal Procedure (Scotland) Act 1975, section 160(1) (now section 101 of the Criminal Procedure (Scotland) Act 1995), providing that the jury is not to be informed of the accused's previous convictions. It had previously been held, in *Cordiner v HM Advocate*,[2] that a breach of that section amounted to a 'miscarriage of justice' within the meaning of section 254(1) of the 1975 Act[3] though it would not necessarily amount in all cases to a 'substantial' miscarriage of justice. In *McCuaig* the Lord Justice-Clerk held that under the newly enacted provisions, 'The matter in my view is now entirely one for the *discretion* of the Court'. That was an extempore opinion and it appears that there was no argument submitted to the High Court as to the true import of the newly enacted section 228(2) of the 1975 Act. The reasoning in support of the conclusion that Lord Wheatley reached there has been described as involving 'an exercise in statutory interpretation which, in the weight it places on the single word 'may',[4] might be described as almost rabbinic in its boldness'.[5] The true function and purpose of the word 'may' in the Criminal Procedure (Scotland) Act 1995, section 118(1) (formerly section 228(1) of the 1975 Act), it is submitted, is not to confer an unfettered discretion on the High Court to 'dispose' (i e finally dispose) of an appeal by doing whichever one or other of the things specified in paragraphs (a), (b) and (c) it chooses. On the contrary, because the High Court is not empowered to do anything other than those things authorised by paragraphs (a), (b) and (c), the effect is that it is *required* to do one or other of these things. On this reading there is no 'discretion' conferred by the word 'may', although there is some flexibility in the construction and application of the words 'miscarriage of justice'.

1   1982 SCCR 125.
2   1978 JC 64 (opinion of the court delivered by Lord Justice-Clerk Wheatley).
3   Which re-enacted the Criminal Appeal (Scotland) Act 1926, s 2(1).
4   In the Criminal Procedure (Scotland) Act 1975, s 254(1), as amended.
5   Sheriff Gordon, Editor, in 1982 SCCR at 129.

7.10   Miscarriage of justice: more recent developments

In later cases the court has tended either to hold that there has been a miscarriage of justice and so to allow the appeal[1] or to hold that there has not, and, therefore, to refuse it.[2] In *Hunter v Lord Advocate*[3] the court (the opinion of the court being delivered by Lord Justice-Clerk Wheatley) held that the trial judge had fallen into error by excluding certain evidence that he should have admitted. The opinion included the passage:

'An error in law by the trial judge in regard to the evidence of a witness does not *eo facto* [i e by reason of that fact alone] necessarily lead to a granting of an appeal. By the terms of section 228 [now 106(1) of the 1995 Act] the appellant has to show that the error resulted in a miscarriage of justice . . . In all the circumstances . . . while we are of the opinion that the trial judge erred in law in the manner complained of, we are also of the opinion that no miscarriage of justice resulted from it. We accordingly refuse his appeal.'

1   *Cordiner v HM Advocate* 1991 SCCR 652.
2   *Binks v HM Advocate* 1984 SCCR 335.
3   1984 SCCR 306.

7.11   Current understanding of miscarriage of justice

The High Court now tends to look rather at the seriousness, importance and materiality of the error that the appeal brings to light. Whatever the character of the error (misdirection, wrongful exclusion of evidence, misconduct by the prosecution, etc), the High Court, in the light of its judgment about the importance of that error in the context of the whole trial, goes on to make the further judgment as to whether or not what went wrong may have affected the understanding and the deliberations of the jury in such a way as to lead them to draw an important inference or inferences adverse to the appellant. If the judgment is that the error was likely to have influenced the jury to reach a material judgment adverse to the appellant it will hold that the ground of appeal has been made out, that the 'alleged' miscarriage of justice was a true miscarriage of justice, and, a miscarriage of justice having occurred, the conviction appealed against must be quashed.[1] In *McGougan v HM Advocate*[2] in which the trial judge misdirected the jury as to what circumstances could be treated as corroborative of guilt, the Lord Justice-Clerk, delivering the opinion of the court, said at page 54:

'Whether or not a misdirection produces a miscarriage of justice must depend upon the circumstances and we readily accept that there may be cases where there is no miscarriage of justice despite the fact that there has been a misdirection by the trial judge'.

The case of *Mumraiz Khan and Aman Khan v HM Advocate*[3] is a striking example of how virtually the same error by the trial judge in relation to each of two accused in one trial was held to have led to a miscarriage of justice in one case, but not in the other. The final decision rests upon the court's assessment of the gravity and possible results of the error, seen in the context of the whole circumstances.[1]

In most recent cases the approach to applying the miscarriage of justice test has been that found in *Cameron v HM Advocate*.[4] An example is *Sutherland v McGlennan*[5] in which both parties and the court accepted that the *Cameron* test applied. The material part was quoted:

'[I]f the court is to find that a miscarriage of justice has occurred in an appeal such as this,[6] it must be satisfied that the additional evidence is at least capable of being described as important and reliable evidence which would have been bound, or at least likely, to have had a material bearing upon, or a material part to play in, the jury's determination of a critical issue at the trial.'

The test was also applied in *Elliott v HM Advocate*[7] on the issue of whether the fresh evidence disclosed by affidavits would have led the jury to hold that there was diminished responsibility, in a murder case. It is noteworthy, however, that in *Mitchell (S.P.) v HM Advocate*[8] Lord Justice-General Hope, delivering the opinion of the court, preferred the analysis set out in *Church v HM Advocate*,[9] at least in relation to the approach to questions of credibility and reliability. Differences between the formulation of the approach were also canvassed in *Campbell (T) v HM Advocate, Kidd v HM Advocate*[1] and *McLay v HM Advocate*[11]. In the *Kidd* case the court said '. . . we do not consider that there was any essential difference of approach between that in *Cameron* and that more fully spelled out in *Church.*' In *McLay*, the court referred to *Kidd* and said 'The upshot is that the test to be applied is the test as explained in *Church*'. Sir Gerald Gordon's commentary suggests that the test actually adopted in *McLay* is the *Cameron* test. It is not clear that the law has been finally clarified.[10]

1   *Kidd v HM Advocate* 2000 SCCR 513, 528, para [23].
2   1991 SCCR 49.
3   1992 SCCR 146.
4   1987 SCCR 608.
5   1999 SCCR 652.
6   I e a fresh evidence case.
7   1995 SCCR 280.
8   1996 SCCR 477.
9   1996 SCCR 29.
10   1998 SCCR 14.
11   2000 SCCR 579

7.12   Miscarriage consisting of incorrect rejection of 'no case to answer' submission[1]

There is a live question as to whether or not a miscarriage of justice may have occurred if the trial judge has incorrectly refused a 'no case to answer' submission and the accused then gives evidence which fills the 'fatal gaps', as they were described by Lord Emslie in *Little v HM Advocate.*[2] In that case the Lord Justice General said:

'In refusing both appeals we wish to observe that in the course of the hearing it appeared that we might require to consider the implications of section 140A [no case to answer] of the Criminal Procedure (Scotland) Act 1975, if we had been satisfied that the trial judge had erred in reject-ing the submissions of no case to answer made on behalf of the appel-lants. As we have pointed out, counsel for Mrs Little accepted that in asking ourselves if there had been a miscarriage of justice we were quite entitled to have regard to the evidence which Mrs Little herself elected to give and lead but, ignoring that concession, the problem would have been how to deal with convictions, fully justified by the whole evidence before the jury, on the assumption that there were fatal gaps in the Crown evi-dence which were only filled by the evidence given by and on behalf of the first appellant and by the evidence given by MacKenzie [a witness led for the defence] . . . In view of the conclusions at which we have arrived we are fortunate that we do not have to resolve this problem in these appeals without the advantage of much more comprehensive exploration of the proper interpretation to be placed on section 140A than was presented on behalf of the appellants. That section, which is entirely novel to our accustomed and well-tried procedure, would appear to echo rules of law long familiar to other jurisdictions, and the problem to which we have referred has, we apprehend, been examined in the courts of England and in courts of the Commonwealth, including the Supreme Court of Victoria, in relation to their own systems of prosecution and criminal procedure. No relevant decisions in these other jurisdictions were cited to us and when the problem requires to be resolved in a criminal appeal in Scotland we would expect to have full discussion of relevant foreign decisions to assist us to appreciate clearly the full implications of the new factor which has been introduced by Parliament into the law of Scotland in the shape of section 140A of the Act of 1975.'

The English cases that the Lord Justice-General had in mind would include *R v Abbott*[3] in which it was held that the error of the trial judge, in not upholding the submission of no case to answer on the basis of the evidence adduced by the prosecution, meant that the jury's verdict could not stand. A feature of that case on the facts was that both accused had gone into the witness box after the trial judge had wrongly rejected the submission of no case to answer; the appellant's co-accused gave incriminating evidence against the appellant and thus provided evidence to warrant a conviction, such evidence having been wholly deficient until then.

The matter has not yet been determined by the High Court in Scotland. The sections of the Criminal Procedure (Scotland) Act 1995 remain, in this respect, in essentially the same terms as before. Because there is only one relevant ground of appeal, namely 'alleged miscarriage of justice', and because errors by the judge who presides at the trial do not necessarily[4] constitute or result in a miscarriage of justice, the fact that the trial judge has fallen into error by not upholding the no case to answer submission does not appear, of itself, to compel the court to conclude that a miscarriage of justice has occurred. The context will have to be considered. So, for example, if the real issue in a culpable homicide trial, resulting from a traffic accident death, was the quality of the accused's driving, but the prosecution evidence fell marginally short of what was necessary to corroborate that the accused was driving the car, the accused's advocate would quite properly make a motion of no case to answer. If the trial judge wrongly rejected it and the accused, acting on legal advice, decided not to rest upon the hope of establishing on appeal that the trial judge was wrong in that respect, and proceeded to adduce evidence from a witness as to the quality of the driving; and that witness incidentally provided the missing but necessary evidence that the accused had indeed been the driver, then, if the jury upheld the prosecution's view of the quality of the driving, and convicted, it is not clear that the High Court would conclude that a miscarriage of justice has taken place purely because the presiding judge had erred in rejecting the no case to answer submission. In such a situation, an error has been made; but a finding that an error has occurred, including one that may have adversely affected the interests of an accused, has never been enough, on its own, to warrant the quashing of a conviction, unless it has been of such a character that it has brought about a miscarriage of justice. The High Court would be acting in accordance with its pragmatic, non-technical traditions if in this type of case it looked behind the procedural forms to judge the reality. Such an approach would not, of course, exclude the possibility of a finding that a miscarriage of justice had occurred, even in a case where the accused, acting on legal advice, has entered the witness box and while there has filled the fatal gap in the prosecution evidence. The court's understanding of the justice of the case might, on this approach, always be more important than any merely procedural or technical consideration. The precise facts of the case might be of decisive importance, as they appear to have been in *R v Abbott*.

However, with the coming into force of the Human Rights Act 1998, article 6 of the European Convention on Human Rights is likely to be invoked in favour of the view that a miscarriage of justice occurs if the court errs in refusing a 'no case to answer' submission and the accused is then advised to give evidence and does so. The jurisprudence of the European Court of Human Rights lays considerable emphasis on the careful observance of fair trial procedures; and it might be argued that a person left facing charges that should have been dismissed as a result of the correct application of the law – notably in relation to corroboration – and who is as a result forced into the witness box where his evidence 'fills the gap' has been deprived of his right of silence.[5] This argument is strengthened by the enactment of the Criminal Justice (Scotland) Act 1995, section 32, which allows the prosecutor to comment upon the accused's failure to give evidence. The situation discussed could arise sharply if the accused faced several charges (as in *Cordiner v HM Advocate*,[6] where several distinct charges were rolled up into one and where the loss of the right of silence is discussed).[7] In such a case, the accused might feel compelled to enter the witness box in order to defend himself against a serious charge that ought to have been dismissed for lack of evidence. He would thus expose himself to questioning – with no right to remain silent – on other charges on the indictment, being charges in relation to which he would have wanted to exercise his right to remain silent. (The European Court of Human Rights itself might, however, consider that the procedural rules governing no case to answer and the related rule of evidence about corroboration (which lies at the root of the Criminal Procedure (Scotland) Act 1995, sections 97 and 160) were matters for the Scottish courts to determine, but the Court is still likely to consider whether or not the proceedings as a whole were unfair).[8] In the light of the ruling in *Thomson v Crowe,*[9] it is now clear that in both solemn and summary proceedings the accused should know at the close of the Crown case exactly what evidence the prosecution is able to rely on.

1 Criminal Procedure (Scotland) Act 1995, s 97(1) (solemn) and s 160 (summary).
2 1983 SCCR 56.
3 [1995] 2 QB 497.
4 *McGougan v HM Advocate* 1991 SCCR 49.
5 See *Murray v United Kingdom* [1996] 22 EHRR 29; *Saunders v United Kingdom* (1996) 23 EHRR 297; *Condron v United Kingdom* 2 May 2000 (unreported).
6 1991 SCCR 671.
7 Lord McCluskey at 671 E-F.
8 *Miailhe v France (No 2)* (1996) 23 EHRR 491, para 43.
9 1999 SCCR 1003.

PARTICULAR GROUNDS OF APPEAL

7.13 Examples of common grounds

Although there is only one statutory ground of appeal, 'alleged miscarriage of justice', there are various particular grounds of appeal which are commonly advanced as a basis for the conclusion that there has been a miscarriage of justice in the proceedings brought under review of the High Court in the appeal. The particular statutory examples of fresh evidence and unreasonable verdict are discussed elsewhere in this chapter. The grounds discussed are not exhaustive of the possible types or categories of appeal. Some examples are given, or suggestions are made, as to how particular grounds may be formulated; but there are no set forms. Clarity, accuracy, brevity, comprehensiveness and coherence are the features of a well-formulated ground.

7.14 Misdirection

Any alleged misdirection by the trial judge must be specifically identified and highlighted in the grounds of appeal. A judge may misdirect a jury by omitting to give a direction that he ought to have given, by giving a direction that he ought not to have given or by giving a direction that is likely to mislead or confuse the jury or in any way violate the accused's right to a fair trial. The examples given below may be referred to, principally for the purpose of illustrating how to formulate the ground of appeal. However, the room for error in a charge is unbounded; accordingly, the practitioner who listens to or subsequently scrutinises the judge's charge to the jury must ask himself when considering the statement of grounds of appeal:

(1) What was the law applicable to the case on which the jury needed directions?

(2) In the light of the applicable law, was the jury given all the directions that were necessary, and given them accurately, fully and clearly?

(3) Did the trial judge deal with all the necessary law and with all the real issues canvassed in the submissions to the jury?

(4) Was any important direction omitted, for example, a direction in relation to concert, provocation, reasonable doubt, onus of proof, self-defence, possible alternative verdicts, the applicability of the *Moorov*[1] doctrine or the definition of the crime or offence and its essential ingredients?

(5) Did the trial judge invite the jury to consider evidence or other material matters on which the Crown did not seek to rely?

(6) If the trial judge gave examples to the jury to illustrate the way the law might fall to be applied, did he do so in a way that was unhelpful, contradictory of his more general statements as to the law, or simply confusing?

(7) In dealing with the evidence, did the trial judge refer to it accurately or misleadingly?

(8) Did the trial judge deal with the evidence fairly or did he give undue weight to certain evidence or insufficient attention to other evidence?

(9) Did the trial judge appear, either expressly or by his choice of language, to seek to impose his own views on matters properly within the jury's province?

(10) Did the trial judge express opinions, however qualified, upon matters not properly falling within his province?

(11) Did the trial judge invite the jury to approach the evidence in a way that was not legitimately canvassed during the trial?[2]

(12) Was the accused's right to find trial under article 6 of the ECHR violated?

If the practitioner asks himself the right questions, the answers should reveal the flaws in a defective charge. The task is then to articulate the answers as grounds of appeal, as coherent criticisms of the charge as printed. Now that the trial proceedings are recorded on audio tapes, it is not unknown for the appellant to suggest that, although what the trial judge said can be read as if it might be a fair statement, it was delivered in such a tone of voice or with such histrionic emphasis that it amounted to an attempt to impose the judge's view upon the jury. In such a case it is highly desirable that the particular passages criticised be identified in the ground of appeal so that they may be listened to by the sifting judges. Some examples of grounds of appeal related to alleged misdirection follow. It is, however, essential to bear in mind that the appeal court will read the charge as a whole in the light of what were the real issues in dispute: 'The court is not disposed to examine out of context isolated sentences in the charge of a judge who presides at a criminal trial.'[3] 'The trial judge can be expected to deal with live issues, not with possible circumstances which are never raised in the trial.'[4] The issue is not whether or not the directions given might have been better expressed; the issue is whether or not there has been a miscarriage of justice.[5] A judge is entitled to have the jury recalled after they have retired to consider their verdict, but before delivering it, so as to correct any error in the charge, thereby reducing the risk that the error might be said to have led to a miscarriage of justice.[5]

1   1930 S.C. 68; 1930 SLT 596.
2   As in *McDade v HM Advocate* 1994 SCCR 627.
3   *Wilkie v HM Advocate* 1938 JC 128 at 131, per Lord Justice Normand. Cf *McPhelim v HM Advocate* 1960 JC 17.
4   Per the Lord Justice-General in *Johnston v HM Advocate* 1997 SCCR 568, at 577.
5   *McIntosh v HM Advocate* 1997 SCCR 68 at 75F.

7.15   Misdirection by omission

In *McTavish v HM Advocate*[1] a conviction of murder was quashed because, although the presiding judge in his charge to the jury reminded the jury of an incriminating reply allegedly made by the accused to the murder charge preferred by the police, he omitted to make specific reference to the fact that the accused in evidence had denied making the alleged reply at all. The successful ground of appeal was framed thus:

'The presiding judge misdirected the jury in regard to the police evidence concerning the events in the police station and the panel's alleged replies to said charge in that he referred the jury to the replies only in the context of whether they had been elicited fairly and failed to put to the jury the fact that the panel denied altogether having made the replies.'

In *McKenzie v HM Advocate*[2] where the presiding judge omitted to give the standard and elementary directions on onus and reasonable doubt, the successful grounds were framed as follows:

'The presiding judge misdirected the jury in respect that: (1) He failed to direct the jury that the onus of proof of the accused's guilt rested on the Crown; (2) he failed to direct the jury that the Crown had to prove the accused's guilt beyond all reasonable doubt; (3) he failed to direct the jury that, in the event of their having any reasonable doubt as to the accused's guilt, the accused should have the benefit of such doubt.'

In *King v HM Advocate*[3] the successful ground of appeal was:

'The trial judge failed to direct the jury that it was open to them to believe the evidence of Peter King [the first accused], or parts of it, and on that basis, insofar as it exonerated James King [the second accused], to acquit him; or even if it created a reasonable doubt about the Crown case against James King, to acquit him'.[4]

In *McBrearty v HM Advocate*[5] a ground of appeal was that the trial judge omitted to direct the jury as to the possibility of a finding of provocation; but the appeal failed, neither the Advocate Depute nor counsel for the defence having mentioned provocation in addressing the jury. There have been many appeals in which the criticism advanced has been that the directions in relation to corroboration,[6] or the applicability of the *Moorov* doctrine[7] were inadequate or erroneous. It could be a serious error to omit to tell the jury that an alternative verdict (e g of reset) was available to it.[8] *MacDonald v HM Advocate*[9] provides an example of a charge seriously flawed by the omission of elementary but essential directions.

---

1   1975 SLT (Notes) 27.
2   1959 JC 32.
3   1985 SCCR 322.
4   For other cases, see *Chalmers v HM Advocate* 1994 SCCR 651; *Webb v HM Advocate* 1996 SCCR 530; *Hughes v HM Advocate* 1997 SCCR 277; *Kearns v HM Advocate* 1999 SCCR 141.
5   1999 SCCR 122.
6   E g *Hutchison v HM Advocate* 1997 SCCR 726; *Callan v HM Advocate* 1999 SCCR 57.
7   E g *Thomson v HM Advocate* 1998 SCCR 657; *Paterson v HM Advocate* 1999 SCCR 750; *Reid v HM Advocate* 1999 SCCR 768.
8   *Steele v HM Advocate* 1992 SCCR 30; *Allan v HM Advocate* 1995 SCCR 234.
9   1995 SCCR 663.

7.16 Misdirection – error of law

In *Macdonald v HM Advocate*,[1] where the presiding judge misdirected the jury in reference to the 'not proven' verdict, the successful ground of appeal was in these terms:

'3. The sheriff misdirected the jury in relation to the not proven verdict. He states that if the not proven verdict did not exist the jury's verdict would almost certainly be that of guilty. This could clearly have been taken by the jury as a judicial indication that the not guilty verdict was not appropriate to this case.'

In *Sinclair v HM Advocate*[2] the sheriff directed the jury that the charges were linked in time, character and circumstances, so that the *Moorov*[3] doctrine could apply. The successful ground of appeal (which made the correct criticism) namely that it was for the jury to resolve that issue, being essentially an issue of fact, was couched in these words:

'The trial sheriff misdirected the jury in that he . . . failed to give adequate and proper directions in relation to the application of the *Moorov* doctrine. In particular, he failed to leave it to the jury to decide whether the connection which the application of the rule requires was proved to their satisfaction (*HM Advocate v Stewart*, 19 March 1981, Crown Office Circular A7(81).'

There are numerous examples of misdirections as to the use that a jury might make of a 'mixed' statement made extra-judicially by an accused person: e g *Thomson (K.) v HM Advocate*,[4] though in that case the misdirection was held to be 'of no practical significance in the context of the trial'.

1 1989 SCCR 29.
2 1990 SCCR 412; see also *Macintosh v HM Advocate* 1991 SCCR 776.
3 *Moorov v HM Advocate* 1930 JC 68.
4 1998 SCCR 683.

7.17 Misdirection regarding corroboration

No person can be convicted of a crime or of a statutory offence, except where the legislature otherwise directs, unless there is evidence of at least two witnesses implicating the person accused with the commission of the crime or offence with which he is charged: *Morton v HM Advocate*.[1] In that case, in which only one witness, the victim, identified the accused as the assailant, it appears that the ground of appeal was that 'the verdict was contrary to the evidence'. That would not be regarded as a sufficiently specific ground today; nowadays, in a case such as *Morton*, it would be necessary to say something such as: 'The trial judge misdirected the jury by saying that there was evidence sufficient to identify the appellant as the person who assaulted Miss X. There was no evidence of identification to corroborate that given by Miss X herself.' The first ground of appeal would be, 'There was insufficient evidence to identify the appellant as the person who assaulted Miss X. There was no evidence from any other witness pointing to the appellant as Miss X's assailant'.

In *Cordiner v HM Advocate*[2] a conviction of rape was quashed because the trial judge directed the jury that they could find corroboration of the complainer's evidence in a possible connection between the accused and an article of the complainer's clothing; the clothing, however, was connected with the crime only by the evidence of the complainer herself. The successful ground of appeal was:

'The Crown sought to rely for corroboration on the identification of a jersey (label number 16) as being the property of the appellant. The jersey was identified by the complainer only and accordingly could not form a separate, independent source as is required to constitute corroborative evidence. The learned trial judge failed to direct the jury that it would not be open to them to rely on such evidence for corroboration. Such failure to give appropriate directions resulted in a miscarriage of justice.'

Another example of fully stated, well-expressed cogent grounds of appeal may be seen in *McGougan v HM Advocate*[3] in which the appellant was charged with using lewd practices towards a very young girl; the trial judge had instructed the jury that they could hold that the appellant's reactions and demeanour could corroborate incriminating admissions made by him. That was held to be a material misdirection. The ground stated was: 'The jury were not directed by the learned trial judge to any relevant elements of evidence which could be taken to corroborate the appellant's statement. This was a material misdirection which led to a miscarriage of justice.' The particular ground of appeal upon which the successful submission was based was slightly less specific than it might have been because it did not specifically mention the trial judge's reference to the evidence about the appellant's reactions and demeanour. It would have been better had it done so. In *Mackie v HM Advocate*,[4] however, the successful ground of appeal was simply stated: 'The trial judge erred in directing the jury that there was sufficient corroborated evidence to enable them to convict the appellant of the charge.'

1 1938 JC 50, per Lord Justice-Clerk Aitchison, delivering the Full Bench opinion; see also *Smith v Lees* 1997 SCCR 139; *Fox v HM Advocate* 1998 SCCR 115.
2 1991 SCCR 652.
3 1991 SCCR 49 at 51–52.
4 1994 SCCR 277, decision disapproved in *Fox v HM Advocate* 1998 SCCR 115.

7.18 Misdirection by withdrawing defence

It is a misdirection to withdraw a plea of self-defence in circumstances in which there is evidence that would entitle the jury to conclude that the accused had been acting in self-defence. In *Surman v HM Advocate*[1], where the ground of appeal was upheld, the ground was stated simply, clearly and without elaboration:

'The learned trial judge erred in law and misdirected the jury by withdrawing consideration of the special defence of self-defence from the jury in so far as it relates to the fatal wound.'

Similar grounds of appeal would exist if the trial judge erroneously withdrew any line of defence, such as provocation or accident or diminished responsibility or involuntary intoxication.[2]

1 1988 SCCR 93.
2 Cf *Ross v HM Advocate* 1991 SCCR 823.

7.19 Conduct of the trial

There are numerous examples of grounds of appeal in which the alleged miscarriage of justice is said to have resulted from some circumstance related to the conduct of the trial. Some examples are given to illustrate how grounds of appeal may be framed to give adequate notice of what is complained of.

7.20 Conduct or comment by the trial judge

In *Tallis v HM Advocate*[1] the sheriff took over the role of cross-examiner of the accused, and, both in that way and by the terms of his charge to the jury, conspicuously failed to demonstrate and maintain his complete impartiality upon the vital issue of the credibility of the accused. The successful ground of appeal was in these terms:

'The sheriff interrupted the cross-examination of the procurator fiscal and proceeded to cross-examine the panel. After the conclusion of the speeches the sheriff adjourned for one and a quarter hours before charging the jury and thereafter the terms of his charge were such as to show a bias and may have constituted a miscarriage of justice resulting in the panel being convicted by a majority of the jurors.'

Though this formulation could have been improved, it gave clear notice of the points to be made and therefore achieved its purpose as a ground of appeal. In *Hutchison v HM Advocate*[2] a witness prevaricated and denied having made a prior statement to the police. The trial judge, in the presence of the jury and on the motion of the Advocate Depute, ordered the witness to be detained and to be brought before the court at the end of the trial; the witness was taken into police custody in court before the eyes of the jury. Similar treatment was meted out to a second witness who was also taken into custody but only after a courtroom struggle with the police. The detailed grounds of appeal may be seen in 1983 SCCR at 505; they merit study as an example of full, clear and coherent grounds of appeal which focus the issue well. They contain a full narrative of events and assertions as to the likely consequences of such events upon the minds of the jurors, concluding:

'In the foregoing circumstances the jury were precluded from fairly assessing the credibility of the said . . . witnesses and the proper weight to be placed upon their evidence in particular in so far as the said evidence exculpated the appellant; accordingly the appellant has been subjected to a miscarriage of justice.'

Reference should also be made, both for entertainment and enlightenment, to the fourth ground of appeal in *Macdonald v HM Advocate*[3] where the complaint was of oppression by the sheriff who, it was said, sought to rush the trial through and expressed the wish that he would be spared 'the usual counsel's disease' of 'long-winded speeches'. The High Court chose to decide the case upon another ground and offered no guidance on the proper conduct of trials in the Western Isles; but the ground of appeal is a model of clarity. There are many cases that illustrate the circumstances in which a trial judge may or may not comment upon the fact that the accused has not given evidence in court.[4] An adverse comment by the presiding judge on the accused's evidence before it is completed can be fatal to the conviction: *Milton v McLeod.*[5]

---

1   1982 SCCR 91.
2   1983 SCCR 504.
3   1989 SCCR 29.
4   See *Stewart v HM Advocate* 1980 JC 103; *Sutherland v HM Advocate* 1994 SCCR 80; *Handley v HM Advocate* 1998 SCCR 584.
5   1999 SCCR 210 (a summary case).

7.21   Conduct of the prosecutor

The prosecutor's conduct may afford a good ground of appeal. So where a prosecutor in his address to the jury commented adversely on the accused's failure to give evidence the ground of appeal was:

'There was a miscarriage of justice under section 228 of the Criminal Procedure (Scotland) Act 1975 in respect that the procurator fiscal depute, in contravention of the terms of section 141(1)(b) of said Act, commented at length on the accused's failure to give evidence to support his special defence on one charge and on his withdrawal of his special defence on the other charge. Although the sheriff directed the jury to disregard these remarks, it was not possible for them not to be influenced by them.'[1]

At the hearing, although the ground of appeal was largely accepted by the High Court, it was concluded that the evidence and the sheriff's charge were such as to warrant the conclusion that no miscarriage of justice had occurred. The prosecutor may now comment upon the accused's failure to give evidence: the Criminal Justice (Scotland) Act 1995, section 32 removed the statutory restriction upon such comment contained in the Criminal Procedure (Scotland) Act 1975, sections 141(1) (b) and 346(1)(b).

1   *Upton v HM Advocate* 1986 SCCR 188.

7.22   Defective representation

In *Anderson v HM Advocate*[1] a court of five judges overruled *McCarroll v HM Advocate*[2] and held that the defective conduct of the defence could violate an accused's right to a fair trial and thus bring about a miscarriage of justice. However, the court was careful to define the circumstances very narrowly. The Sutherland Committee recommended that the law should continue to be as laid down in *Anderson*. The important considerations relating to a ground of appeal based upon defective misrepresentation are summarised here:
1.   The defective representation must have resulted in a failure to present the defence that the accused has instructed, thus depriving the accused of his right to present his intended defence and therefore of his right to a fair trial.
2.   The defence advocate must act on the basis of the instructions he had been given. He is not permitted to present a

defence 'contrary to the instructions he has received as to the basic nature of it'.

3. The defence advocate has a measure of discretion as to how the defence is to be conducted. For example, a decision whether or not to attack the character of Crown witnesses is likely to be within the ambit of his discretion. Similarly, the defence advocate often has to decide if he should lead all the alibi witnesses whose names have been intimated; he will be taking essentially tactical decisions in relation to such a matter in the light of the quality of the potential witnesses and their criminal record.[5] Such tactical decisions are most unlikely to be regarded as amounting to a failure to present the accused's defence.

4. If a question of fact arises in the appeal as to the nature of the defence or the effect of it on the conduct of the defence advocate, the appeal court may exercise its powers under the Criminal Procedure (Scotland) Act 1995, section 104, to hear evidence or to remit for inquiry to a fit person, if satisfied that the complaint could otherwise meet the stringent tests required by *Anderson*.

5. In all cases when a complaint is made, and leave is granted, the Clerk of Justiciary will advise the advocates and/or solicitors criticised, provide them with copies of the grounds of appeal and invite them to respond.

6. The court has to be satisfied that there has been a miscarriage of justice. Even if the defence advocate has been guilty of an error which has resulted in a failure to place before the court additional evidence that was capable of supporting the defence advanced, that might not lead to a miscarriage of justice; it may well be that further evidence which merely added to evidence in support of the appellant's defence and which was open to significant criticism as to its credibility might not result in a miscarriage of justice (*Allan* v *HM Advocate*).[3] The burden upon an appellant who alleges defective representation and who has been professionally represented throughout the proceedings is a very severe one. Where questions of inadequate representation are put in issue, the submission is likely to fail unless the appellant can show what information would have been revealed if the preparation of the case had been done adequately. The appellant must demonstrate the relevant link between whatever complaints might legitimately be made against the solicitor or counsel and the presentation of the defence in court. It has also been held that once senior counsel has

come into the case a solicitor was entitled to look to him for advice and guidance as to what he considered necessary for the preparation of the case (*McIntosh v HM Advocate* (No 2)).[4]

1   1996 SCCR 114.
2   1949 JC 10.
3   1999 SCCR 923.
4   1997 SCCR 371, 395.

7.23   Other misconduct by the defence advocate

Misconduct by counsel or solicitor acting for an appellant's co-accused, for example by making improper and prejudicial remarks to the jury about the appellant in the course of his address, could also give rise to a good ground of appeal. An example of how such a ground may be worded is to be found in *Pike v HM Advocate.*[1] The relevant ground for the appellant, Mrs Pike, was:

'That a miscarriage of justice may have occurred by reason of the remarks made by counsel for the fifth-named panel, Mrs Finlay . . . in his address to the jury and in the absence of any evidence to support the said remarks (or notice of intention to lead such evidence) to the effect that:
 (i) the evidence indicated a scheme of deception played upon the fifth-named panel by her co-accused, including the appellant;
(ii) the statement to the police by the fifth-named panel could be compared with that of the appellant to show the lack of guilty knowledge on the part of the fifth-named panel and, by inference, the existence of such knowledge in the appellant.'

If there was substance in such a ground of appeal one would expect the ground of appeal to be associated with a complaint that the trial judge had failed to give adequate directions to the jury in connection with the matter (as it was in *Pike*). It is not uncommon or improper for the same underlying criticism to figure more than once in distinct grounds of appeal.

1   1987 SCCR 163.

7.24   Incompetent proceedings

In *Gallagher v HM Advocate*[1] the Crown brought a charge against the accused under the Coinage Offences Act 1936, section 9(1) and indicted the accused in the sheriff court where he was convicted. No objection was taken by the panel to the competency of the trial although the statutory penalty was penal servitude, a penalty that could not be imposed in the sheriff court. The sheriff remitted the panel to the High Court for sentence and a sentence of three years' penal servitude was imposed by a single judge, despite a plea that the whole proceedings were fundamentally null. The High Court of Justiciary upheld an appeal against conviction and sentence upon grounds stated as follows:

'(1) That the sheriff and jury had no jurisdiction to try the indictment on which the appellant was convicted, in respect that the minimum sentence which could be imposed by the court on conviction was, under section 9(1) of the Coinage Offences Act 1936, three years' penal servitude. (2) That, in view of a fundamental nullity in the proceedings in the sheriff court, it was incompetent for the High Court to impose any sentence on the appellant . . .'

It should be remembered, however, that although an issue of fundamental nullity may be raised at any time, and may be noticed and raised by the court itself, questions of the competency or relevancy of the indictment must be raised at a preliminary diet and may not be raised later except by leave of the court on cause shown.[2] But if such a point is raised at a preliminary diet, and repelled, it may be raised again on appeal. The intermediate diet cases[3] illustrate how a procedural error can be fatal to the proceedings. The problem canvassed in those cases was removed by the Criminal Procedure (Intermediate Diets) (Scotland) Act 1998.

1   1937 JC 27.
2   Criminal Procedure (Scotland) Act 1995, s 72(1) and 79.
3   *Mackay v Ruxton; Dingwall v Ruxton* 1997 SCCR 790; *Kerr v Carnegie* 1998 SCCR 168; *Vannet v Miligan* 1998 SCCR 305.

7.25   Evidence: wrongful admission or exclusion; comment

There are numerous examples of appeals taken against convictions on the ground that evidence which should have been excluded was admitted or that evidence which should have been admitted was excluded. *Brady v HM Advocate*[1] is an example of an (unsuccessful) appeal against a refusal to admit evidence which, it was argued, should have been admitted. The ground was 'After debate outwith the presence of the jury, the presiding judge refused to allow evidence to be led of earlier specific incidents of violence by the victim or other person and/or property. In the circumstances of the case and in the interest of justice, it was appropriate that an exercise of discretion by allowing said evidence should have been made in favour of the accused'. *Tonge v HM Advocate*[2] provides examples of grounds in a successful appeal relating to the wrongful admission of evidence, the evidence consisting of a response by a detained suspect made in reply to a police accusation which had not been preceded by a common law caution. The grounds were:

'1. That the trial judge misdirected the jury in that he did not direct them that on the evidence the statement alleged to have been made by the applicant to the investigating police officers was made in circumstances which rendered the statement inadmissible as evidence. 2. That the trial judge erred in not sustaining the objection made on behalf of the applicant to the statement made by the applicant to the investigating police officers.'[3]

In effect, the same point (no common law caution) lay behind both grounds; and number 2 fell to be considered first. It was that ground upon which the appeal was allowed.

Sandlan v HM Advocate[4] contains examples of various grounds of appeal taken relating to alleged misdirections by the trial judge as to the evidence, the wrongful admission of evidence over objection, and the trial judge's failure to afford counsel for one of the accused an opportunity to cross-examine witnesses on matters on which they had given evidence incriminatory of the appellant. *Bates v HM Advocate*[5] also contains (at page 341) fully stated grounds of appeal in relation to the admission of evidence and includes a statement as to the course that the trial judge should have followed. In *McNee v Ruxton* (a summary case) the court held that the sheriff erred in excluding legitimate cross examination:

'what the sheriff has done is to prevent a relevant line of cross-examination from being developed in regard to matters which were material to conviction.'[6] That would express the ground of appeal well, although the ground of appeal would have to add some specification to identify the line of cross-examination and the materiality. There may be a miscarriage of justice if the trial judge comments adversely upon the defence case, e g by describing the defence account of events as 'this tale'.[7] It may be a material misdirection to comment inappropriately upon the fact that the accused did not give evidence.[8] The presiding judge must be careful to try to ensure that the accused gets a fair trial when the accused is unrepresented, even if the absence of representation appears to be the result of his own fault, behaviour or choice. The judge must be careful to give him every opportunity to bring out his defence and to prevent the Crown from taking advantage of the accused's lack of expertise.[9] If the trial judge refers to the evidence in his charge to the jury, he must be careful not to refer to it inaccurately, particularly in relation to any material matter; such a mistake is likely to be regarded as leading to a miscarriage of justice, even if the judge has carefully instructed the jury to rely not on his references to the evidence but on their own recollection.[10]

1 1986 SCCR 191.
2 1982 SCCR 313.
3 1982 SCCR 313, 336.
4 1983 SCCR 71.
5 1989 SCCR 338.
6 1997 SCCR 291, 293.
7 *Hunter v HM Advocate* 1999 SCCR 72.
8 *Sutherland v HM Advocate* 1994 SCCR 80.
9 *Bullock v HM Advocate* 1999 SCCR 492. See also *Venters v HM Advocate* 1999 SCCR 441.
10 *Cairns v HM Advocate* 1999 SCCR 552; *Crawford v HM Advocate* 1999 SCCR 674; *Shepherd v HM Advocate* 1996 SCCR 679.

7.26 Irregularities affecting the proceedings

There are many examples of improprieties occurring in the course of proceedings and giving rise to appeals. Of their nature they are usually unprecedented and seldom repeated; so there is no regular style or form for writing a ground of appeal based on some such incident. The ground must simply narrate succinctly what it was that occurred, why it was, or might have been, prejudicial to the interests of the accused or of justice and, usually, its context. So where the trial judge communicated with the jury after they had retired to consider their verdict, by sending them messages via the clerk of court about important matters which should have been the subject of direction given in open court, the High Court held that a miscarriage of justice had resulted: *Cunningham v HM Advocate*;[1] the grounds of appeal in *Cunningham* were very detailed and should be studied in full[2] but two of them are quoted here to illustrate how to frame grounds of appeal to fit the circumstances.

'1. It is contended that a miscarriage of justice occurred in the proceedings at the appellant's trial in each of the following respects:
  (a) After the conclusion of the judge's charge to the jury, and during the course of their deliberations, they received advice or instructions as to

their powers and obligations, not directly from the judge, by way of any further charge delivered in court and in the presence of the accused in response to issues there raised by the jury, but indirectly from or through the clerk of court, outwith the presence of any person other than the clerk and the jury, or one or more of them, in response to questions raised by the jury (or one or more of them) with the said clerk; the said questions being conveyed by the clerk to the judge, and the judge's response being likewise conveyed to the jury (or one or more of them) in terms verbatim or otherwise to the appellant unknown. It is respectfully submitted that the said procedures constitute a miscarriage of justice; that the verdict of the trial court should be set aside; and that the convictions following thereon should upon review be quashed.'

The second, a supplementary ground of appeal, read:

'In any event, as narrated in the foregoing grounds of appeal, the clerk of court was on more than one occasion present with the jury after they had been enclosed, contrary to section 153(2) of the Criminal Procedure (Scotland) Act 1975; and visited the jury, contrary to section 153(3) thereof. He also communicated with the jury, not or not only in giving a direction or in response to a request under section 153(3)(b) thereof on behalf and with authority of the presiding judge, contrary to the said section 153(3). These circumstances constituted a material breach of said section 153 and accordingly the appellant should be acquitted in terms of section 153(4) of said Act and his conviction should be quashed.'[3]

Another case which gave rise to a successful appeal on a similar ground was *McColl v HM Advocate*[4] where the ground was: 'There was a miscarriage of justice in that the clerk of court communicated with the jury and gave the jury certain advice outwith the presence of any other person in breach of both sections 145 and 153 of the Criminal Procedure (Scotland) Act 1975 (as amended).' This was an interesting case because, in effect, counsel for the appellant gave the High Court his own account of what had transpired. The whole matter was investigated by obtaining reports from the clerk and the trial judge and even a precognition of the clerk of court. This process left several matters unclear but disclosed enough to enable the court to find that a miscarriage of justice had occurred and to quash the conviction.

In *W v HM Advocate*[5] the trial judge, before pronouncing sentence, interviewed alone a social worker who had prepared a report on the appellant. That gave rise to a ground of appeal in the following terms:

'There was a miscarriage of justice in that, having heard the plea in mitigation which sought disposal by way of a probation order, the presiding judge adjourned the case in order to speak in chambers with the social worker who had prepared the social enquiry report. Said meeting took place outwith the presence of the appellant, defence counsel and the advocate-depute. On his return to the bench the presiding judge made no reference to what had been discussed in chambers but proceeded to sentence the appellant. Said conduct by the presiding judge was improper and oppressive.'

The court stated that it was not appropriate or desirable for a judge to interview a social worker in private when considering sentence; but the sentence imposed was quashed upon a different ground.

In *Thomson v HM Advocate*[6] the trial judge, having understood that the jury would not be able to reach a verdict within a reasonable time in the evening, adjourned the trial and instructed that arrangements be made for the jury to remain in seclusion and to be accommodated overnight. When no suitable accommodation could be found, the judge, who was no longer in the court building, directed the clerk of court to send the jurors home, with appropriate instructions about not discussing the case with anyone. The clerk of court did so; but outwith the presence of the accused and while the trial was adjourned. It was held on appeal that this procedure was in breach of section 99 of the Criminal Procedure (Scotland) Act 1995 and that the verdict should be set aside. Authority was granted to the Crown to bring a new prosecution in accordance with section 119 of the 1995 Act. The opinions also deal with the law about communicating with a secluded jury.[7]

1   1984 SCCR 40.
2   1984 SCCR 40 at 43–4.
3   See also *Kerr v HM Advocate* 1999 SCCR 763.
4   1989 SCCR 229.
5   1989 SCCR 461.
6   1997 SCCR 121.
7   *Kerr v HM Advocate* 1999 SCCR 763.

7.27   Verdict – unreasonable or ambiguous

It is a good ground of appeal that the recorded verdict is incompetent[1] or does not make sense because it is self-contradictory or incomprehensible or ambiguous[2] and confused or that it does not disclose a crime known to the law of Scotland.[3] Similarly, if a verdict goes beyond the terms of the indictment, that will afford a good ground of appeal. A verdict given in defiance of a direction by the trial judge may be appealed. It is, of course, open to the trial judge to take whatever steps are appropriate in open court to discover if the patent flaw in the orally delivered verdict reflects some superficial error which can be put right before the verdict is recorded[4] or if it discloses some irremediable confusion which is fatal to the verdict: cf *White v HM Advocate*[5] where the relevant ground of appeal was: 'That the trial judge erred in law in allowing to be recorded a verdict from the jury that was in direct conflict with directions he had given to them'. The High Court said that the trial judge should have reminded the jury of his original directions and sent them out again to consider their verdict. The convictions were quashed.

In *McGeary v HM Advocate*[6] it was said that the proper course to take is to draw the jury's attention to the defect in the verdict which they have returned, doing so before it is recorded, and to provide them with an opportunity of reconsidering it before it is recorded. The trial judge may instruct the jury to retire to the jury room to think about the matter so as to be sure that their intentions are properly understood and expressed. In *Cameron (J.P.) v HM Advocate*[7] the jury foreman announced verdicts on several charges; the trial judge recognised that the verdicts were patently inconsistent. The appeal court agreed that the interests of justice had required that the patent confusion be resolved and held that the trial judge had properly taken steps to remove the confusion. The best time to ascertain exactly what the jury intended their verdict to be is after they have announced it orally and before the clerk of court records it for reading over to them. The appropriateness of dealing with the matter at that stage is clearly illustrated by *Ainsworth v HM Advocate*[8] where the appeal court had to reconstruct the verdict. The Lord Justice-General said:[9]

'There is no fixed rule about what should be done when a jury returns verdicts which are inconsistent with each other or demonstrate by their verdict that they have failed to apply the directions which have been given to them by the trial judge. That part of their verdict that is directly affected by this failure can of course be dealt with by quashing the conviction in part on the ground that there was a miscarriage of justice. The question whether that failure affects their verdicts on other charges or, as in this case, other parts of the same charge has to be dealt with by examining the facts and circumstances of each case.'

In *MacKay v HM Advocate*[10] it was observed that, if the jury's verdict is confused and it is necessary to make grammatical changes, that should be done in the presence of the jury and should be done before the jury are asked to confirm the verdict as recorded in writing by the clerk of court. But if the jury indicate that the verdict as delivered is their final verdict, it must be accepted as such.[11] *Salmond v HM Advocate*,[12] where the jury in an attempted murder case returned a verdict of 'guilty by reason of reckless indifference, with extreme provocation', provides a good example of a ground of appeal fully stated but with commendable brevity: 'The jury's verdict of guilty of attempted murder under provocation being incompetent, a miscarriage of justice has resulted.' The court set aside the conviction and substituted an amended verdict, holding the appellant guilty of assault (to the danger of life etc) under extreme provocation.

1 *Salmond v HM Advocate* 1991 SCCR 43.
2 *Hamilton v HM Advocate* 1991 SCCR 282.
3 *Sayers v HM Advocate* 1981 SCCR 312.
4 Cf *Took v HM Advocate* 1988 SCCR 495.
5 1989 SCCR 553.
6 1991 SCCR 203, 205.
7 1999 SCCR 476.
8 1996 SCCR 631.
9 At 635A.
10 1997 SCCR 743.
11 *Kerr v HM Advocate* 1992 SCCR 281.
12 1991 SCCR 43.

7.28 Conviction – perverse and unreasonable

In the previous statutory provision[1] there was no express reference to reviewing a verdict on the ground of its apparent unreasonableness. The Sutherland Committee discussed this matter at paragraphs 2.59–2.70 of its Report and recommended an express statutory provision. Parliament adopted the test formulated in paragraph 2.70 and enacted the Criminal Procedure (Scotland) Act 1995, section 106(3)(b), which – read short – provides: 'a person may bring under review of the High Court any alleged miscarriage of justice . . . based on – (b) the jury's having returned a verdict which no reasonable jury, properly directed, could have returned'. This is an objective test. This ground of appeal has not yet been successfully invoked. Such a ground of appeal was advanced in *Rubin v HM Advocate*:[2] where it was submitted that 'The quality, character and strength of the evidence against the pannel when viewed as a whole was insufficient to justify the conviction of the pannel'. The particular appeal was dismissed, despite the gravest doubts expressed by the court about the reliability of a principal witness for the Crown; but the Lord Justice-General said: 'I do not, however, bearing in mind Lord

Keith's reservation of opinion in *Dow v MacKnight* 1949 JC 38 [at 56], require to consider and decide whether there could ever be circumstances sufficiently exceptional in which an appellate court might properly quash a conviction upon that ground.'

As there is now express statutory provision, and given that now it is possible to hear additional fresh evidence and to grant authority to bring a new prosecution, and given the growing familiarity of the civil courts in judicial review cases with the concept of a decision so unreasonable that no reasonable person called upon to decide it could have decided it in the way it was decided, it is at least conceivable that the High Court of Justiciary may be more ready in a suitable case to retreat from the notion, hitherto underlying the consideration of solemn appeals, that the conclusions, or supposed conclusions, of the jury on each and every issue of fact are sacrosanct and inviolable whatever the weight and coherence of the evidence. The report of the trial judge could be of great importance in assisting the court to assess such a ground of appeal.[3] Older cases that bear upon this matter include *Macmillan v HM Advocate*,[4] *Webb v HM Advocate*,[5] and *Slater v HM Advocate*.[6] *Higgins v HM Advocate*[7] is an unsatisfactory case but it serves to illustrate the traditional reluctance of the High Court to interfere with the verdict of a jury on a matter of fact, including credibility. In *King v HM Advocate*,[8] where there was a clear, vitally important irreconcilable conflict between a body of evidence pointing to guilt and a body of evidence pointing to innocence, it was held that the jury were entitled to choose which body of evidence to accept and which to reject. The new ground of appeal is fully discussed in a helpful article by PW Ferguson in 1999 SLT (News) at 125.

1 Criminal Procedure (Scotland) Act 1975, s 228(2).
2 1984 SCCR 96.
3 See *Farook v HM Advocate* 1991 SCCR 889.
4 1927 JC 62.
5 1927 JC 92.
6 1928 JC 94.
7 1956 JC 69.
8 1999 SCCR 330.

7.29 Sentence – grounds of appeal; examples

There are many possible grounds of appeal against sentence. They include incompetency,[1] excessiveness, inappropriateness,[2] failure to back-date or to take account of the so-called comparative principle,[3] taking account of irrelevant matters.[4] The practice note of

29 March 1985[5] applies to grounds of appeal against sentence. Accordingly it is not enough just to say in the ground of appeal: 'The sentence imposed was excessive in all the circumstances'. In a summary appeal against sentence[6] the court declined to entertain an appeal where the stated ground was: 'The sentence is excessive. No previous convictions libelled.' The circumstances must be set forth in the ground of appeal. If the ground is incompetency the character of the alleged incompetency must be spelled out. The test of adequacy will be whether or not the grounds of appeal have given sufficient notice to enable the sentencing judge to understand the complaint made and to comment fully upon it. But even in the unusual type of case where the substantial ground of appeal is that since the conviction and sentence there has been such a marked improvement in the appellant's behaviour that the court should give him an opportunity to maintain the improvement[7] – a matter upon which the sentencing judge may well be unable to comment – it is still correct practice to condescend upon the alleged new circumstances, if only to allow the Crown an opportunity to seek information about them to place before the court if asked to do so, or the court to order further inquiry under the Criminal Procedure (Scotland) Act 1995, section 104(1) or section 182(5). In *Jackson v HM Advocate*[8] the appellant had been sentenced to life imprisonment in 1984; he was a discretionary life prisoner. When the Prisoners and Criminal Proceedings (Scotland) Act 1993 came into force a certificate was granted that he should serve 16 years of his sentence before being eligible for parole. He then appealed against his life sentence. After obtaining medical reports the court allowed the appeal, quashed the life sentence and replaced it with a hospital order with an unlimited restriction on discharge.

1   Cf *Noble v Guild* 1987 SCCR 518 (summary).
2   *McRae v HM Advocate* 1987 SCCR 36.
3   *Bates v HM Advocate* 1989 SCCR 338; *Allan v HM Advocate* 1990 SCCR 226.
4   *Khaliq v HM Advocate* 1984 SCCR 212.
5   Cf 2.27 above.
6   *Campbell v MacDougall* 1991 SCCR 218.
7   As in *Rennie v MacNeill* 1984 SCCR 11.
8   1998 SCCR 539.

7.30   Sentence – deportation etc

The same considerations as to the giving of adequate notice and specification apply in respect of grounds of appeal relating to incidental orders or penalties such as deportation,[1] forfeiture, disqualification or the like. Thus, in a summary case, *Willms v Smith*,[2] where the sheriff recommended deportation of a German who pleaded guilty to an assault of punching and admitted one minor previous conviction, the successful grounds of appeal, which stated the circumstances briefly but fully, were:

'The decision of the sheriff to recommend deportation to Her Majesty's Government is harsh and oppressive[3] for the following reasons:

(1) The offence in itself did not merit such a recommendation.

(2) The appellant is married to a British citizen, who is unwilling to live in West Germany because of language difficulties. If the appellant were to be deported, the parties would therefore be separated.

(3) The social inquiry report available to the court when sentence was imposed showed the appellant to be both a caring and educated person who had given his wife much assistance and support in her attempts to overcome problems which she had encountered.'

---

1   Immigration Act 1971, s 6(1),(5) (as amended).
2   1981 SCCR 257.
3   The test since 1981 has been not whether the sentence was 'harsh and oppressive' but whether it was excessive or inappropriate.

8. Bail and interim regulation

8.01 Bailable crimes and offences

All crimes and offences, including murder and treason, are now bailable.[1] The Lord Advocate and the High Court have the right to admit to bail any person charged with any crime or offence. This right is preserved by the Criminal Procedure (Scotland) Act 1995, section 24(2). The extra-statutory right of the High Court preserved by section 24(2) cannot be exercised by a single judge of the High Court.[2] It has to be exercised by the High Court on a petition to the *nobile officium*.

Section 26 of the 1995 Act, which specified circumstances in which bail was available, was repealed by the Bail, Judicial Appointments etc (Scotland) Act 2000, which was brought into force on 11 August 2000. The provisions of section 26, and the restriction applicable to murder and treason, could have been incompatible with article 5(3) of the European Convention on Human Rights.

1 Criminal Procedure (Scotland) Act 1995, s 24(1) (amended, with effect from 11 August 2000 by the Bail, Judicial Appointments etc (Scotland) Act 2000).
2 *Milne v McNicol* 1944 JC 151.

8.02 First instance applications for bail

Solemn

In solemn proceedings, applications for bail are usually presented in the form of a printed petition either before or after full committal and the court's decision is recorded on the application.[1]

Summary

In summary proceedings, applications for bail are made orally to the court when the complaint calls before the court. The court's decision is recorded in the minute of proceedings. After the initial stages, the rules and procedures for bail in summary procedure are virtually the same as for solemn procedure.[2]

Section 1 of the Bail, Judicial Appointments etc. (Scotland) Act 2000 inserts a new section 22A into the 1995 Act requiring the sheriff to entertain and determine a bail application on the first occasion on which a person is brought before the sheriff on petition or in respect of a complaint, though he may defer the decision for up to 24 hours. The new section applies even if the person is in custody for another matter. If no decision is taken within that period, the person is to be liberated; but he is not liberated from the custody (if any) consequent on the other matter. A new section 23A allows a person to be admitted to bail, whether under section 22A or under section 23, even if he is already in custody because he has been refused bail in respect of another matter or because he is serving a sentence of imprisonment.

1 See *Renton and Brown*, para 10-04.
2 See *Renton and Brown*, para 10-01 and Criminal Procedure (Scotland) Act 1995, s 23(6).

8.03 Appeal in respect of bail: solemn cases

Where in any case whatsoever, an application for bail is made and is refused by any sheriff,[1] or where the applicant is dissatisfied with the conditions of bail, he may appeal to the High Court, and the High Court may, in its discretion, order intimation to the Lord Advocate.[2] In practice, the Justiciary Office intimates all bail appeals to the Crown Office together with the date of the hearing. The court which has refused bail or has granted bail on conditions has power to review its decision, including the conditions of bail: see the Criminal Procedure (Scotland) Act 1995, section 30(2) and *Gilchrist, Petitioner.*[3]

If an application for bail is granted by the sheriff, whether before or after committal until liberation in due course of law, the public prosecutor has the right of appeal to the High Court against the decision or the conditions.[4] If the prosecutor appeals, the accused is not liberated until the Crown appeal has been disposed of, with the exception contained in section 32 – which provides for liberation after 72 hours from the granting of bail if the appeal is not disposed of and the court has not granted an order for the applicant's further detention in custody.[5] Sundays and public holidays do not count in computing these time limits. If the prosecutor's appeal is refused the High Court may, but rarely does, award expenses against him.[6]

1 CP(S)A 1995, s 23(2); but see the important decision in *Burn, Petitioner* 2000 SCCR 384 for the requirements which the Crown must satisfy in seeking to oppose the grant of bail prior to committal until liberation in due course of law.
2 Criminal Procedure (Scotland) Act 1995, s 32 has to be construed as indicated by s 307(1), ie 'bail' means release on conditions.
3 1991 SCCR 699, a summary case under the similarly worded s 299 of the Criminal Procedure (Scotland) Act 1975.
4 CP(S)A 1995, s 32(2).
5 CP(S)A 1995, s 32(7).
6 CP(S)A 1995, s 32(6).

8.04 Appeal in respect of bail: summary cases

Similarly, in summary proceedings, when a court has refused to admit a person to bail or has admitted to bail on conditions, it has power on an application by that person to review its decision and to alter it on cause shown.[1] This provision does not affect a person's right of appeal in relation to the refusal of bail or the conditions.[2] The right of appeal against the refusal of bail in summary proceedings, or against the bail conditions, is contained in the Criminal Procedure (Scotland) Act 1995, section 32(1). An appeal lies to the High Court which may in its discretion order intimation to the prosecutor. In practice, the Justiciary Office intimates to the Crown Office.

The prosecutor also has a right of appeal to the High Court against a bail decision by the court of summary jurisdiction or an order by such a court ordaining an accused person to appear. If the prosecutor appeals, the accused is not liberated at once; the provisions regarding his release if the appeal is not disposed of within 72 hours from the granting of bail are the same as those applicable in solemn proceedings: see paragraph 8.03 above.[3] If the prosecutor's appeal is refused, the High Court may, but rarely does, award expenses against him; but otherwise no fees or expenses are awarded or exigible in respect of any appeal regarding bail or ordaining to appear.[4] Section 32(2) also applies when an appeal is taken by the prosecutor against the fact that a person has been ordained to appear.[5]

1 Criminal Procedure (Scotland) Act 1995, s 30(1) and (2).
2 CP(S)A 1995, ss 30(4) and 32.
3 CP(S)A 1995, s 32(2) and (7).
3 CP(S)A 1995, s 32(2).
3 CP(S)A 1995, s 32(2)(c).

8.05   Bail appeal pending sentence or disposal

Under the Criminal Procedure (Scotland) Act 1995, section 201, in both solemn and summary proceedings the court has the power to adjourn the hearing for the purpose of enabling inquiries to be made or of determining the most suitable method of dealing with the case and the court has power to remand the accused in custody or on bail. The court has similar remand powers under section 200 in respect of a person about whose physical or mental condition the court wishes to have inquiry made. The remanding court cannot review its own decision;[1] but the decision can be appealed.

The accused who is so remanded can appeal against a refusal of bail or against the conditions imposed. Any appeal must be made within 24 hours of his remand by presenting an application to the High Court. There is no form prescribed for such a note of appeal, but it is usual to present a petition briefly narrating the history and giving in outline the reasons why bail should be granted. The High Court, either in court or in chambers (but almost invariably in chambers), may, after hearing the parties: (1) review the order appealed against, and either grant bail on such conditions as it thinks fit or (in section 201 cases only) ordain the accused to appear at the adjourned diet; or (2) confirm the order of the inferior court.[2]

1 *Long v HM Advocate* 1984 SCCR 161.
2 CP(S)A 1995, ss 201(4) and 200(9).

8.06 Procedure in bail appeals

In practice, all bail appeals to the High Court in respect of the grant or refusal of bail, or the conditions, or an order ordaining an accused to appear (all referred to as 'bail appeals') are dealt with in the same way by the High Court. A diet for the hearing of an appeal is normally fixed within two working days of the receipt by the Clerk of Justiciary of the necessary papers. When a bail appeal is marked, the clerk of the court of first instance should obtain from the local solicitor acting for the accused the particulars of that solicitor's Edinburgh solicitor, if he has one. If the appeal is marked by the Crown, the clerk of the inferior court should note the exact time of the marking of the appeal and telephone the Clerk of Justiciary to intimate the necessary details – these steps are necessary because of the strict time limits that apply.

All bail appeals, including applications for interim liberation pending the determination of an appeal and Crown appeals, are put out before a single judge at 9.30 a m. Although he usually sits unrobed in a small room, the room is a public court. After the parties have been heard the appeals are usually disposed of at once without any reasons being given in writing. If either party, or the judge, needs further information the case will usually be continued for 24 hours for that purpose. Those appearing are expected to be brief, frank and to the point but ready to answer questions from the judge about the accused person's criminal record and personal circumstances.

8.07 Later review of a bail decision

The High Court can review its earlier decision on a question of bail: Criminal Procedure (Scotland) Act 1995, section 30(2).[1] But in so far as the parts of a decision on bail are separable, if the

High Court has dealt with one part only, e g whether or not to grant bail, or whether or not to impose a particular condition, other parts, e g different conditions, may be reviewed by the court to which the application was first made.[2]

1   Cf *Shanley v HM Advocate* 1946 JC 150.
2   *Ward v HM Advocate* 1972 SLT (Notes) 22, commenting on *HM Advocate v Jones* 1964 SLT (Sh Ct) 50.

8.08   Applying for bail pending determination of appeal (solemn procedure)

It is very common, pending determination of an appeal, to apply for bail (usually referred to in this context as *interim* liberation). The High Court may, if it deems fit, admit the appellant to bail pending the determination of his appeal; but only on his application.[1] Even at this stage, all crimes and offences are bailable as of right, except murder and treason.[2] The Lord Advocate has the right to admit to bail any person charged with any offence, including murder and treason.[3] The High Court, in the exercise of its *nobile officium*,[4] may also admit to bail a person charged with murder or treason.[5] Only a quorum of three or more judges of the High Court may exercise this power.[6]

Any application for bail following conviction is made on Form 15.2-D and it must narrate correctly that on a date specified the applicant lodged an intimation of intention to appeal, or a note of appeal, to the High Court of Justiciary. Although the right to seek bail arises on the intimation of an intention to appeal,[7] the application should not normally be made until the note of appeal containing the grounds of appeal has been lodged.[8] Where bail is sought by a person who has lodged only an intimation of intention to appeal, his written application must state clearly why bail is being applied for at that stage, and the court may refuse to entertain the application in the absence of any such statement.[9]

The relevant facts in support of grant of bail must be set forth in Form 15.2-D. These will be the usual facts relevant to grant of bail, such as having a fixed address, a supportive family, a job, a modest criminal record, no or few previous bail contraventions. In addition, there will be assertions that there are substantial grounds for the appeal, and/or that there is a likelihood that if the appellant remains in custody he will have served much of his sentence before his appeal is determined. In the case of a note of appeal against sentence, the form for the note of appeal is Form

19.3-A, which allows for applications for bail or other interim relief.

The application is heard and determined along with the ordinary bail appeals in the Supreme Court, Edinburgh, by the bail judge. The appellant may make the application personally or through counsel.[10] The Crown makes no representations to the bail judge in respect of applications for interim liberation, unless there is some special procedural circumstance of which the court should be made aware. If the application cannot for some administrative reason be properly dealt with at once it is normally continued or re-heard later the same day or on the next lawful day.

The decision of the court is given at once orally by the judge. If the single bail judge grants the application, the Justiciary Office sends a fax to the prison where the applicant is held, intimating that bail has been granted. This enables him to be released without delay. Before release he must sign an 'Acceptance of Bail Conditions' form supplied to him by the prison authorities. If the single judge refuses the application, the Clerk of Justiciary sends a notification of the decision on Form 15.3-A. He also sends Form 15.3-B. By completing this form and returning it within five days to the Clerk of Justiciary the appellant can appeal against the refusal of bail. If he does not do so, the refusal by the single judge is final.[11]

An appeal court, consisting of three judges, who may include the judge who refused bail,[12] will hear and determine the appeal if one is taken. If the appellant is not legally represented, he has the right to appear personally at the appeal hearing. If he is legally represented then technically he requires the leave of the court to be present, but in practice the appellant is always brought to attend the appeal. The Clerk of Justiciary has the responsibility of placing the application before the court and of notifying the applicant if his application to be present has been granted or refused. If it is granted the Clerk of Justiciary must also notify the prison governor and the Secretary of State.[13] An applicant who is admitted to bail must, unless the High Court otherwise directs, appear personally in court on any day or days fixed for the hearing of the appeal, whether or not he is legally represented. If he does not attend, the court will usually decline to consider the appeal and may dismiss it, though it may choose to determine it.[14] The court is slow to excuse a failure to be present when the case is called,[15] because the failure to appear is a breach of a condition of bail (and punishable under section 27).

1 Criminal Procedure (Scotland) Act 1995, s 112(1).
2 CP(S)A 1995, s 24(1); but see *Walsh, Petitioner* 1990 SCCR 763; CP(S)A 1995, s 26 and para 8.01 above; see also style No 6 in Appendix.
3 CP(S)A 1995, s 24(2).
4 Cf *Milne v McNicol* 1944 JC 151.
5 *Walsh, Petitioner* 1990 SCCR 763.
6 *HM Advocate v Renicks* 1998 SCCR 417.
7 CP(S)A 1995, s 112(1); but see *Smith v McCallum* 1982 SCCR 115.
8 *Smith v McCallum* 1982 SCCR 115 the so-called 'guidelines' case; but cf CP(S)A 1995, s 112(5), making it clear that a person who has lodged notice of intention to appeal has a right to seek bail. See also *Ogilvy, Petitioner* 1998 SCCR 187.
9 Practice Note, 18 March 1994, 1994 SLT (News) 132.
10 CP(S)A 1995, s 103(8).
11 CP(S)A 1995, s 103(8).
12 CP(S)A 1995, s 105(6). Whether this proposition can survive the full coming into force of the Human Rights Act 1998 is very doubtful.
13 CP(S)A 1995, s 105(5).
14 CP(S)A 1995, s 112(4).
15 *McMahon v MacPhail* 1991 SCCR 470.

8.09 Interim liberation (summary procedure)

A convicted person who is in custody and appeals against conviction only or against conviction and sentence by application for a stated case under the Criminal Procedure (Scotland) Act 1995, section 176, or appeals against sentence only by a note of appeal under section 186, can apply to the convicting court for bail (interim liberation).[1] An application for bail must be disposed of by that court within 24 hours after the application for bail has been made.[2] It is made by completing the appropriate section of the form, either Form 19.2-A (stated case) or Form 19.3-A (note of appeal against sentence).

The court 'disposes' of the application by deciding whether to grant it or refuse it; adjourning consideration of that issue is not a disposal: *Gibbons, Petitioner*,[3] a case under section 28(2) of the previous Criminal Procedure (Scotland) Act 1975 which is now reproduced in the Criminal Procedure (Scotland) Act 1995, section 23(7). The wording of section 177(2) of the 1995 Act, 'An application for bail shall be disposed of within 24 hours after such application has been made', is different from that in section 23(7) where the wording is: 'An application under subsection (5) or (6) above shall be disposed of within twenty-four hours *after its presentation to the judge*, failing which the accused shall be liberated forthwith' [emphasis added].

It has not yet been decided by the High Court whether the rule that applies in section 23(7) cases – ie that the 24-hour period starts to run from the time when the application is presented to the sheriff or judge[4] – applies to section 177(2). *Renton and Brown* expresses the opinion that application to the court does not mean lodging with the clerk of court; and that accordingly the 24 hours start to run when the application is placed before the judge or sheriff.[5] This is probably correct, but in *HM Advocate v Keegan*[6] Lord Cameron drew attention to the long-standing distinction between 'presentation' and 'lodgement of written applications' with clerks of court, so there could still be room for argument. The better view, it is submitted, is that the application is not 'made' until it is put before the justice or sheriff.

In any event, section 177(2) contains no provision to the effect that if the matter is not disposed of within the prescribed period the appellant is to be liberated forthwith, so the consequences of failure to dispose of the matter within the prescribed time limit are less clear. One consequence is that the appellant is effectively deprived either of his liberty or of his right of appeal against the refusal of bail. Since the statute gives him no remedy for such failure or its consequences he may present a petition to the *nobile officium* against the failure to dispose of the application.

It appears quite clear from the whole context, but especially from Form 19.2-A and Form 19.3-A themselves, that the application for bail has to be in writing: cf heading (4) of Form 19.2-A and heading (3) of Form 19.3-A. If, in disposing of the application, the court refuses bail or imposes conditions and the appellant wishes to appeal against the refusal, or against any condition, the appeal to the High Court is by a note of appeal written, within 24 hours, on the complaint and signed by the appellant or his solicitor.[7] If such appeal is not taken in this way within twenty-four hours after the judgment of the court disposing of the application the right of appeal is lost.[8]

Once such a bail appeal is lodged, a certified copy of the complaint and proceedings is transmitted to the Clerk of Justiciary. The High Court, or any judge thereof (invariably a single judge), after hearing parties, has power to review the decision of the inferior court and to grant bail on such conditions as the court or single judge thinks fit, or to refuse bail.[9] No fees or expenses of any kind are exigible from or may be awarded against an appellant in custody in respect of such a bail appeal to the High Court.[10] The Crown has no right of appeal against the grant of bail pending determination of an appeal.

If, having been granted bail, the appellant does not thereafter proceed with his appeal, the inferior court has power to grant warrant to apprehend and imprison him for such period of his sentence as remained unexpired when he was released on bail, and the period of imprisonment runs from the date of his imprisonment under that warrant of the inferior court.[11] If an appellant who has been granted bail does not thereafter proceed with his appeal (against conviction or conviction and sentence) but, at the time of the abandonment of the appeal, is serving a term of imprisonment imposed subsequently to the conviction appealed against, the inferior court has power to order that the sentence, or any unexpired portion thereof relating to the conviction, should run from such date as the court may think fit, not being a date later than the date on which the term or terms of imprisonment subsequently imposed expired.[12]

The relevant subsection envisages the exercise of discretion by the sheriff or justice. So, where the inferior court is contemplating an order under section 177(6), intimation of this intention must be given to the appellant to allow him to make representations to the court and to put before that court any information to be advanced as relevant to and necessary for the proper exercise of that discretion. This was decided in *Proudfoot v Wither*,[13] where the High Court intimated that the appropriate way of dealing with a case in which the lower court was contemplating such an order was to give intimation to that effect to the (former) appellant to allow written submissions to be made by him or his solicitor to the inferior court; it would then be for that court to decide if a hearing was necessary before determining how the discretion was to be exercised. This decision has now been given statutory effect by section 177(7).

1 Criminal Procedure (Scotland) Act 1995, ss 177(1) and 186(10).
2 CP(S)A 1995, ss 177(2) and 186(10).
3 1988 SCCR 270.
4 *HM Advocate v Keegan* 1981 SLT (Notes) 35; *Lau, Petitioner* 1986 SCCR 140.
5 *Renton and Brown* para 10-04.
6 1981 SLT (Notes) 35.
7 CP(S)A 1995, ss 177(3) and 186(10).
8 *Fenton, Petitioner* 1981 SCCR 288.
9 CP(S)A 1995, s 177(3).
10 CP(S)A 1995, s 177(4).
11 CP(S)A 1995, s 177(5).
12 CP(S)A 1995, s 177(6).
13 1990 SCCR 96.

INCIDENTAL PROCEDURES AND INTERIM REGULATION

8.10   Interim relief pending appeal

If a person is to pursue an appeal against conviction or sentence or both he will normally want to suspend or delay the penal consequences of the court's decision on guilt or punishment until at least the final determination of the appeal on its merits. There exist procedures for achieving this purpose. It is important to take care to observe the timetables and the detailed procedural requirements laid down by statute. Although it is hoped that in a text such as this it is possible to describe these procedures accurately, they may be altered from time to time, and there is no substitute for going to the statute itself each time until one is totally familiar with the steps to be taken, and when and how to take them. It may be necessary, in special circumstances, to make an application for *interim* relief in the course of proceedings by way of petition to the *nobile officium*, which is more fully discussed in Chapter 6.

8.11 Disqualification, forfeiture, loss of licence deportation etc

If, when he is convicted in solemn proceedings, a person is disqualified or some forfeiture or disability attaches to him by reason of his conviction then, subject to the Criminal Procedure (Scotland) Act 1995, section 121(3), the disqualification, forfeiture or disability does not attach for the period of four weeks from the date of the verdict. If he proceeds with the appeal, whether against sentence alone or against conviction or both, then (subject to section 121(3)) disqualification, forfeiture or disability does not attach until the appeal is determined.[1] Similarly, if, upon conviction, any property, matter or things which are the subject of the prosecution or connected therewith are to be, or may be, ordered to be destroyed, the destruction or forfeiture or the operation of an order for destruction or forfeiture of such property etc is suspended for four weeks; or, if the appeal proceeds, whether by intimation of intention to appeal or by note of appeal, until the note of appeal is determined.[2] An appeal prevents the making of a deportation order.

Section 121(3) provides, however, that if the enactment that makes provision for disqualification or forfeiture, or similar order upon conviction itself contains express provision for the suspension of the disqualification, forfeiture etc pending determination of the appeal[3] the particular express provision then governs the matter. Thus, sections 38(2) and 41(2) of the Road Traffic Offenders Act 1988 provide expressly for the situation of an appellant who on conviction has been disqualified from driving. The court by or before which a person was convicted may, upon the application of the appellant, suspend the disqualification pending an appeal against the disqualifying order.[4] The High Court has a similar power to suspend the disqualification if, and on such terms, as it thinks fit.[5] The court that suspends the disqualification must send notice of the suspension to the Secretary of State.[6]

1 Criminal Procedure (Scotland) Act 1995, s 121(1).
2 CP(S)A 1995, s 121(2).
3 Immigration Act 1971, s 6(6).
4 Road Traffic Offenders Act 1988, s 39(2).
5 RTOA 1988, s 41(2).
6 RTOA 1988, ss 39(3) and 41(3).

8.12 Suspension of disqualification from driving pending appeal

There are special procedural rules as to suspension of disqualification from driving where an appeal is pending in solemn proceedings: they are contained in the Criminal Procedure Rules.[1] If the sentencing court was the sheriff court, the appellant applies to the sheriff using Form 15.11-A, attaching a copy of the note of appeal which must be endorsed as having been received by the Clerk of Justiciary. If the sentencing court was the High Court, or if an application to the sheriff using Form 15.11-A has been refused, the application is made by petition to the High Court using Form 15.11-B, which must be lodged with the Clerk of Justiciary. In either event the note of appeal must have been lodged before the petition is submitted. Proof of service (on the procurator fiscal (Form 15.11-A), or on the sheriff clerk and the Crown Agent (Form 15.11-B)) should be attached to the petition: see paragraphs 3 and 4 of the Forms.

The petitioner or his solicitor must, on lodging the petition, send a copy of it to (1) the Crown Agent, and (2), if the sentencing court was the sheriff court, the clerk of that court. The court may order further intimation and may dispose of the application in open court or in chambers. The application will be dealt with by a single judge whose decision is not subject to review or appeal. On an order being made on the petition under the Criminal Procedure Rules 1996, Rule 15.11(3), the Clerk of Justiciary has to intimate as required by Rule 15.12(4). Rule 15.12(6) specifies what the Clerk of Justiciary has to do on determination of the appeal. Rules 15.11 and 15.12 should be referred to for details of all incidental aspects of these applications.

1 Act of Adjournal (Criminal Procedure Rules) 1996, SI 1996/513, Rule 15.11.

8.13 Suspension of certain sentences pending determination of appeal

The Criminal Procedure (Scotland) Act 1995, section 121A(1) sets out that where an intention of intimation to appeal or, in the case of an appeal under section 106(1)(b)–(e), 108 or 108A of the Act, a note of appeal is lodged, the court may on the application of the appellant direct that the whole, or any remaining part, of a relevant sentence shall be suspended until the appeal, if it is proceeded with, is determined. Section 121A(4) provides that the term 'relevant sentence' means any one or more of the following, namely a probation order, a supervised attendance order made under section 236(6) of the Act, a community service order or a restriction of liberty order.

Form 15.12.A-A and Rule 15.12A of the Criminal Procedure Rules 1996 relate to suspension of certain sentences pending determination of an appeal. The person whose sentence has been suspended, in whole or in part, must appear personally in court on the day or days fixed for the hearing of the appeal. If he does not do so, the court has the wide range of powers specified in section 121A(3) of the 1995 Act, to dispose of the appeal as it thinks fit. If suspension of a driving disqualification is sought in summary appeals by means of bill of suspension then Rule 19.9 (appeal by stated case) and Rule 19.10 (appeal by bill of suspension) of the Criminal Procedure Rules apply.

8.14 Failure of accused to attend trial and subsequent procedures

An accused person who has been committed for further examination and granted bail on the standard conditions in terms of section 23(1) of the Criminal Procedure (Scotland) Act 1995 might fail to appear for his trial. If so, and a warrant is granted for his arrest, the procedure for obtaining bail after his detention is set out in *Love, Petitioner*.[1] It used to be thought that a petition to the *nobile officium* of the appeal court was the appropriate method of obtaining bail but it was there held that the correct course is for the person to apply to the appropriate sheriff for bail in terms of section 23(5) of the 1995 Act. If bail is refused the appellant may apply to the High Court in terms of section 32(1) of the 1995 Act.

1   1998 SCCR 161, SLT 461.

8.15   Other provisions

The Road Traffic (New Drivers) Act 1995 contains new provisions relating to the revocation of licences and restoration of licences without re-testing in certain cases: see sections 2, 5, 8 and 10. No new procedural rules have been made in respect of the operation of these new statutory provisions; so existing forms and procedures should be used, adapted as necessary.

Appendix

1. Bill of advocation

HIGH COURT OF JUSTICIARY

Unto the Right Honourable
The Lord Justice-General, The Lord Justice-Clerk
and Lord Commissioner of Justiciary

1. BILL OF ADVOCATION

HOYERS (UK) LIMITED, a company incorporated under the
Companies Acts and having its registered office at Leeds Road,
Huddersfield, Yorkshire, — <u>COMPLAINERS</u>

against

STEWART R HOUSTON, Procurator Fiscal, Lanark,
<u>RESPONDENT</u>

HUMBLY SHEWETH

That the complainer is under the necessity of complaining to your
Lordships of a pretended interlocutor pronounced at Lanark on 3
May 1991 by Douglas Allan, Esquire, Sheriff of South
Strathclyde, Dumfries and Galloway at Lanark upon a complaint
at the instance of the respondent, charging 'Hoyer International
Limited' and another as therein set forth with a contravention of
the Control of Pollution Act 1974, section 31(1), whereby the
Sheriff granted the motion of the respondent to allow the complaint to be amended incompetently, erroneously and contrary to
law, as it will appear to your Lordships from the annexed statement of fact and note of the pleas in law.

WHEREFORE the complainer prays your Lordships letters of
advocation in the premises at his instance in common form; and
in the meantime to grant warrant to the Clerk of the Sheriff Court
at Lanark, or other custodier of the proceedings at the instance of
the respondent against the complainer and another, and interlocutors following thereon, to transmit the same to the Clerk of
Justiciary; and on consideration of the said proceedings to advocate the same, to recall the interlocutor complained of, to remit to
the Sheriff of Strathclyde, Dumfries and Galloway at Lanark to
proceed with the complaint as accords and to find the complainer

entitled to expenses; or to do further, or otherwise in the premises as to your Lordships shall seem proper.

ACCORDING TO JUSTICE, Etc,

2. STATEMENT of FACTS for COMPLAINER.

STAT. I.   The complainer is Hoyers (UK) Limited, a company incorporated under the Companies Acts and having its registered office at Leeds Road, Huddersfield, Yorkshire.

STAT. II.   On 20 November 1990 a complaint at the instance of the respondent charging 'Hoyer International Limited', Leeds Road, Huddersfield, Yorkshire and was sent by recorded delivery post to Hoyer International Limited, Leeds Road, Huddersfield, Yorkshire. A copy of the complaint is annexed hereto. The said 'Hoyer International Limited' was cited to answer said complaint in the Sheriff Court at Lanark on 12 December 1990.

STAT. III.   There is no company in existence registered under the Hoyer International Limited, nor did one exist at the relevant time.

STAT. IV.   On 10 December 1990, Messrs, Ford and Warren, solicitors, Leeds wrote to the respondent purporting to intimate a plea of not guilty on behalf of 'Hoyer International Limited'. On 12 December 1990 said plea of not guilty was recorded by the court and a trial diet was fixed for 18 February 1991. On 6 February 1991, the complaint called again, when a solicitor purported to appear on behalf of Hoyer International Limited and there was presented to the court a joint minute of acceleration purporting to be signed on behalf of the Hoyer International Limited accelerating the diet from 18 February, 1991 until 6 February 1991. On 6 February 1991, the trial diet was adjourned until 23 April 1991.

STAT. V.   On 23 April 1991 the respondent moved the Sheriff in terms of Section 335 of the Criminal Procedure (Scotland) Act 1975 as amended to amend the complaint by amending of the first accused from 'Hoyer International Limited' to that of the complainers namely 'Hoyers (UK) Limited'. The motion was opposed by the complainer. After hearing argument for the respondent and on behalf of the complainer, the Sheriff reserved judgement and adjourned the trial diet until 3 May 1991.

STAT. VI.   On 3 May 1991 the Sheriff issued his judgement, granted the motion for the respondent by amending the name of the first accused in the said complaint by deleting 'Hoyer International Limited' and substituting therefor 'Hoyers (UK) Limited' and adjourned the trial diet to a date to be fixed.

3. PLEAS-IN-LAW FOR COMPLAINER

1. The motion for the respondent being incompetent and the Sheriff's interlocutor being incompetent, erroneous and contrary to law, the interlocutor should be set aside.

2. *Separatim, esto* the motion for the respondent and the Sheriff's interlocutor were competent (which is denied), the Sheriff erred in the exercise of his discretion by granting the motion.

3. *Separatim, esto* the Sheriff was correct to grant the motion for the respondent (which is denied), he erred in the exercise of his discretion by failing to dismiss the complaint.

ACCORDING TO JUSTICE,

APPENDIX
1. Complaint
2. Copy Productions

2. Bill of advocation

HIGH COURT OF JUSTICIARY

Unto the Right Honourable
The Lord Justice-General, The Lord Justice-Clerk
and Lord Commissioner of Justiciary

BILL OF ADVOCATION

for

The Right Honourable Lord Fraser of Carmyllie,
Her Majesty's Advocate, <u>COMPLAINER</u>

against

DAVID MECHAN, Prisoner in the prison of Barlinnie, Glasgow,
<u>RESPONDENT</u>

HUMBLY SHEWETH

That the complainer is under the necessity of complaining to your Lordships against a decision of the Right Honourable Lord Morton of Shuna dated 28 June 1991 whereby the said Lord Morton of Shuna at a preliminary diet following upon the service on the respondent of an indictment at the instance of the complainer for trial in the High Court of Justiciary sitting at Glasgow on 8 July 1991 sustained a plea in bar of trial by the respondent on the ground that the respondent had suffered gross or grave prejudice due to undue delay in the complainer bringing proceedings against the respondent and dismissed the said indictment and that unjustly, erroneously and contrary to law will appear to your Lordships from the annexed statement of Facts and notes of plea-in-law;

WHEREFORE the complainer prays your Lordships for letters of advocation in the premises at his instance in common form; and on consideration of the proceedings at the instance of the complainer against the respondent to advocate the same; to recall the decision complained of and to do further or otherwise in the premises as to your Lordships may seem proper.

ACCORDING TO JUSTICE

STATEMENT OF FACTS FOR THE COMPLAINER

1.   The respondent has been indicted at the instance of the complainer on two charges of assault and robbery. The crime libelled in charge 1 is alleged to have been committed on 3 January 1990. The crime libelled in charge 2 is alleged to have been committed on 6 February 1990. The said indictment has been served upon the respondent for trial at the sitting of the High Court at Glasgow commencing on Monday 8 July 1991.

2.   The respondent was arrested on 17 February 1990 and was cautioned and charged in respect of charge 1 upon the said indictment. On 21 February the respondent was placed on an identification parade and was identified by the complainer in charge 1. The respondent was also viewed by the complainer on charge 2 of the said indictment but was not identified by him.

3.   On 28 December 1990 Crown Counsel, following upon the seat of a report from the Procurator Fiscal, instructed that the respondent be indicted with both the said crimes. An indictment was prepared for the sitting of the High Court of Justiciary at Glasgow on 4 February 1991 and a copy sent to the respondent's agents. The said indictment was not properly served upon the respondent and did not call at the said sitting of the High Court on 4 February 1991.

4.   On 15 February 1991 a petition warrant was granted for the arrest of the respondent in respect of the 2 charges on the present indictment. The respondent appeared on the said petition at Glasgow Sheriff Court on 12 April 1991. This case was then continued for further examination and on 19 April 1991 he was fully committed on the said petition.

5.   Following upon service of the indictment upon the respondent for trial at the sitting of the High Court of Justiciary at Glasgow commencing on Monday 8 July 1991 the respondent, by Minute of Notice under section 71(1) of the Criminal Procedure (Scotland) Act 1975, submitted a plea in bar of trial on the ground that he had been severely prejudiced due to the inexcusable delay of the complainer in taking proceedings. The said plea was argued before the Right Honourable Lord Morton of Shuna at Edinburgh High Court on Friday, 28 June 1991 and at the conclusion of the hearing his Lordship sustained the plea in bar of trial and dismissed the indictment.

6.   The complainer submits that the said decision of Lord Morton of Shuna was unjust, erroneous and contrary to law.

There was in the circumstances no undue delay on the part of the complainer and, further, if there was any undue delay the respondent failed to demonstrate that he had suffered gross or grave prejudice thereby such as to warrant dismissal of the indictment without the charges having been brought to trial.

PLEA-IN-LAW FOR THE COMPLAINER

The said decision being unjust, erroneous and contrary to law, it should be recalled and the indictment remitted to an assize for trial.

ACCORDING TO JUSTICE

3. Bill of advocation

HIGH COURT OF JUSTICIARY , SCOTLAND

Unto the Right Honourable the
Lord Justice-General, the Lord Justice-Clerk
and Lords Commissioners of Justiciary

BILL OF ADVOCATION

for

X Y, <u>COMPLAINER</u>

against

PROCURATOR FISCAL, PERTH,
<u>RESPONDENT</u>

HUMBLY SHEWETH:

That the complainer is under the necessity of complaining to your Lordships against a decision of the Justice in the District Court of Perth and Kinross on the 6th March 2000, whereby the said Justice, after hearing the evidence of five witnesses, granted a motion by the Respondent's depute to adjourn a Trial to 11th April 2000, erroneously and contrary to law as will appear to your Lordships from the annexed statement-of-facts and note of plea-in-law;

WHEREFORE the complainer prays your Lordships for letters for advocation in the premises at his instance in common form; to grant warrant for serving a copy of this bill and deliverance thereon on the said X Y respondent; and in the meantime to grant warrant ordaining the Clerk of the District Court at Perth to transmit the whole of the said proceedings complained to the Clerk of Justiciary: and on consideration of the said proceedings to advocate the same; to recall the order complained of or to do otherwise or further in the premises as to your Lordships may seem proper.

ACCORDING TO JUSTICE, etc.

STATEMENT OF FACTS FOR THE COMPLAINER

STAT. 1.   That a plea of not guilty was tendered on 21 July 1999 when the case was continued to an Intermediate Diet on 21 September 1999 and the Trial Diet on 5 October 1999. A list of Witnesses for the Respondents was supplied to the complainer's agents on 2 September 1999 and contained two witnesses, namely:- a police constable Brian Anderson, Tayside Police Office Perth, and Allan Pettigrew, Tayside Police Office Perth.

STAT. 2.   That the case was called for Intermediate Diet on 21 September 1999 when the complainer appeared and maintained his plea of not guilty. The Crown at that stage indicated that they were prepared for trial. On 5 October 1999 the case called for trial, and the Crown then made a motion to adjourn the trial on the basis that they had no witnesses present and could not explain the absence of the witnesses. Although there was opposition the motion of the Crown was then granted by the Magistrate with the new Trial Diet being fixed for 8 November 1999. Prior to the next Trial Diet the Crown indicated again that they were not prepared for trial and they moved to adjourn. This motion was also acceded to and a new Intermediate Diet was fixed for 10 January 2000, and a new Trial Diet fixed for 24 January 2000. On 10 January 2000 the case called once more as an Intermediate Diet, and the Crown confirmed that they were prepared for trial adding that an additional three witnesses would be cited, advising further who those witnesses would be, confirming that they were available for the trial. On 24 January 2000 the case called for trial and the complainer's agent who was to conduct the trial was then taken unwell and the case was adjourned to a new Trial Diet, same being fixed for 6 March 2000. On this day the case proceeded to trial.

STAT. 3.   That at the trial on 6 March 2000 evidence was lead by the Respondent's depute from PC Brian Anderson who identified the complainer as the driver of motor R236 TWB which vehicle was alleged to have been seen on 6 April 1999 on the Perth to Dundee road travelling at the speed of 96 miles per hour. He also gave evidence as to the operation of the VASCAR unit employed to detect speed. He did not give any evidence as to any procedure in terms of section 1 of the Road Traffic Offenders Act 1998 having been adopted by him, and in the course of examination he could not remember the terms of said section 1 caution and he could not recall whether he had his *aide memoire* with him at the time. Moreover   he   could   not   remember   specifically   his involvement in any such caution. This witness was followed in evidence by PC Allan Pettigrew, the corroborating officer who gave evidence of the same facts but who was able to refer to a caution being given to the accused, same being given by the first witness, that being in terms of section 1 of the Road Traffic Offenders Act. This witness's evidence was followed by a witness who had not been formerly identified to the defence as a witness, said witness speaking to the measurement of the measured half mile used to calibrate the VASCAR unit. His evidence was followed by PC Hope who gave evidence as to the checking of the speedometer in the police vehicle. Following him evidence was led from PC Taylor in respect of the speedometer accuracy of the police vehicle in question.

STAT. 4. That after the evidence of PC Taylor the Respondent's Depute indicated that she might wish to re-call witness P.C. Brian Anderson. She did not explain why she felt it necessary to recall the witness nor the reason why there was a point which was pertinent to the facts and issues which she had not taken from him when he was originally called. The complainer's agent made clear to the Justice that the jeopardy to the complainer of continuing the trial given that she had already received complaints from the complainer's employers about being absent from work. As a consequence of this the Justice refused the motion made to the court by the Respondent's Depute to adjourn the trial that day. The complainer made it clear that he was quite prepared to see the trial to its completion on that date and was prepared to sit late also if this would be required. The Magistrate gave the Respondent approximately 1 hour to endeavour to locate the witness PC Brian Anderson. The case recalled at approximately 3 o'clock p m and the Respondent's depute indicated that the witness could not be located and moved the court to adjourn the trial to a future date on the basis that she was not prepared to close her case. In recalling the witness the Respondent's Depute did neither explain why she wished to recall the witness nor why it was essential in her view that she should do so. The motion was opposed by the complainer's agent, and it was argued that there was no good reason for this adjournment, as none had been advanced, nor was there any explanation being given as to why it was necessary for the Crown to recall the witness which motion in any event could have been opposed. The Respondent did not argue that there had been omission on his part nor any oversight, nor that something material had developed in the course of the examination of subsequent witnesses which would justify the recall of a witness who had previously been discharged from his citation. It was also advanced that granting the adjournment would further prejudice the complainer's right in this regard and that he would in any event lose money from his employment if indeed he did not lose his employment altogether. In light of the fact that the Magistrate had previously refused to adjourn the proceedings in total without any reason having been advanced by the Crown, there was no more merit in the application for the adjournment at the later stage in the proceedings than there had been previously.

STAT. 5. That the Justice granted said motion for an adjournment and a further diet of trial has been fixed for 11 April 2000.

STAT. 6. That said decision of the said Justice was oppressive, erroneous and contrary to law. Said Justice failed to give due weight to the oppressive nature of the Crown's conduct and failed to have proper regard to the interests of the complainer.

PLEA-IN-LAW

1. The said decision of said Justice being oppressive, erroneous and contrary to law should be reversed.

IN RESPECT WHEREOF

4. Bill of suspension

HIGH COURT OF JUSTICIARY

Unto the Right Honourable
The Lord Justice-General, The Lord Justice-Clerk
and Lords Commissioners of Justiciary

BILL OF SUSPENSION

for

THOMAS ANTHONY CURRIE, presently a Prisoner in the
Prison of Barlinnie, Glasgow, <u>COMPLAINER</u>

against

JOHN G. McGLENNAN, Procurator Fiscal, Kilmarnock,
<u>RESPONDENT</u>

HUMBLY MEANS AND SHOWS your servitor, THOMAS
ANTHONY CURRIE, Complainer.

THAT the complainer under the necessity of applying to your
Lordships for suspension of a pretended warrant dated on or
about the 10 day of July 1989 whereby Sheriff Croan, Esquire,
Sheriff of North Strathclyde at Kilmarnock granted warrant to the
respondent, following upon a petition at the instance of the
respondent dated 6 July 1989, to compel the complainer to take
part in an identification parade, most wrongously and unjustly as
will appear to your Lordships from the annexed statements of
Facts and note of pleas in law.

THEREFORE the complainer prays your Lordships to grant
warrant for serving a copy of this bill and deliverance thereon on
the said John G. McLennan the respondent, and further to grant
warrant ordaining the Clerk of the Sheriff Court at Kilmarnock to
transmit the whole proceedings complained of to the Clerk of
Justiciary; to suspend the said pretended warrant *simpliciter* and to
find the complainer entitled to expenses; or to do otherwise or
further in the premises as to your Lordships may seem proper.

ACCORDING TO JUSTICE

STATEMENT OF FACT FOR THE COMPLAINER

1. That on 5 June 1989 the complainer, the said Thomas Anthony Currie and others appeared at Kilmarnock Sheriff Court on a petition at the instance of the respondent, charged with murder and were committed for further examination in custody.

2. That on 13 June 1989 the complainer and others appeared at Kilmarnock Sheriff Court on a second petition at the instance of the respondent charged with murder and contravention of the Misuse of Drugs Act 1971, section 4(3) and were committed until liberated in due course of law.

3. That on 10 July 1989 the respondent presented a petition in Kilmarnock Sheriff Court, craving warrant for Officers of Strathclyde Police to take said Thomas Anthony Currie and others from Barlinnie Prison, Glasgow to 'D' division, Police Headquarters, Baird Street, Glasgow for the purpose in taking part in an identification parade to be viewed by two named witnesses.

4. That by interlocutor dated 10 July 1989 the learned Sheriff granted a warrant in the terms sought by the respondent.

5. That the complainer respectfully submits that the learned Sheriff erred in the granting of said warrant and that he failed to give proper weight to the interests of the complainer and that in the whole circumstances of the case said warrant is unlawful and oppressive.

PLEA-IN-LAW FOR THE COMPLAINER

The learned Sheriff's said decision to grant said warrant as craved being unjust, erroneous and contrary to law should be recalled.

IN RESPECT WHEREOF

5. Bill of suspension

HIGH COURT OF JUSTICIARY

Unto the Right Honourable the Lord
Justice-General, the Lord Justice-Clerk and
Lords Commissioners of Justiciary

BILL OF SUSPENSION

for

X Y, <u>COMPLAINER</u>

against

Procurator Fiscal, Glasgow, <u>RESPONDENT</u>

HUMBLY MEANS AND SHEWS YOUR SERVITOR, ALEXANDER HAMILTON, COMPLAINER:

That the complainer is under the necessity of applying to your Lordships for suspension of pretended convictions and sentences said convictions and sentences being most wrongeous and unjust as will appear to your Lordships from the annexed statement of facts and note of pleas-in-law.

THEREFORE the complainer prays your Lordships to grant warrant for serving a copy of this bill and deliverance thereon on the said Procurator Fiscal, the respondent: further to grant warrant ordaining the Clerk of the Sheriff court at Glasgow to transmit the record relating to said proceedings to the Clerk of Justiciary; to suspend said convictions and sentences *simpliciter*; and to suspend said convictions and sentences ad interim; to grant interim liberation; to find the complainer entitled to expenses; or to do further or otherwise as to your Lordships shall seem proper

ACCORDING TO JUSTICE, etc

STATEMENT OF FACTS FOR THE COMPLAINER

1. That at a diet of trial on 18 October 1999 the complainer was found guilty at the Sheriff Court of Glasgow of contraventions of sections 23(4)(a), 4(3)(b) and 5(2) of the Misuse of

Drugs Act 1971 and he was sentenced in *cumulo* to 4 months' imprisonment.

2. That the trial diet was provided over by a temporary sheriff.

3. That a temporary sheriff is not an 'independent and impartial tribunal' within the meaning of article 6(1) of the European Convention of Human Rights ('the convention').

4. That the decision of the respondent to proceed to trial before a temporary sheriff was an act within the meaning of section 57(2) of the Scotland Act 1998.

5. That in terms of section 57(2) the Lord Advocate as represented by the respondent has no power to act in a way which is incompatible with any Convention right.

6. That by proceeding in the manner described the respondent acted in a way which was incompatible with the complainer's right to a hearing by an 'independent and impartial tribunal'. Such an act was incompetent.

7. That the complainer's right having been violated by the act of the respondent his convictions and sentences should be suspended.

8. *Separatim.* Since a temporary sheriff is not an 'independent and impartial tribunal' within the meaning of article 6(1) of the Convention it follows that justice could not be seen to be done in a trial before such a sheriff and accordingly the complainer's convictions and sentences should be quashed.

PLEAS – IN – LAW

1. That the complainer's right to a hearing before an independent and impartial tribunal having been violated the convictions and sentences following thereon should be suspended *simpliciter*.

2. That justice not having been seen to be done the convictions and sentences following thereon should be suspended *simpliciter*.

IN RESPECT WHEREOF

6. Petition to the *nobile officium*

HIGH COURT OF JUSTICIARY, SCOTLAND

Unto the Right Honourable the Lord
Justice-General, the Lord Justice-Clerk and
Lords Commissioners of Justiciary

PETITION

of

A B
to the NOBILE OFFICIUM

of the

HIGH COURT OF JUSTICIARY

HUMBLY SHEWETH:

1.   That the Petitioner appeared on Petition at Dumbarton Sheriff Court charged with conspiracy and murder, alleged to have been committed between 17 and 21 February 1999. A copy of said Petition, which is dated 20 January 2000, is appended hereto. On 28 January 2000 the Petitioner was fully committed thereon , until liberated in due course of law. In light of the nature of the charge no application for bail was made at that appearance or at the prior appearance when she was committed for further examination.

2.   That the petitioner, who has no previous convictions, now seeks to be admitted to bail.

3.   That in terms of section 24(1) of the Criminal Procedure (Scotland) Act 1995 the crime of murder is not bailable but that in terms of section 24(2) thereof, your Lordship's court has the right to 'admit to bail any person charged with any crime or offence'. The petitioner, in the absence of any other remedy open to her to secure her bail, is accordingly under the necessity of making this application to the Nobile Officium of the High Court of Justiciary.

THE PETITIONER THEREFORE PRAYS THE COURT: To hold that there are no good or substantial grounds for refusing bail: that it is in the interests of justice that bail be granted and accordingly to admit her to bail on such conditions as to Your Lordships shall seem appropriate: and to decern: or to do further or otherwise in the premises as to your lordships shall seem proper.

ACCORDING TO JUSTICE

7. Petition for special leave to appeal

PETITION FOR SPECIAL LEAVE TO APPEAL

IN THE PRIVY COUNCIL ON APPEAL FROM THE
HIGH COURT OF JUSTICIARY
APPEAL COURT

Under the Scotland Act 1998 Schedule 6 paragraph 13(a)

between

XY ... Petitioner

and

HER MAJESTY'S ADVOCATE ... Respondent

TO THE RIGHT HONOURABLE THE JUDICIAL
COMMITTEE OF THE PRIVY COUNCIL

THE HUMBLE PETITION OF THE ABOVE NAMED PETI-
TIONER SHEWETH:-

1   That your Petitioner prays for special Leave to Appeal to
the Judicial Committee of the Privy Council from the judgement
of the High Court of Justiciary sitting as the Court of Criminal
Appeal, (The Lord Justice-General, Lords Coulsfield and
Nimmo-Smith) dated 18 February 2000 dismissing your
Petitioner's application for Leave to Appeal against a determination of a devolution issue dated 18 February 2000.

2   That the principal grounds on which this Petition proceeds
are:–
   i. That the Court of Criminal Appeal erred in its analysis of
      facts in making such determination and thereby violated
      your Petitioner's right under article 6-1 of ECHR and the
      Scotland Act 1998.
   ii. That the Court of Criminal Appeal erred in its analysis of
      facts in making such determination and thereby violated
      your Petitioner's right under article 6-1 of the European
      Convention on Human Rights (ECHR) and the Scotland
      Act 1998.
   iii. That the Court of Criminal Appeal, in refusing Leave of
      Appeal to the Judicial Committee of the Privy Council

acted contrary to natural justice and to the provisions of ECHR and the rights guaranteed to your Petitioner therein under article 6-1 aforesaid.

3. That by interlocutor dated 17 January 2000, Lord Osbourne, after hearing argument at a preliminary diet on 13 January 2000, upheld a devolution issue Minute of X Y, relating inter alia to delay in bringing him to trial on indictment in the High Court. Copies of said interlocutor, Minute and the indictment presently faced by your Petitioner are annexed hereto and referred to for their terms brevitatis causa. That part of said Minute which relates specifically to an alleged breach of article 6(3)(d) of ECHR was not insisted upon on behalf of your Petitioner at said preliminary diet. Lord Osborne also upheld a similar Minute in relation to your Petitioner's co-accused, Ryan Renicks, a copy of which is annexed hereto and referred to for its terms brevitatis causa.

4. That Lord Osborne, in relation to the question of delay, found that the Crown had no power to proceed with the present indictment in the context of the delay which had occurred in the proceedings against your Petitioner, who had not been dealt with within a reasonable time, as required by article 6-1 of ECHR. Lord Osborne granted the Crown Leave to Appeal against his decision ex proprio motu. A copy of the Opinion of Lord Osborne is annexed hereto and referred to for its terms brevitatis causa.

5. That the Crown lodged an Appeal against Lord Osborne's decision, which appeal was argued before the Court of Appeal on 1 February 2000. A copy of the Crown Note of Appeal is annexed hereto and referred to for its terms brevitatis causa. In addition to oral argument, the Court was provided with a brief outline argument on behalf of your Petitioner, a copy of which is annexed hereto and referred to for its terms brevitatis causa.

6. That Lord Osborne prepared a Report in respect of said Crown Note of Appeal which indicated inter alia that it was his view that the Crown sought to raise matters at Appeal upon which they had not relied at the preliminary diet. A copy of said report is annexed hereto and referred to for its terms brevitatis causa.

7. That the Court of Criminal Appeal upheld the Crown Appeal, overturning the said decision of Lord Osborne. Copies of the Opinions of the said members of the Appeal Court are annexed hereto and referred to for their terms brevitatis causa.

8. That your Petitioner moved the Court of Criminal Appeal

to grant Leave to Appeal against their decision to Your Lordship's in terms of Rule 13 of Schedule 6 to the Scotland Act 1998. The basis upon which such leave was sought were that the issue in question was of extreme importance to your Petitioner and raised important matters for the administration of justice in Scotland, that your Petitioner contended that the analysis of facts upon which the Court of Criminal Appeal's decision proceeded was wrong and unreasonable, that the case was one which was suitable for appeal to Your Lordships, and that your Petitioner had had the benefit of detailed and carefully reasoned decision in his favour from Lord Osborne at first instance. The apparent basis upon which the Court of Criminal Appeal refused your Petitioner Leave to Appeal against the determination of 18 February 2000 was that another appeal would further delay your Petitioner's trial in circumstances in which it would still be open to him to appeal against any conviction in respect of the time taken for the proceedings to be concluded.

It is respectfully submitted on behalf of your Petitioner that such refusal of leave denies your Petitioner the right to exhaust an available remedy and vindication of his right under said article 6-1 of ECHR not to be brought to trial at all in circumstances where he has not been dealt with in a reasonable time. In terms of section 57(2) of the Scotland Act 1998 the question is one of the competency of the Crown's act in proceeding to trial.

A copy of the interlocutor of the Court of Criminal Appeal refusing Leave to Appeal is annexed hereto and referred to for its terms *brevitatis causa*. That your Petitioner was brought to trial timeously in 1996, but that unexplained and unreasonable delay in the subsequent Appeal proceedings by virtue of the Trial Judge's failure to produce a report for the Appeal in accordance with his statutory duty to do so, and until eventually being ordered to do so within seven days on 21 October 1997 only after your Petitioner was forced, in the light of no progress being achieved, in spite of lengthy correspondence, to Petition the Nobile Officium of the High Court to obtain such order. That any report produced by the Trial Judge was brief and inadequate with the result that further procedure was necessary to clarify matters, culminating in a procedural diet on 10 July 1998 where certain parts of the trial proceedings were ordered to be extended. As a consequence of the initial delay by the Trial Judge, further delay resulted from one of the original trial shorthand writers claiming to be unable to decipher his notes due to passage of time, resulting in further delay as the Justiciary Office attempted to deal with that matter in correspondence. For these reasons, your Petitioner's ultimately successful Appeal, although no fault of his own, was not disposed of until June of 1999. The Opinion of the court of Appeal on that case refers to the Trial Judge causing 'initial delay'. Copies of the original indictment, agents' correspondence, your Petitioner's Note of Appeal and Grounds of Appeal, your Petitioner's Petition to the Nobile Officium of the High Court, the Trial Judge's Report, the interlocutor of the Court of 10 July 1998, correspondence between the Justiciary Office and said shorthand writer and the Opinion of the Court in respect of your Petitioner's successful appeal against conviction are annexed hereto, and referred to for their terms brevitatis causa.

9. That the history of your Petitioner's case is summarised in said Opinions of Lord Osborne, said Opinions of the Court of Criminal Appeal, said Minute on behalf of your Petitioner, said devolution Minute on behalf of your Petitioner's co-accused Ryan Renicks, said brief outline argument on behalf of your Petitioner, and a brief summary timetable of events since your Petitioner's original conviction on 22 October 1996. The latter two documents were presented to the Court for ease of reference in following oral argument at the Court of Criminal Appeal Hearing on 1 February 2000. Copies of said Opinions, Minutes and documents are annexed hereto and referred to for their terms brevitatis causa.

10. That the Court of Criminal Appeal has erred, having regard to the ECHR jurisprudence and Scottish Authorities to which it was referred, in its analysis of the delay which has occurred in the conduct of your Petitioner's case, and has erred in law in finding that there has been no breach of your Petitioner's rights in terms of article 6(1) of the ECHR. In particular, and without prejudice to the foregoing generality, your Petitioner contends that the Court of Criminal Appeal overstates the complexity of the matters which would have required to be dealt with in the Trial Judge's Report and understates the period of abnormal delay in production of any report, in circumstances where the Lord Justice General's guidelines provide that such reports should normally be provided within SIX WEEKS. Your Petitioner further contends that the Court of Criminal Appeal's analysis gives insufficient weight to the inadequacy of the report subsequently produced and the directly consequential delays which resulted. It is submitted that the Court of Criminal Appeal's apparent exclusion of the necessity for the provision of transcripts due to the brevity of the Trial Judge's Report and the difficulties in their provision from the definition of 'conduct of the judicial authorities' is artifi-

cial and unreasonable in the circumstances. Your Petitioner also submits that the granting of Leave to Appeal is appropriate having regard to the fact that the Court of Criminal Appeal disapproved most of the propositions focussed by the Crown in their Note of Appeal and largely based its decision on a fresh analysis of the facts primarily emanating from the Bench in the course of the Crown's presentation of the Appeal . Reference is made to *HM Advocate v Little* 1999 SCCR 625, *Stogmuller v Austria* (1969) 1 EHRR 155, *Proszak v Poland* 16 December 1997, RJC 1997 – VIII, *Kenmache v France* (1991) 14 EHRR 520, *Vernillo v France* (1991) Series A, NO. 198 20 February 1991, *Eckle v Federal Republic of Germany* (1982) 5 EHRR I, *Mowat v HM Advocate*, Opinion of Appeal Court, 25 June 1999, *Bunkate v Netherlands* (1993) 19 EHRR 477 *Buchholz v Federal Republic of Germany*, 3 EHRR 597, *Dougan v UK* 1997 SCCR 57, *Boddaert v Belgium* (1992) 16 EHRR 242, *McNab v HM Advocate* 2000 SLT 99, *HM Advocate v McKenna*, unreported, 15 December 1999, *Zimmerman and Steiner v Switzerland* 1983 EHRR 17.

11.   That your Petitioner submits that in the whole circumstances the unexplained delay which resulted in his case not being dealt with in a reasonable time is properly analysed at around two years and 9 months, which in the context of the case is a clear breach of article 6.1 of ECHR.

12.   That in the foregoing circumstances it is in the interests of justice that your Lordships grant special Leave as prayed, having regard in particular to the importance of the determination of the issue in question for your Petitioner, the important considerations which are raised in relation to the conduct of the administration of justice in Scotland, and to the fact that your Petitioner has at an earlier stage in the proceedings had the benefit of a favourable decision in a careful and fully reasoned judgement of the presiding Judge at the preliminary diet.

YOUR PETITIONER THEREFORE HUMBLY PRAYS that your Lordships may be graciously pleased to grant him special Leave to Appeal against the judgment of the Court of Criminal Appeal of the High Court of Justiciary dated 18 February 2000 and its determination of the devolution issue aforesaid or for such further or other right in the premises as to your Lordships may seem fit.

AND YOUR PETITIONER WILL EVER PRAY ETC

Index

When using this index, it should be remembered that appeals in *solemn* cases are dealt with in chapter 2, and appeals in *summary* cases are dealt with in chapter 3. Accordingly the index itself does not always indicate whether the entries relate to a *solemn* or to a *summary* appeal, other than by showing the chapter number as '2' or '3'. Similarly, the powers of the court in *solemn* cases are dealt with in paragraphs 6.01 to 6.13 and the powers of the court in *summary* cases are dealt with in paragraphs 6.14 to 6.20.